W9-ATP-160

Illinois Artillery Officer's Civil War:
The Diary and Letters of John Cheney

Edited by
Gordon Armstrong

"Illinois Artillery Officer's Civil War: The Diary and Letters of John Cheney," edited by Gordon Armstrong. ISBN 1-58939-767-3.

Published 2005 by Virtualbookworm.com Publishing Inc., P.O. Box 9949, College Station, TX 77842, US. ©2005, Gordon Armstrong. All rights reserved. No part of this publication may be reproduced, stored in a retrieval system, or transmitted in any form or by any means, electronic, mechanical, recording or otherwise, without the prior written permission of Gordon Armstrong.

Manufactured in the United States of America.

John Cheney's diary bears the dedication to:
My dear wife Mary

I dedicate this volume to:
My good friend and distant cousin Kay O'Brien, and
My dear wife Nancy Espersen

Table of Contents

Editor's Note

John Cheney of Dixon, Illinois served in the Army of the Tennessee as captain of Battery F, 1st Illinois Light Artillery. Later on he was promoted to major and became a corps chief of artillery. Cheney was engaged in the Western Theatre – Tennessee, Mississippi, Alabama and Georgia – between February 1862 and August 1864.

This book draws on 318 entries from John Cheney's war diary and 100 letters he wrote home to his wife Mary. The letters start February 1862 while the diary starts November 1862. There is a June 1863 to November 1863 gap in the diary. The diary and letters also have gaps corresponding to furloughs, sick leaves and recruiting service at home. When the letters are redundant with the diary, those letters are omitted or more heavily edited. Letters tend to supply more detail than the dairy.

John Cheney was an educated man. The approach taken in editing his writing was to preserve his content, style and tone, but increase readability. Edits included punctuation, changes in capitalization, spelling out some abbreviations, breaking up run-on sentences, and creating paragraphs. Spelling errors were corrected. Words that could not be deciphered are shown as [__].

In Cheney's letters to his wife Mary, he sometimes responded to content in her letters to him. Since we do not have Mary's letters, John Cheney's comments often have no context for us. For example, "What is Hall doing in Dixon?" If the context or meaning could not be inferred, such one-sided material was edited out. Cheney's letters also reported on the health status of a long string of Dixon, Illinois soldiers whose wives and mothers Mary knew. Those long lists are edited out while more specific health reports remain.

John Cheney referred to a group, e.g., army, as a plural noun. He said "the army are" rather than "the army is." Cheney also said "we done it" and he used "ain't." Those grammatical errors remain.

For those not familiar with the practice, dates are sometimes listed with "ult." or "inst." rather than the name of the month. "Ult." is an abbreviation for the Latin *ultimo* meaning the month before the current one, and "inst." for *instant* meaning the current month.

Another practice to be aware of is the absence of the modern notion of in-law when referring to family members. John Cheney referred to his wife's family members and his own the same way, e.g., "Brother Tom" (his brother Tom Cheney) and "Brother James" (his brother-in-law James Briggs).

Cheney mentioned the names of numerous soldiers and others he came in contact with. If the person could be identified, details were listed in a footnote the first time the person was mentioned, and that person was included in the People Index. If the people were well known, e.g., generals, or if they couldn't be identified, they didn't get a footnote and are not in the index. The names of Confederate soldiers and politicians are set in italics.

Acknowledgements

For help with the background research I thank: the staff of the National Archives in Washington, DC; the staff of the Illinois State Archives and the people who made a wealth of their information available on the Internet; Stella Grobe of the Lee County Historical Society, Dixon, IL; the staff of the New England Historic Genealogical Society, Boston, MA; Joe Stabile of Sioux City, IA; Louise Fox of Senatobia, MS; Edward Fields of the Davidson Library, University of California, Santa Barbara; and Debbie Steffes of the Morris (Illinois) Area Public Library.

For their encouragement I thank: Fred Kiger, Jeff Clark, Ernest Dollar and Malcolm MacDougall.

For her careful review of the manuscript, I thank Judy Hobbs.

Chapter 1 - Family Background Pre-War

Following the attack on Fort Sumter April 12, 1861 and Lincoln's call for troops April 15, Illinois began raising regiments. On April 21 the 5 foot 9 inch, slim built John Terrill Cheney attended a recruiting meeting at the courthouse in Dixon, Illinois. He volunteered for Company A, 13th Illinois Infantry. That unit raised more men than it needed and Cheney withdrew his name the next day. On September 24, John Cheney volunteered again, this time with authorization to raise an artillery company.

Cheney was born February 25, 1830 in Holderness, New Hampshire in the section that is now the separate town of Ashland. Located in Grafton County, Ashland is in the middle of the state in the Pemigewasset River valley and the foothills of the White Mountains. John was the son of Person Cheney and Ann Morrison, both of New Hampshire and old stock New England families. Person Cheney was in the paper manufacturing business at a Holderness mill belonging to his uncle John Pattee. Person and Ann Cheney had five sons and two daughters.

John Cheney about 1850

Person Cheney's brother Moses lived in Holderness and also worked at the paper mill. Moses was married to Abigail Morrison, the sister of Ann Morrison. That is two Cheney brothers married two Morrison sisters. Moses Cheney and his wife Abigail (John's uncle and aunt) were very active in the anti-slavery movement and the Underground Railroad. It is hard to know what influence they had on their nephew, but John

Cheney developed a strong anti-slavery attitude.

In addition to local schooling in Holderness, New Hampshire, he attended the Newbury Institute,[i] Newbury, Vermont a progressive Methodist secondary school.

The 1850 Census lists the 20-year-old John Cheney's occupation as storekeeper. On August 6, 1852 he received a license from the town of Holderness, New Hampshire to "sell wine and spirituous liquor for mechanical and medical purposes."

On November 28, 1850, John Cheney married Mary Briggs. Mary was born February 14, 1830 in Boston, Massachusetts, the daughter of John Briggs and Nancy Franklin. The latter (Mary's parents) were born in England, removed to Massachusetts about 1829 and later moved to Holderness. John and Nancy Briggs had three sons and five daughters.

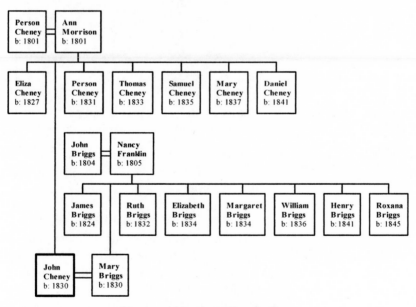

Cheney / Morrison Family Tree

---

[i] Newbury Biblical Institute, founded in 1839, was the first Methodist seminary in the U.S.

John and Mary's first child, son Royce, was born in Holderness on July 28, 1854.

John & Mary Cheney with Royce about 1855

John Cheney participated in the New Hampshire militia where he received his first training in artillery. At an 1892 Civil War reunion, Cheney related his early militia experience.

> In the State of New Hampshire, all male citizens between the ages of eighteen and forty-five were required to do military duty, at least three days in each year... Our regiment, the 13th New Hampshire, had no artillery, and a few of us got up a company of artillery, and our state magnanimously gave us one piece (a six-pounder) and with a nice uniform and a good drill-master, we went at it.

In 1856 John Cheney and family left New Hampshire, apparently accompanied by Mary's mother Nancy (Franklin) Briggs and 3 of Mary's unmarried sisters – Elizabeth, Margaret and Roxana. Mary's father, John Briggs had died in 1848.

The family settled briefly in Grand Haven, Michigan where John Cheney was a hotel proprietor at the Spring Lake House. By about 1858 they had relocated to Dixon, Illinois. Also in Dixon at about that time was John's brother Person Cheney and his family.

Dixon is located in the northern part of Illinois about 100 miles west of Chicago. In the 1860s the town was on the Illinois Central Railroad's main line running from Cairo at the southern tip of Illinois to Galena in the northwest corner of the state. Trains also ran from Dixon to Chicago on the Galena & Chicago Union Air Line (later Chicago & Northwestern).

In April of 1860 Cheney & Co. (John and his brother Person) opened and ran the Waverly House Hotel. That hotel was owned by the railroad and located by the depot in what was formerly called the Dement Town section of Dixon.

The 1860 Dixon Census for John Cheney lists him as landlord in an "eating house." His household, in addition to his wife Mary and son Royce, included his brother Person Cheney with wife Harriet and their son Charles. Also in the household was John Cheney's mother-in-law Nancy (Franklin) Briggs and sisters-in-law Margaret and Roxana Briggs. By the time of the 1860 Census, sister-in-law Elizabeth Briggs (known as Lib) had married James Vesper, also living in Dixon. James Vesper volunteered to serve in Cheney's Battery. Another of Mary Briggs Cheney's sisters, Ruth (Briggs) Shepard, moved to Dixon at some later date.

John and Mary Cheney's second child, daughter Grace, was born July 8, 1861. By the time of his September 1861 enlistment, John Cheney was no longer in the hotel business and had moved out of the Waverly House. John was, at that time principally a grain dealer, among other enterprises. Person Cheney continued to manage and live at the Waverly House Hotel.

Chapter 2 - Entering the Army

Drilling at Camp Butler and Benton Barracks
January 14, 1862 to March 30, 1862

Background

Cheney was successful in recruiting an artillery company and on January 14, 1862 Cheney's Battery – Battery F, 1st Illinois Light Artillery – departed Dixon to begin its training at Camp Butler, Springfield, Illinois, and then further training at Benton Barracks, St. Louis, Missouri. Among the volunteers in Cheney's Battery was Henry Benn[i] who had gained artillery experience in the Mexican War. At Camp Butler, Benn, who became a 1st lieutenant, taught Capt. Cheney artillery drills at night using checker pieces.

Headquarters, 1st Regt. Ill. Light Arty.
Camp Butler, Feb. 8, 1862

My dear Wife,

It is Sunday morning and I thought after delaying so long, I would take my time and write you a good long letter. I should have written you sooner, but have been very busy as our lieutenant colonel was not here, and we had to "paddle our own canoe." There is no artillery here except our company. There being no higher officer of artillery, I am in command, a position at once honorable, but very far from being easy. We had good luck in coming down. Arrived at 10 o'clock. It rained when we got here and we did not get to bed till 1 o'clock in the morning.

Yesterday Lieut. Burton[ii] and myself went to Springfield (6 miles) and back on foot. Thirty of our men with Lieut. Benn went to Springfield to guard the arsenal. They have cannon and sabers to drill with and board at a hotel.

---

[i] Lieut. Henry L. Benn of Grand Detour, IL, Battery F, 1st Illinois Light Artillery

[ii] Lieut. Josiah H. Burton of Dixon, IL, Battery F, 1st Illinois Light Artillery

On the reception of the news from Fort Henry,[i] Governor Yates[ii] ordered 34 guns. Lieut. Benn took a detachment of our men and went out at 10 o'clock and gave them the guns. They acquitted themselves admirably. Our barracks are very comfortable, and the men healthy and good-natured. The officers' quarters are very comfortable. We have 3 rooms, stove etc. etc.

I felt bad to leave home. I had known of it so long and so fully made up my mind that it would be a bad job to do, that I thought I could go without much trouble of mind. But in this I was disappointed. I looked around for Royce but could not find him. I often think of him and as often wish he was a little older thus I could have him with me.[iii] Then the family would be equally divided if such a thing is possible. How is Gracie? I hope her cough is better by this time.

Our men seem to be pleased with me and my every wish is complied with. I feel proud of them. When they get their uniforms (which will be in a day or two) they will compare favorably with any company of volunteers that I have ever seen.

The Deacon is well; he's just come in and filled his pipe. Sends his love to all. Kiss Royce and Gracie a thousand times for me. As often as you get lonesome and think your lot a hard one, think of the cause in which I am engaged, the glorious success that is now attending our arms, and hope for my speedy return when the joy of meeting will repay for the separation.

I have not learned yet when we will be mustered in and cannot tell when we will get paid. I do not yet know how I am to get my uniform,[iv] but doubt not there will be a way open at some time. Let me know how you are getting along and take good care of your health. The 46th Regiment[v] looks very fine and is really a good regiment.

Affectionately yours,
Jno. T. Cheney[vi]

~ ~ ~ ~ ~

---

[i] Confederate Fort Henry on the Tennessee River (in Tennessee) was captured February 6, 1862

[ii] Illinois Gov. Richard Yates (Republican)

[iii] Officers such as Cheney could bring a son with them to war. Such children had no official status in the army.

[iv] Officers purchased their own uniforms, swords etc. while enlisted men had them issued

[v] The 46th Illinois Infantry had many soldiers from Dixon, IL

[vi] Jno is an abbreviation for John

Camp Butler
Feby. 13, 1862

Dear Wife,

I have anxiously waited for a letter from you, as I know you must have written me before this time. I have not heard a word from home since I left. I am reminded that tomorrow will be your birthday's anniversary. I wish I could be at home. I want very much to hear from you all. How is Gracie?

You will have learned that the 46th have gone to Tennessee. We expect marching orders in the course of 10 days. I am a little afraid of not getting a chance to come home before leaving, but shall come if possible. We have just held our election and James[i] is elected sergeant, something that he little expected. We have just got the uniforms for the men. I assure you that they are very much pleased with them, as they are neatly trimmed and every way superior to the infantry. I have not got mine yet and don't know as I shall. If not I hope to be able to do just as good service without it, as with it, though I should feel a little better to dress as the rest do.

It has been very muddy here, but is now colder and the mud pretty well dried up. My health was never better. Have plenty to do. I want you to do the best you can in the way of writing, as I don't expect to get more than half of the letters you send. I will come home if consistent but if not let me know how you get along and also how our Eastern[ii] friends are.

We have 3 cases of measles; all doing well. No Dixon boys sick. I have written this very hurriedly and hardly know what I have written. Keep good cheer, for all will be well. Good night.

Your affectionate husband,
John

Battery F was officially mustered into service February 25, 1862; coincidently John Cheney's 32nd birthday.

[i] Sergt. James M. Vesper of Dixon, IL, Battery F, 1st Illinois Light Artillery; the husband of Lib (Briggs) Vesper, who in turn is the sister of Mary (Briggs) Cheney

[ii] Eastern friends were those in New England, especially New Hampshire

~ ~ ~ ~ ~

Springfield, Ill.
Feby. 26, 1862

Dear Wife,

I am driven almost to death with work and have not seen time to get my sword or to write. I am well. Expect we will move on Friday. Have had a present of an officer's overcoat from Allen. I am very anxious to hear from home. As soon as I get to St. Louis[i] will write to you all particulars.

Don't worry about me for I am as well and tough as I ever could wish to be. Keep good courage. I am as confident, as I am of my existence, that Gracie is better, but it seems to me that Royce is a little unwell. Am I right?

Will wait till I get my sword and sash before I get a miniature[ii] taken. Love to all.

Affectionately your husband,
John T. Cheney

~ ~ ~ ~ ~

Camp Butler
Mch. 2, 1862

Dear Wife,

We are still doing guard duty at Camp Butler. Expect to be relieved tomorrow and as soon as we can get ready, go to St Louis. The prisoners[iii] at this camp are as curious looking a sect of mortals, as I ever saw. Most of them are dressed in butternut colored cloth; evidentially homemade. They are somewhat sickly; 4 died yesterday and 2 today. They say generally, they would gladly fight for the Stars and Stripes and I believe they tell the truth. I really wish you could be here to see them.

I have received your letters regularly. Be assured I have been delighted to hear that Gracie has been out into the sitting room and to know when she was. I know you must be nearly exhausted by this time, but take hope, as Gracie gains, you will.

---

[i] St. Louis, MO is the site of his next posting – Benton Barracks
[ii] Miniature is a small photograph
[iii] Camp Butler was a training facility that became a prisoner of war camp receiving 2,000 Confederates taken at the Battle of Fort Donelson, TN February 13-16, 1862

Your timely hint to me is not without its effect. Be assured that I shall not be guilty of any act that will ever throw discredit upon so good a family as I have. I will write for the paper[i] as soon as I have time to write as I want to.

I have walked from the arsenal to Camp Butler today and will walk back in the morning. We had a hard thunderstorm last night and are having a rainy day today. My health is very good. I did not know how much enthusiasm I had, till I have tried it. I hope you will continue to write every day and direct[ii] to Springfield till you get word to send to St. Louis.

Give my love to all the friends, and to Pers[iii] and Hat[iv] in particular as they now, if ever, need the sympathies[v] of friends. I was quite glad to learn that Royce was not sick. I have written all that I can think of that will interest you, except pay, which is about $146 per month as near as I can learn.

Affectionately your husband,
Jno. T. Cheney

~ ~ ~ ~ ~

Springfield Arsenal
Mch. 7, 1862

Dear Wife,

I will write you a few lines and send[vi] by Lieut. Burton. We are now together. Have been separated since I got back from home till today. We do not know when we shall go away. They are having some difficulty in getting artillery horses. I have expected to hear from you, but suppose you have written and sent to St. Louis. You cannot imagine how I long for a letter from home. How is our dear little Gracie? I hope you are better than when you last wrote. I suppose Royce has almost got so he can write to me! Tell him to try it. Burton will tell you all the particulars about us. I have bought no sword as yet, and probably shall not till we get to St. Louis.

---

[i] "Republican and Telegraph" was the Dixon, IL paper – the issues from the Civil War years are not available

[ii] Direct here means address the letter

[iii] Person Cheney of Dixon, IL; John Cheney's brother. Pers did not enlist in the army due to his health.

[iv] Harriet Cheney, the wife of Person Cheney

[v] Charles, the son of Person and Harriet Cheney, died Feb. 15, 1862

[vi] Lieut. Burton was returning to Dixon on leave

Enclosed you find a letter from Bullock.[i] I wish you to read it and send it to Pers, and tell him to have it published in the "Republican and Telegraph." I hope a like history[ii] may never ever be written of me. I would rather my head be taken off and be sent home headless, than to be at home with the stigma <u>coward</u> attached to my name. Still I may run.

Our men are generally healthy. We have just drawn our battery[iii] and have it nicely mounted in front of our camp. It looks fine. We have just drawn the last of our equipments. Burton is here and I must close, as I have no more time.

Affy. your husband,
John

~ ~ ~ ~ ~

Headquarters, 1st Regt.
Springfield Arsenal
Mch. 12, 1862

Dear Wife,

You letter of 7th inst. came duly to hand. Be assured I was delighted to hear that Gracie was so much better. I hope you will get her miniature, and yours and Royce's taken soon. Perhaps you could do so and send them by Lieut. Burton.

I want you to let me know from time to time just how you are getting along. Don't deny yourself of any comfort in the world for there is no necessity for it.

The weather is very pleasant indeed here. Mud almost dried up. Our company are making so fine progress in their drill. We do not know as yet when we are to leave. It is reported that the ladies of Springfield are going to present our company with a banner. I do not know that it is true, but if it is, it will be a very pretty compliment for our company, among entire strangers as we are.

---

[i] Lieut. (later Capt.) Hezekiah H. Bullock of Dixon, IL, Co. I, 46th Illinois Infantry

[ii] The history was apparently related by Bullock about someone else rather than being about Bullock

[iii] Battery F originally was a 4-gun battery equipped with James Rifles – a rifled (as opposed to smoothbore) cannon with 3.8 inch bore firing a 6 pound projectile

I am not much surprised at John Stevens'[i] action at Ft. Donelson. I do not know that I should not do the same thing under like circumstances, but it seems to me that I would thank my men to shoot me if I did.

I expect Royce is learning to write very fast, and will expect to hear from him soon. We are having less sickness than at any time since we left Dixon. Give my love to all inquiring friends. I will get my miniature taken as soon as I get my sword and sash. Expect that will be when we get to St. Louis. Write often and long. Don't fret about me, but make yourself happy as possible, and all will be well. I wish I could step in and see you.

Affectionately your husband,
John

~ ~ ~ ~ ~

Headquarters, 1ˢᵗ Reg. Lt. Artillery
Springfield Arsenal
Mch. 14, 1862

Dear Mary,

We leave this evening at 6 o'clock for St. Louis. Direct to "Benton Barracks." I do not know when we go further or where we go. I will write you again on Sunday from St Louis.

Our boys are much pleased with the idea of leaving and generally in good health and spirits. I have considerable business to do and must cut my letter short. Don't fret about me for I am all right and expect to be. Write often and give me all the news. My love to all the friends.

Affy. your husband,
John

~ ~ ~ ~ ~

Benton Barracks, Mo.
March 16, 1862

Dear Mary,

It is Sunday evening and agreeable with my promise I will write you. Lieut. Burton has just come back. Says he has a package for me

---

[i] Capt. John Stevens of Dixon, IL, Co. H, 46ᵗʰ Illinois Infantry. The 46ᵗʰ left Camp Butler February 11, 1862, arrived at Ft. Donelson February 14, and saw action the 15ᵗʰ. John Stevens was wounded at Shiloh April 6, 1862 and later died of that wound.

from you, which is in his trunk at St. Louis. He has gone to St. Louis and will return tonight. I will not send this till he comes, then I will finish the letter. I have got my sword, sash and belt, and in a day or two I will get my daguerreotype[i] taken and send to you.

John Cheney's sword belt and sash

Benton Barracks are the most beautiful that I have ever seen, only that just now it is a little muddy. The boys are in fine spirits. I believe it is healthier here than Springfield. I cannot tell when we shall leave but probably very soon. If we were sure of remaining here 2 weeks I would certainly like to have you and Royce and Grace come down. Would you like to come? It would be such a treat to you to see 13,000 men in a body. I wish you would write me if you wish to come to me if we get stationed where we can stay long enough for you to do so.

We expect our pay next week when I will send you some money. My quarters are first rate. Everything in neat order, well-ventilated rooms. A hydrant just back of the quarters from which we get good water. We have the promise of horses and sabers soon. I hope you will manage to enjoy life as well as possible, and never fret for my safety, for whatever is, is right. All the fears, hopes and wishes of friends will

---

[i] Daguerreotype is a photographic image on a silver coated plate; largely obsolete by 1862.

not change the matter. It may seem strange for me to talk thus to you, but it is all true. Although I write you so, I don't expect you to do as I wish you to. I know you can't help a continual anxiety about me, any more than I can about you.

I often think of the snow banks in Dixon when I look out and see the green grapes about here. St. Louis is a very fine city. I think I would about as soon live there as any place I know of. I have written to the "Republican and Telegraph," which you will see in print. I will keep you posted in our movements. My labors are continual and arduous. If you don't hear oftener than once a week you will not be surprised.

My love to each and all, Marg,[i] Royce, Gracie in particular. Don't deny yourself of anything you may want.

I have waited till Monday morning. Burton could not get his truck yesterday and I have not got your letter. This is one of the loveliest mornings I ever saw. A regiment of cavalry have just left for Pilot Knob.[ii] They look splendidly, and their music is soul stirring. I will write again in a very short time. My sheet is full and I must stop now. Good cheer now Mary.

Your own,
John

~ ~ ~ ~ ~

---

[i] Margaret Briggs of Dixon, IL, the sister of Mary (Briggs) Cheney
[ii] Pilot Knob, Missouri is about 85 miles south of St. Louis

Letterhead on March 20, 1862 letter

Benton Barracks
March 20, 1862

Dear Wife,

On Monday evening I received your letter. Also your miniature with Royce and Gracie's. I was never more pleased in my life, as you looked as though you was not fretting yourself very much considering the circumstances. Little Gracie looks so good too. And Royce is getting to be so much of a boy. Mary you don't know how much I prize these pictures. Money would not buy them. I am so glad that you got them taken in season to send by Lieut. Burton. I have one of those very uncomfortable fellows on my eye; it's a sty. So that I will not have mine taken till it gets well. You may expect it in about 4 or 5 days after receiving this.

We do not know yet when we will go away, but not for some week or ten days probably. We are still getting along well, and enjoying good health. I have been to St. Louis today. Have got our mules for transportation, and expect our horses in a few days. I think so much of those pictures Mary that I don't know what to say of them. You will get a view of Benton Barracks from this sheet.

Tell Lib[i] she must not get desponding. She ought to have too much good sense, to say nothing of the aid she may receive from the spirit world, to fret about us. We are well provided for, doing the best we ought to do for the cause of humanity, and the progress of truth and justice. If we fall, what is it? Nothing to mourn over, but on the contrary to be proud of.

Lib: For my sake, for the sake of Jim, for the sake of friends about you, for the sake of the eternal laws of progression that we all believe in. For the sake of the friends in spirit life who would willingly assist you in doing so, keep up good spirits. Be cheerful and happy, always believing that whatever is, is right. We are always cheerful, and only wish that you may be so, trusting to that everlasting chain of events that must come, do what we will, and believing that the Glorious Giver will do all things well. It may seem to Lib that I ought not to suggest so much to her, guided as she is by superior intelligence, but I can only say I feel constrained to say this much.

Mother:[ii] I suppose you are in good spirits. God bless you, as He will.

Margaret: I expect you are not fretting much. You ought not to.

Royce: I suppose you find plenty of business to do in the way of sliding etc. to make life pleasant. Be good boy.

Jed and Tate:[iii] You are one unbroken family. Thank God it is so and enjoy life, as you ought to, which I have no doubt you do.

Pers and Hat: Your little Charlie is in Heaven with angels. Swallow the apparently bitter cup without a murmur. Thank God that you are to see him again entirely far from the many ailments of which he used to complain.

Gracie: When the rest get blue, just look up and laugh and talk them out of it.

I will write you again next Sunday. Now Mary let me hear from you often and let nothing disturb you. I will come back, now mind that.

Affectionately your husband,
John T. Cheney

~ ~ ~ ~ ~

[i] Elizabeth (Briggs) Vesper of Dixon, IL, wife of Sergt. James Vesper; Elizabeth is the sister of Mary (Briggs) Cheney

[ii] Nancy (Franklin) Briggs, mother of Mary (Briggs) Cheney; John Cheney's mother-in-law

[iii] Jed and Tate are young men, say teenagers, who seem to be family of some type but whose relationship to the Cheney or Briggs families is not clear

Dear Mary,

I had a good warm bath this morning. Had the company inspected. Had my dinner of roast beef, boiled rice, bread and butter, potatoes and tea. And now will write to you. Since I last wrote you I have been busy getting ready to move whenever we may be ordered. We only lack our horses, which I expect we will get this week. I have been to St Louis, and there saw some twenty cannons taken from the Secessionists and a large stack of muskets. They look as though the men who had handled them had been pretty roughly used. Some of the guns had been shot in the muzzles, splitting them and other marks of bad usage. One caisson[i] had received a shot right under the driver, and must have come very close to his legs if it did not hit him. Such is war.

The weather is fine. The walking is very good. It is a splendid sight to look out and see the troops on parade. I do not hardly dare to advise you to come down here, as we are so likely to move soon.

Col. Dubois, chief of artillery, sent to the commandant of the post, day before yesterday, for 3 of the captains of batteries, best in order for service, to report to him at St. Louis. Of 14 batteries, Capt. Cogswell's[ii] of Ottawa, Capt. Bouton's[iii] of Chicago and Capt. Cheney's, were selected. We immediately reported ourselves and were instructed to put ourselves in shape for moving. He says a large force will be sent toward the Rocky Mountains. He now proposes to send 3 batteries and ours is one of them. The whole may be changed, as it is impossible to tell what a day may bring forth. So far as I am concerned I hope to be put where we are most needed, be it where it will. I do not think we will get away in less than a week or ten days. If you wish to come down and think you can stand it, do so. I wish you would. If I had money I would send it to you, but if you come I will have plenty of money to send you back when we leave. I yesterday got an order from Gen. Halleck for our payment and we will be paid this week.

If you conclude to come, telegraph me and I will meet you at the depot. If I should fail to go to the depot to meet you, you can go to Barnum's Hotel and they will telegraph me. I do want to see you again before leaving, but you must exercise your own good judgment about

---

[i] Two wheeled vehicle for carrying artillery ammunition; attached to a limber similarly to the way a cannon is attached to a limber

[ii] Capt. William Cogswell of Ottawa, IL, Cogswell's Battery, Independent Illinois Light Artillery

[iii] Capt. Edward Bouton of Chicago, Battery I, 1st Illinois Light Artillery

coming. Should you conclude to come and anything happens that we were gone when you came, I could fix it with Maj. Carnell so that you could get money to get home. I think we will be 10 days. The boys are still well and anxious to move along toward the seat of war. A movement that will tell, will soon be made. I hope that by fall we may all return to our families and friends with a happy country.

Remember me to all the friends and our family in particular. I will go to St. Louis tomorrow and have my ambrotype[i] taken and sent to you by mail. Lew Smith is here selling those bulletproof vests. I think they are a good thing and may buy one. Now Mary remember the oft repeated wish that you be of good cheer. Believe that if possible our last days shall be our best.

I am trying to imagine how you are spending the Sabbath but cannot form a conception. I hope that this moment you are surrounded by friends and enjoy-

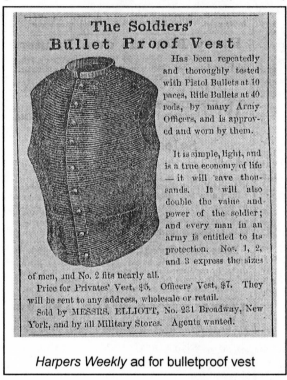

Harpers Weekly ad for bulletproof vest

ing yourself first rate. I think of no more to say to you today, only tell me if Gracie says any little words yet and if Royce is getting so as to write.

Your husband,
John T. Cheney

~ ~ ~ ~ ~

---

[i] Ambrotype is a photographic image made on a glass plate cased in front of a dark background

Dear Wife,

I have spent the day in riding on horseback to St. Louis and surroundings – fortifications, water reservoir, etc. It has been a very
pleasant day indeed. The roads are excellent. The country is beautifully
romantic. I often thought of the local area at home and wished you
were here to go about with me. Lieut. Burton accompanied me. We
both have good horses. My horse is a beauty; will canter like a rabbit
and jumps ditches like a fox. I think I am getting to be a very fine rider.
I feel quite tired tonight on account of having rode so far, and it being
comparatively new business for me. Otherwise I am in excellent health.

It is impossible for me to say with any certainty where we will go
or when we will be ordered away. We have not got our horses shod yet,
nor have we been paid. E. B. Stiles and Charlie have visited the
company today, but I was absent. The boys say that he is coming up
again. If he does I will go to St Louis with him and get my ambrotype
taken, and send by him as it will be more likely to go safely than by
mail.

I received a Dixon paper today of the 20th. Suppose Pers sent it.
Wish he would send me a New Hampshire paper occasionally. Lieut.
Burton is writing to his wife. Any news that I may forget to write, you
may learn from her. Between you both, you will be each left pretty well
posted. Lieut. Burton is a good officer, liked by the men, and I am well
satisfied will give a good report of himself.

You forgot to say how Mother was when you wrote. Tell Mother I
knew we had the prettiest girl in the country some time since, and am
glad to know that she thinks so. I wrote to Royce and suppose you have
read it before this. I look anxiously for the mails and am delighted to
hear from you Mary, and hope you will spend a large portion of your
time in writing me. You don't say anything about Nero,[i] how is he?

Henry Chappell[ii] went out Friday to help break our mules and
foolishly mounted a wild one. He was thrown and broke his ankle. He
will get over it, but it will be some time yet before he can do service.
He is in the hospital. Everything that can be done for him is done, and
he is quite comfortable. He does not wish his father to know of it, but I
suppose he will find it out some way. If he does and should inquire of
you concerning him, tell him all about him. I would write his father but
Henry don't wish me to do so.

---

[i] Nero is John Cheney's dog
[ii] Pvt. Henry Chappell of Dixon, IL, Battery F, 1st Illinois Light Artillery

Last evening the boys got two fiddlers and we all turned in. We had a good civil little dance, everything conducted in good order – ladies with uncovered heads, gents with caps on. You can see my dear that camp life is not without its pleasures. I am going to make time pass just as pleasantly as possible. I am glad to know that you are (just what I have known for so many years) possessed of good common sense, and doing as I am trying to do, make the best of a bad job.

I feel tonight that you are thinking of and perhaps writing to me and trying to persuade yourself that all is well. I often wish Jed and Pers were with us. I am more and more convinced that it would be the best thing they could do for their health to come into camp, beside the satisfaction of doing something for the maintenance of the government. Though they are doing much toward making those contented and happy that we have left behind. "Verily they shall have their reward,"[i] is that quoted right? They may perhaps consider it a treasure laid up in Heaven on which I believe there is no cash dividend paid.

Well Mary I have written you a long letter and it seems to me that it don't amount to much. But after all, if it is with you as it is with me, you will never get tired of reading. If I could just look in and see you all tonight, what a satisfaction it would be. Perhaps if I was near enough to look in, you would give me an invitation to come in, which I would accept.

Tell Lib never to fear for Jim. We are fast friends and shall be while life shall last. We started together in unity, have remained so, and will return so. I am very glad to know that you are all together and think you may dwell together in unity and have a merry time.

Frank Whaley[ii] has just stepped in and wishes to be remembered to you all. Frank is a very efficient orderly.[iii] I am satisfied that I could not have made a better selection. So far as I know there is a good feeling in the company toward the officers. If you hear any reports, wish you to let me know. Remember me to all our friends. Don't forget to do a large amount of writing.

As soon as I get paid I will send you some money. Don't be modest about calling on Smith for money for he will let you have it. Does Nero stay with you? What room do you sleep in? How much money

---

[i] Verily I say unto you, They have their reward. Matthew 6:2

[ii] Probably Pvt. Johnson Whaley of Brooklyn, IL, Battery F, 1st Illinois Light Artillery

[iii] Orderly is a soldier who carries orders or provides other services for a superior

have you got? Are you glad the sheet is full? Good night Mary and may God bless you.

Your own,
John

Capt. John Cheney about 1862

Summary

John Cheney served out of a combination of duty and honor. It was his patriotic duty to fight for the "cause of humanity and the progress of truth and justice." His country had provided him the benefits of security and democracy. Now his country was in trouble; it was being dismantled by the seceding states. Cheney saw it as his moral obligation to fight to restore the Union.

To fail to do your duty or worse to be a coward, was a source of dishonor. Honor had an internal component but was also about one's public reputation. Cheney did not want to dishonor his family. He was candid about his lack of certainty about how he would perform in the danger of combat. He didn't anticipate that he would act in a cowardly fashion, but he couldn't rule it out until he actually experienced action.

At this point in his service there was a good deal of novelty and excitement in being a soldier. Cheney was healthy and could enjoy riding around on a good horse. He saw new places and new things.

Chapter 3 - Off to the Front in Tennessee

April 12, 1862 to April 28, 1862

Background

Gen. Albert Sidney Johnston, following defeats in Kentucky in the winter of 1861/62, fell back to Corinth, Mississippi to regroup. Corinth was important as the crossroads of the Mobile & Ohio Railroad and the Memphis & Charleston Railroad.

After the Union victory at Fort Donelson, February 13-16, 1863, Maj. Gen. Grant moved his Army of the Tennessee up the Tennessee River to Pittsburg Landing and Crump's Landing in Savannah, Tennessee, about 25 miles northeast of Corinth. Maj. Gen. Buell and his Army of the Ohio marched west from Nashville, Tennessee to join Grant. Grant and Buell planned to attack *Johnston* at Corinth.

On April 6, 1862 *Johnston* moved out of Corinth and attacked Grant before Buell arrived. Grant was unprepared and for the first day of the Battle of Shiloh, Confederate forces carried the day. *Johnston* was killed and *Gen. P. G. T. Beauregard* took command. Buell arrived in time to reinforce Grant when the battle resumed April 7th and Union forces prevailed. *Beauregard* returned to Corinth.

Battery F departed Benton Barracks, Missouri. They traveled from St. Louis by steamboat going south on the Mississippi River, then east on the Ohio River and then south on the Tennessee River past Fort Henry, to Pittsburg Landing, Tennessee. They arrived on April 9, 1862 just missing the Battle of Shiloh. Cheney's Battery became part of Maj. Gen. Lew Wallace's 3rd Division in Maj. Gen. Grant's Army of the Tennessee. Under Capt. Cheney were Lieuts. Benn, Burton and Smyth.

Pittsburg Landing, Tenn. River
April 12, 1862

Dear Wife,

I will try and give you some idea of what has transpired here since I wrote you last. I wrote you at Fort Henry. Nothing of particular interest transpired on the trip from there except that we found 3 intelligent contrabands[i] at Ft. Henry who had run away from their masters, 60 miles across the country, stolen a boat load of Secesh[ii] corn and took it to our troops. We liked their looks pretty well and took them along with us as servants. I am of the opinion that they have ceased to be slaves.

We were told that a Rebel battery was planted between Fort Henry and Savannah. We hove to and tied up to trees under a high bluff to stay for the night. We threw out pickets[iii] on each side of the river so as not to be taken by surprise. Ed O'Brien had charge of one squad and they had a fine time. We planted our guns on each side of the boat, loaded our side arms[iv] and were pretty well prepared for the reception of the enemy.

Lieut. Smyth[v] and myself spread our blankets on the upper deck in the open air. We were soon asleep when we were awakened by a hurricane that tore the trees (to which we were fastened) out by the roots. One fell across the bow of the boat doing no damage of any account. The wind was of short duration and we were soon all right

---

[i] The legal status of run-away slaves that came into the Union army lines was problematic. Four slave states (Delaware, Kentucky, Maryland, and Missouri) remained in the Union and the Fugitive Slave Law was in effect. Prior to the Emancipation Proclamation January 1, 1863 slaves who ran away from owners in Confederate states were not free. They were deemed contraband. Contraband of war is forbidden items or goods that could be used for war, e.g., muskets, ammunition, saddles. International laws recognized the right of parties at war to seize contraband from neutral parties to prevent it from falling into the hands of one's enemy. Since the Confederacy used slaves to build military fortifications, the position was taken that slaves (legally property) could therefore be held by the Union army to prevent them from being used to aid the Confederate war machine. Once under the protection of the Union army, contrabands were employed repairing roads and bridges, transporting supplies, building fortifications, and as cooks and servants.

[ii] Secesh is a shortened form of Secessionist, meaning the South, Southerners

[iii] Picket is a soldier posted to give warning of an approaching enemy

[iv] The artillery were not issued muskets. Officers and sergeants carried pistols.

[v] Lieut. Samuel Smyth of Elkhorn, IL, Battery F, 1st Illinois Light Artillery, later captain of Battery A

again. No enemy visited us. In fact they have all been driven back and were concentrating at Corinth.

We heard of the battle at Savannah[i] and were sorry that we were too late to take a part in it. I am not competent to give you an account of the battle. No person can form an idea of its magnitude without being here to look over the battle ground. Donelson sinks into utter insignificance when compared with it. On Sunday morning at 7 o'clock when most of our men were quietly eating their breakfast, they were rushed upon by the enemy. Bullets flew thick and fast, tents completely riddled, and soon their artillery commenced a raking fire. Our men were soon drawn up in line of battle when the tug of war came.

Our forces were driven. It almost seems that the enemy might have driven our army into the river had they had 2 hours more daylight. But thanks to Gen. Buell and his noble army who threw away their whole equipment, except arms and ammunition, and arrived here in season to give them Hell on Monday morning. On Sunday we were whipped, our batteries taken. But on Monday they were repulsed, our batteries retaken. 49 pieces of the enemy's guns taken, hundreds of their horses killed and thousands of the rebels made to bite the dust. The gunboats opened a terrible fire on them mowing down whole companies. Trees 2 feet in diameter are completely cut off by their shots and the air filled with fragments of their bursting shells.[ii]

I rode over the ground yesterday to see the fragments. You are perhaps aware that the fighting was in the timber. Well there is not a tree but that is riddled with bullets and broken. Muskets, cannon, caissons, shells, harness, torn hats, caps, coats, pants, cartridge boxes, haversacks, knapsacks, dead horses, etc. etc. cover the ground. It is a horrible sight. But the devilish Rebels were forced to retreat, and have lost more men in killed and wounded, than we have. Though they have taken more prisoners than we have.

Gen. Grant is censured for letting the enemy take us by surprise. I think it is high time that such men be removed. Gen. Halleck arrived last night and will take command in person so we may affect better things. Our men fought bravely and only fell back when it would have been folly for them to have done otherwise.

The Rebels' canteens contained whisky and gunpowder. What do you think of furnishing such stuff to men? Well they fought desperately and evidently are well drilled. Since we came here it has rained

---

[i] Battle of Shiloh – Savannah, TN is just north of Pittsburg Landing
[ii] Shell is a hollow cannon projectile filled with a small bursting charge and fuse that fragments the shell; it was used at longer range

continuously and it would now be impossible for either army to move. Therefore we cannot tell when the fight will be resumed though it is highly probable the next fight will be at Corinth which is some 22 miles from here and 18 miles from the river. My own opinion is that it will be some two weeks hence and we whip them.

I feel more like fighting now that I am in Secesh, than ever before. I am now getting a good ready to do the best I can. I would rather leave a widow than return to you with the stigma coward forever attached to my name. So expect me to fight and trust that I may come out unharmed. I feel confident that I will not fail.

I have visited Capt. Stevens. He has had a leg amputated just below the knee and is doing well; left yesterday for Savannah. Capt. Marble[i] is wounded in the leg, but will not lose the leg. Have not seen him as he left for Savannah before we arrived. I visited Col. Kirk[ii] yesterday, found him wounded in the breast. He will recover and said to me "I will be with you at Corinth boys." Maj. Levenway's[iii] boys[iv] had left.

The 34th fought bravely and also the 46th. Officers and men all did themselves honor in both regiments. Col. Davis[v] is believed to be fatally wounded. I have not heard a word from home since March 20th and I assure you that I feel anxious to hear. My health is very good indeed. The boys are generally well and eager for an engagement with the Rebels.

If Pers had come along as a sutler[vi] he could have made a fortune. I really wish he had come, as the sutlers are generally swindlers. It would be a luxury for our boys to trade with a man who had a little of the milk of human kindness in his breast.

Good courage wife and angels guard and guide you and our beloved children.

Your John

~ ~ ~ ~ ~

---

[i] Capt. John M. Marble of Bloomington, IL, Co. E, 46th Illinois Infantry
[ii] Col. Edward N. Kirk of Sterling, IL, 34th Illinois Infantry
[iii] Maj. Charles N. Levenway of Dixon, IL, 34th Illinois Infantry
[iv] 34th Illinois Infantry
[v] Col. John A. Davis of Rock Run, IL, HQ, 46th Illinois Infantry
[vi] Sutler is a civilian merchant licensed to sell food and small items to troops

Sunday evening, April 13, 1862

My dear Wife,

I thought, as the mail does not leave till tomorrow, that I would write you a few lines more. It has stopped raining and been a very beautiful day, although the mud is very deep. It is impossible for us to move. It is said that the mud dries up very soon. It is probable that we will move in two or three days. You may expect to hear of another battle.

I have spent the day rather curiously for me. Got up in the morning and raised the walls of the tent to air it. Spread the bed clothes outdoors to air them. Ate my breakfast of hard bread, coffee, beans, and pork. Washed my shirt and drawers. Took my horse and rode over to the 34th Regt. where I met Capt. Dysart[i] and several Nachusa[ii] boys. Came back on the outskirts of the late battle ground, and now have just changed my flannel. So you see that I have passed the day rather profitably.

I often thought of you and wished you could be here to see the sad havoc that was made last Sunday and Monday. Still I know that you are much better off at home. Last Sunday when our men were retreating the Rebels cried "Bull Run." On Monday when the devilish Rebels were retreating and being mowed down by the score and hundreds, our boys cried "Fort Donelson." So you see the tables were turned upon them in good shape.

It is impossible to form any correct opinion of the number of killed and wounded, but it is immense. The Rebels lay on acres of ground so that you could walk on them without stepping on the ground. This would seem almost incredible.

I have received your letter of April 3rd. I suppose you have long since this, got the photographs and money. We may be in service 4 months without getting any more pay, so you will do well to keep money enough for your own use if you do not pay up all that I suggested. Use that of Deacon's if you need it. Be sure to keep yourself and Royce and little Gracie well clothed. Don't deny yourselves of anything you need.

---

[i] Capt. Alexander P. Dysart of China, IL, Co. C, 34th Illinois Infantry
[ii] Nachusa boys are men from Dixon, IL. Nachusa was the Indian name of John Dixon, founder of the town.

I received a letter from Father[i] and Mother[ii] today, and it was a real good one I assure you. Capt. Cogswell of Ottawa has just got moved in beside us and is covered with mud, and almost starved. The boys have got some supplies and a hot cup of coffee for him. I have a cup at my side also, that goes good. It is 10 o'clock. I think of no more of interest and will bid you good night and God bless you. I will be back all right. Give my love to all the folks and take good care of yourself. Always remember that you cannot enjoy good health without a contented mind. My dear wife be cheerful and happy.

Your husband,
Jno. T. Cheney

~ ~ ~ ~ ~

Pittsburg, Tenn.
April 18, 1862

My dear Wife,

I wrote you last Sunday and suppose you have received my letter ere this. I also wrote you a line today and sent you $40, and $25 for Lib from Jim. Mr. Petrie took it and promised me he would call and see you and deliver it to you. I suppose it would be a great satisfaction to see anyone who had seen me on the battlefield. Therefore I requested him to call and doubt not you will have seen him before you receive this.

I have spent the week drilling. Have been in the saddle almost continuously. We were out this afternoon and there came up a shower of rain and drove us into camp. After washing myself thoroughly, sit down to write to my better half. This morning Lieuts. Burton and Smyth and myself started early for the front. Rode to without the encampment, and within a short distance of the enemy's pickets. We found the 34th Regiment. Met Capt. Dysart and Adjt. Leavitt[iii] (Pers will know him). I also met Mr. Forsyth[iv] of Dixon; Dr. Hewitt[v] of Franklin Grove. They were all well and it seemed pleasant to meet them. We then went to the 46th and saw Col. Jones,[vi] Bullock (who is now a

---

[i] Person Cheney Sr. of New Hampshire, born February 12, 1801, John Cheney's father
[ii] Ann (Morrison) Cheney of New Hampshire, born February 14, 1801, John Cheney's mother
[iii] Adj. David Leavitt of Sterling, IL, 34th Illinois Infantry
[iv] Lieut. Francis Forsyth of Dixon, IL, Co. D, 34th Illinois Infantry
[v] Asst. Surgeon George W. Hewitt of Franklin Grove, IL, 34th Illinois Infantry
[vi] Lieut. Col. John J. Jones of Fulton City, IL, 46th Illinois Infantry

Lieutenant), Mr. Ludlay, Mr. St. John, Capt. Pride[i] and others of the regiment. They are all well. It is reported that Capt. Stevens is dead and I am of the opinion that it is true. It is also reported that Col. Kirk is dangerously wounded. I hope the Colonel may recover as he has the reputation of being one of the most efficient officers in the service. Col. Davis is also a gallant officer, as also Col. Jones. Billy Howell[ii] is killed. Our section of Illinois has reason to be proud of her officers and men. I take delight in saying that I come from Illinois. Tell Pers that it is not probable that any more fault will be found with Gen. Fremont about gunboats, for they done terrible execution in the engagement.

I saw this morning for the first time a cotton press and the thought came to my mind instantly "that's what's the matter." We went through 3 farms in which wheat had been growing but was trodden into the ground. Some of the buildings have been burned and others used as prisons and hospitals. This may seem hard but if you were here you would rejoice to know that the Rebels had been driven from their houses. They may learn that we are long suffering, but terrible when endurance has ceased to be a virtue. My own feelings are, send away the women and children and wherever we march do the greatest amount of injury possible believing this to be the most speedy way of terminating the war.

We are daily receiving heavy siege guns. It is expected the next fight will be mainly artillery as we have some 600 pieces. I think (relying on what I can learn from those who ought to know) that the next battle will be at Corinth. We will beat them badly. It is reported that there has been considerable fighting between the pickets this afternoon, but it is almost impossible to know whether or not it is true.

I have not heard a word from you since the 3rd of April. I think there must be some delay in the mails as I know you have written me at least 5 times since then. I wish you to direct to me in future, "Cheney's Battery, 1st Reg. Ill. Lt. Artillery."

The boys are most all well. Some of them have what is termed here in camp, the Tennessee Quick Step or in other words the diarrhea. I never could spell it without a dictionary before me. I have had it and have never lost an hour from service. Have got rid of it by taking some rhubarb and was never better in my life. Tell the doctor that we have less sickness in our company that any other company that I know of. I attribute it to my acquaintance with him.

---

[i] Capt. David S. Pride of Oregon, IL, Co. I, 46th Illinois Infantry
[ii] Lieut. William H. Howell of Geneva, IL, Co. I, 46th Illinois Infantry, killed April 6, 1862 Shiloh, TN

I have just been to supper and will tell you what I had. A nice piece of fried lean ham, some stewed beans, crackers, butter, cheese and hot coffee. So you see that I have made a good supper. The fruit trees are in full blossom and look fine. The greatest disadvantage that we labor under is that a bad stench is created by the decaying of dead horses that have not been properly buried. However they are remedying it as fast as possible. I am not discouraged in the least but on the contrary am passing my time rather pleasantly. Don't want to come home till this job is completely and everlastingly finished so that our children may never be called upon to be separated from family and friends as I have been. I have never regretted for a moment that I have done as I have, hard as it was. When I get back Mary, home will be sweet. Never fear for me for I am training myself for coolness. You never saw a letter from me that is written with more steady nerve than this, although I am momentarily expecting orders to march to the front. I have changed very much in that respect since I left. So much so that I believe I can command my company in an engagement with as much coolness as I now write you. This may not sound well in other ears than yours. I only say it that you may not fear that I will become enraged and blindly rush into danger thereby sacrificing myself and perhaps my company and battery.

Remember me to all, Mother, Brother, and Sisters and our little folks. I expect Royce is making good progress with his studies and getting to be a tall boy. Gracie is getting so that she can almost creep and makes company for you all. All of you must keep in good spirits as we do, and all will end well.

It now looks as though it is going to rain some time and I fear we will have another muddy time again. Mary you never saw any mud yet. It is reported that several mules have been left in the mud and nothing to be seen but their ears. My sheet is full and I will bid you a good night. May you always be cheerful.

Affy. your husband,
John T. Cheney

Tell Pers that I must call my letters to you, to him also as I cannot find time to write to him yet.

J. T. C.

~ ~ ~ ~ ~

Pittsburg Landing, Tennessee
Sunday evening, April 20, 1862[i]

My dear Wife,

I have as yet received no letter from you that has been written since the 3rd of April. When I consider that we are only 4 days travel apart it seems very hard not to hear. Still I hope that ere long mail communication will be more regular than it has been, so that I can hear often. I wrote you on Friday evening and at the time, Bullock and Ballard[ii] were with me. It rained and was very dark, so they concluded to stay all night. We sat and talked till 10 o'clock, then lay down. Were talking when we heard what sounded like the retort from a musket, followed by the cry of "I'm shot" etc. We immediately went out and found John Nightlinger[iii] from Mendota, a member of my company who was acting as a corporal of the stable guard. He had been out to see that the horses were all right (lantern in hand). When within about 30 feet of my tent was shot in the hand making a very severe wound. It is a very mysterious affair, but supposed that the shot was prepared for a lieutenant in a Kentucky regiment, and Nightlinger was mistaken for him. We are trying to unravel the mystery but am fearful we will not succeed. I hope Nightlinger will not lose his hand. Still there is some danger of it.

It has rained continuously since Friday and apparently will continue to rain for a long time to come. The mud is dreadful. It will be impossible for our artillery to move forward. The roads are very bad indeed. You may be curious to know how I have spent the day. Well in the morning I put my flannel and stockings to soak, washed my towels, sewed the button on my pants, read the latest paper we could get (April 16), smoked and talked, took a walk to the river and back, and am improving the time before supper in writing. Lieut. Benn had just come into tent and says 75 Secesh prisoners have just passed toward the landing, that our pickets have just taken and brought in. So you see the pickets are pretty close on to each other. The Deacon has just come in. He has a little touch of the Tennessee Quick Step but is now nearly all right again, being a believer in rhubarb which has cured him.

---

[i] This letter is dated Sunday April 22, but Sunday was April 20. It mentions Nightlinger getting shot. Cheney's Monday April 21 letter says he took Nightlinger to the hospital boat. So this letter is the day before, i.e., Sunday April 20.

[ii] Lieut. James Ballard of Plainsfield, IL, Co. I, 46th Illinois Infantry

[iii] Pvt. John Nightlinger of Sublette, IL, Battery F, 1st Illinois Light Artillery

I wish Pers would get and send to us about 25 lbs. each of dried apple and dried peaches, 5 lbs. of good tea. I will stop now and countermand the order. Tell him not to send them as we can buy them here, and might not get them if he sends them. Yesterday I went to visit our colonel and found him a true gentleman - born in Hampton, New Hampshire. It seemed after talking with him a while as though I had known him a long time. My health continues good. If we could only see the sun and I could get a letter from home, I would be pleased.

The Tennessee River is a beautiful one. It only wants the enterprise and energy of bankers to make the country on its borders one of superior loveliness. You would be surprised to see the difference between even Tennesseans and Illinoisans. The difference between the improvements on their farms etc. Their houses are generally log and their dialect a cross between a Negro and a --- I don't know what.

I have not heard from you since I sent the photographs. I thought them very good only that my pants were badly wrinkled. Still I did not dress myself as for church. I presume they will suit you just as well. You may think strange of Lieut. Burton's sending more money home than I did. Well the reason was I was only paid as an officer 2 months or from the time we had 80 men, whereas lieutenants received pay from the time we had 40 men. The next time I can beat him. We have to buy our own provisions (the officers) and it costs us something. Still we get along cheaply.

I am filling this sheet with nothing of very great importance. Still the room is left on the sheet and as there is nothing particularity driving, I may as well be writing as looking out to see the almost intolerable rain and mud. Our poor horses have to stand out and take the storm, as it is impossible to get shelter for them.

I would like very much to step in and sit down to your table tonight, and take a good cup of tea with you all. Then take the old armchair and sit down, put my feet upon another chair or two chairs if handy, and smoke. Mother wouldn't we have a smoke! Don't think that I am dissatisfied or babyish for I am not, for that is what I always enjoyed, and would be particularly pleased with it tonight.

I have just sent to the sutlers for a dozen eggs and will have some boiled eggs, crackers and a cup of tea, then have my smoke. I don't drink any liquor or beer and find that I am as well off so far as most any of them. Still if I had good brandy or cherry bounce,[i] it would do me good, and I should drink it. Whisky sells at $1.00 per pint and will kill

---

[i] Cherry bounce is drink made of a mixture of cherries with rum, whiskey or other alcohol, and sugar

further than James' Rifled guns at that. I have got me a pair of long legged boots that come above my knees, a pair of Indian rubber leggings and poncho. So you see I am well protected from the weather. I will keep writing till I hear from you and hope Gracie is better than when you wrote last. Always tell me just how you all are and I will do the same. Remember me to all of the friends and particularly to our own family which includes all relatives. Good night Mary. I am coming back all right.

Affectionately yours,
John

~ ~ ~ ~ ~

Pittsburg Landing, Tennessee
Monday April 21, 1862

My dear Wife,

The boys have all gone to bed and I thought I would write you a few lines. The day has been a very stormy one. I have spent it in getting John Nightlinger to a hospital boat, reading papers, studying etc. Have got a kettle full of live coals before me to dry out the tent. Have just made and drank a cup of tea. Have my pipe lighted and on the whole am very comfortable. I think I have told you that we have 3 contrabands. Well Tom (one of the sharpest of them) discharged a musket in violation of orders this morning, and was sent to the guard house. We have trained him so that he believes he came from Dixon and knows all the localities in northern Illinois. In answer to the questions, he told them he came from Dixon, belonged to Capt. Cheney's Battery, was in the fight at Fort Donelson[i] etc. etc. They released him and sent him back again. So much for Negro wit.[ii]

The roads are so very bad that it will be impossible for our army to move for some days yet. I am writing to you very often and can only say I will continue to do so just as long as I have time. I see no prospect of a change in the weather. You can conclude that when the letters stop coming, we have fine weather. Some of our boys are unwell, but none of them much sick. We have a good surgeon by the name of Andrews[iii]

---

[i] Battery F was not at Fort Donelson – that Battle was Feb. 11-16, 1862, while they were still in Illinois at Camp Butler
[ii] John Cheney, while a stanch abolitionist, possessed the racial stereotypes and prejudices of his day
[iii] Surgeon Edmund Andrews of Chicago, IL, 1st Illinois Light Artillery

from Chicago, who is very attentive to the men. My own health is first rate.

I do not hear a word from home yet. Still I live in hope that at some time not far distant, I shall. Give my love to the dear ones at home and keep good cheer. Good night my dear.

Affy. your husband,
Jno. T. Cheney

~ ~ ~ ~ ~

Field of Shiloh
April 28, 1862

My dear Wife,

It has been one week this evening since I wrote you. I have been busy drilling, moving, making out reports, payrolls etc. We moved yesterday morning to this spot 4 miles nearer the enemy. Are now in the front in Gen. Lew Wallace's division. We got orders today to cook 3 days rations and form in line of battle immediately. I called the boys out to see how many were willing to go and work when we should meet the enemy. They all were eager for the fight. In 15 minutes the order was countermanded, and we were ordered to be in readiness to leave on an hour's notice. I have no doubt but that you will hear of some fighting by the time you will receive this.

I have not heard a word from you since I came here and it is getting almost intolerable to wait so long. If I could only hear from home I should feel better. If it even contained bad news, I would be relieved in a measure from suspense. My health is first rate yet, and the health of the boys are generally well. The weather is good again which is some satisfaction.

We have just heard of the victory at New Orleans and you may be assured that the boys are having a good time over it. It is also now reported that *Beaury*[i] is retreating toward Memphis. If so we will probably make a forced march for Memphis. Doubtful things are uncertain, so we cannot tell what we may do or where we may go. If we can only have good weather, I care not where we go or when, but I dislike so much rain.

I wish you to direct "Cheney's Battery, Wallace's Division, Tenn. River, In the field." I hope you will have better luck in getting my

---

[i] *Beaury* is Confederate *Gen. Beauregard*, commander of the Army of Mississippi at Corinth

letters than I do in getting yours. Give my love to all the friends and the babies. God bless them in particular. Hope Gracie is well again.

Bennett[i] has just got a letter from Dixon dated 24th April and Burton has one dated 13th day of April, and none for me. I feel worse than before they got theirs. Still I will do as I have learned to do; make the best of it. If we leave you will not probably hear from me again under 10 days. Good cheer and hope will keep you all right. Good night Mary and may God bless you and ours.

Affy. your husband,
Jno. T. Cheney

Summary

While John Cheney had just missed participating in the Battle of Shiloh, he did see its destruction and grisly remains. The prospect of carnage such as Shiloh made him introspective. The battlefield strengthened his desire to get on with the fight he had signed up for. His spirits and his health were good.

Cheney expressed no regard for Southern civilian property. He espoused the practice, later made famous by Sherman, of creating hardship for civilians in order to reduce the Confederacy's resolve to wage war.

---

[i] Pvt. Frederick W. Bennett of Dixon, Battery F, 1st Illinois Light Artillery

Chapter 4 - Advance on Corinth, Mississippi

May 7, 1862 to May 29, 1862

Background

On April 29, 1862 Maj. Gen. Halleck began his deliberate and defensive advance on Corinth. Halleck commanded the Army of the Tennessee (Grant), the Army of the Ohio (Buell) and the Army of the Mississippi (Pope).

Cheney's Battery continued to be part of Maj. Gen. Lew Wallace's 3rd Division in Grant's Army of the Tennessee.

Army of the Tennessee in the Field
Near Corinth, Mississippi
May 7th 1862[i]

My dear Wife,

Your kind letter of 19th ult. was received on the 3rd inst. Who brought it I do not know as it came through the division postmaster to me. It is the first letter I have received from you since we left Benton Barracks. You may be assured that never could a man feel better pleased to hear from home than I was. I should have answered it sooner only that we received marching orders on the morning of the 4th.

We started at 9 o'clock AM and at about 10 o'clock the rain poured in torrents. The roads were already bad, and the rain made them almost impassable for artillery. However we worked all day and at night had got 3 miles. We pitched tents at dark. I went and cut 4 crotched stakes, put some poles across them, spread my blanket and had as good a night's rest as I ever had on the best bed in the house. It rained all night but fortunately in the morning the sun shone and we were again on the march, cutting our way through timber, bridging streams etc. That day (5th) we made 3 miles more and are now very

---

[i] Note this letter is actually dated April not May. But on April 7, 1862 Cheney and the Battery were in the middle of a steamboat trip to Pittsburg Landing. The postmark on the cover is May 13 at Cairo, Illinois.

comfortably encamped in the timbers on high ground. We are 12 miles from Corinth and expect marching orders at any moment.

The great battle would undoubtedly have been fought ere this, only for the horrid conditions of the roads. I feel very anxious for the contest to come, as it will be over the sooner. We all have the utmost confidence in the success of our arms in the coming contest. If we succeed it does seem as though the backbone of the Rebellion is broken. Our boys are in fine spirits and it is no uncommon remark that our boys look so healthy. Lieut. Burton is very healthy and is emphatically an efficient and energetic officer. Some of the boys have just returned from a foraging[i] expedition and brought a nice 250 lb. porker in, so fresh pork for breakfast.

There are a thousand little incidents in camp that I would gladly relate had I the time to do so, but when I get home we will talk it all over. You have probably heard that Henry Horn[ii] is sick. Well he is gaining and will soon be with us. As I have never received a line from you except the one of the 19th, of course I know but little of what has transpired since I left. However I hope your letters will get along sometime.

It is getting dark and I must close. Keep good courage and go about more; time will pass more pleasantly. Give my love to all the friends and the dear little ones in particular.

Affectionately yours,
Jack

~ ~ ~ ~ ~

Army of the Tennessee in the Field
May 8, 1862

My dear Wife,

Your letter of the 18th and 27th ult. came to hand today. I am glad to know that you have at last heard from me. You say that you suppose I am very busy, but hope I will find time to write. Well Mary I believe this is the 10th letter I have written to you since I came to Pittsburg. I wrote you yesterday and hardly know what to write tonight, but could not refrain from writing something, as I am so pleased to learn that you are in better spirits. I began to think I would not hear from you till I got home. Then when I did hear; I feared you would not hear from me, so

---

[i] Foraging is scouring the local towns and farms for food for the troops or horses
[ii] Bugler Henry Horn of Dixon IL, Battery F, 1st Illinois Light Artillery

you would be worried almost to death. But it is all right now and I hope we will be more fortunate in future.

Our advance is within 3 ½ miles of Corinth and a dance is expected to commence at almost any moment. This time we are not to be surprised as Gen. Halleck is here and on the alert, ever watchful, and making preparations on a magnificent scale to give them fits. We learn from the Chicago and St Louis papers that Corinth is being evacuated by *Beaury*, but we know nothing of it here. On the contrary we believe he is preparing to give us the best he has got.

We are in the 3rd Division under Gen. Lew Wallace. His division constitutes a part of the army of the reserve, so you see we shall not open the ball, but will be called to face any of the enemy who may attempt to flank us. We are under a wide awake, fighting general, and will be bravely led. I hope we may as bravely follow. It has been very pleasant for the past two days. If it continues fair, my opinion is that within 48 hours we will see the elephant.[i] I long for the contest to come, as it will the sooner be over, and I want to see "how the cat will jump." Lieut. Benn (I believe I wrote) met with an accident. Shot his finger badly and has gone down the river on a hospital boat. Lieut. Smyth is also sick in hospital at Hamburg,[ii] with bilious[iii] fever, not dangerously. So you see Lieut. Burton and myself are the only commissioned officers now with the company. If we get into a fight and any success attends our efforts, no old soldier[iv] can claim any credit. We are going to fight successfully and come out all right.

You may perhaps be curious to know what prices we pay for the luxuries of life. Well butter 40 cts., crackers 25 per lb., eggs 30 cts. per dozen, cheese 25 per lb., dried apple 20 cts., and other things in proportion. The Deacon says the way they make lemonade is to anchor a box of lemons and 10 lbs. of sugar about a mile up the river and then dip it out at the landing for 3 weeks at 10 cts. per glass. I think the Deacon more than half right. We are badly cheated by sutlers. Still the goods must be had and we are obliged to pay what they ask us.

Give my love to all friends and keep all right in mind, then your physical health will be good. I feel so relieved to know that we can hear from each other again, that I hardly know what to write. Now don't fear to look at the papers, but on the contrary look with confidence expect-

---

[i] The expression "see the elephant" here means be in combat for the first time
[ii] Hamburg Landing, Tennessee on the Tennessee River is a short distance upriver from Pittsburg Landing
[iii] Bilious is liver dysfunction; might include jaundice
[iv] Lieut. Benn was a veteran of the Mexican War

ing to hear a good account of us. My own health is good. Henry Horn has gone down the river to some hospital we don't know where. They left word that he was better and would soon be back. Willett O. Loveland,[i] Mrs. Watson's son, is with them and is getting better. We are all in good spirits and though we want for many little luxuries, still we complain not. We really lack, but little, having all that is really necessary for health and comfort.

You write me for some of my hair. Well you will be obliged to wait for it to grow as I keep it close to my head. I would have to shave close to my head and then not get enough to make a shadow. I'll tell you what is best to do under all the circumstances, viz.[ii] for you and I to keep cool and let my hair grow.

I sent some money by a Mr. Petrie of Ogle County on the 20th and he told me he would call and hand it to you. I hope he has done so before this. I have been out to the front examining the rifle pits and find that precautions have been made on such a scale that we cannot be driven.

As we move along toward Corinth we find graves in which the Secesh buried their dead on their retreat. Their losses must have been severe, as also were ours. Lieut. Col. Jones has gone to the hospital boat sick, but not dangerously.

I had for supper tonight fried ham, mashed potatoes, black tea, sugar, cold rice, doughnuts, butter and hard bread. So you see I am not suffering for the want of food. We have a good cook by the name of Carey.[iii] He is an old Englishman and neat as wax.[iv] I could get my washing done by the colored boys, but I prefer to do it myself. Then I know it is done well. I will do as I have done, write as often as I can and know you will do likewise. Good Night Mary.

Yours,
John

~ ~ ~ ~ ~

---

[i] Pvt. Willett O. Loveland of Dixon, IL, Battery F, 1st Illinois Light Artillery

[ii] Viz is a Latin abbreviation meaning "namely"

[iii] Carey could be either Benjamin or George Carey – both of Dixon, IL and privates in Battery F, 1st Illinois Light Artillery

[iv] 'neat as wax' alludes to the fact that the wax cells of bees exemplify neatness and good order

My dear Wife,

I received your letter of the 29th ult. last night and was as ever delighted to hear from home and friends. Jim also received one, of one day later date in which she – Lib – acknowledges the receipt of the money we sent. There has been considerable skirmishing[i] the first week, and some pretty sharp, though there has been no general engagement as yet. We expect a hard fight. Both armies will fight with desperation, as on its result depends in an excess measure, the time which the war will continue. The weather is fine though it is getting very hot. The roads are getting very good. If a general engagement comes off before another rain, we will have a fair show to get our troops along, and have an equal show with them.

I am glad to hear that Margaret is at home again and hope she will stay, as she is much company for you and Gracie. See that she has what she needs. I got part of my pay for recruiting; all that I ever will get. And my wages up to March 1st. So that I am now entitled to about $300 up to May 1st, which I will get very soon after the battle at Corinth.

You ask if I do not think the war will soon be ended, if we succeed in taking Yorktown[ii] and Corinth. Well Mary I think it must, as I do not see how they can keep their army together after such reverses. We learn that Yorktown is ours and it now remains for us to give them Jessie[iii] at Corinth, which we are determined to do.

I wish you would say to the doctor that Jim and I do not propose to die, as long as we can possibly prevent it. I am glad to hear that you are in better spirits. I am glad to hear that you have faith to believe that all will be well in the end. We have now with us a member of the Sanitary Commission from Ohio; Dr. Prentice from Cleveland. He is provisioning us with many things that we need, such as socks, preserved fruit, rhubarb, lemons, salt and lots of luxuries. God bless him. Our own state has sent boat loads of such things, but not a man of the Commission has been seen in our division, as not a dimes worth of provisions have we received from them. This may be strange to you at home sending, as you are, so many luxuries. What becomes of them God knows, but He has not told us. The doctor only needs to know that we are Union men and in the Federal Army, which ensures us some of his stores.

---

[i] Skirmishing is combat between small groups of detached troops
[ii] Yorktown, Virginia was taken as part of Maj. Gen. McClellan's unsuccessful Peninsula campaign aimed at Richmond
[iii] "Give them Jessie" was an expression used at the time

The boys are generally well although some of them are hobbled with the Quick Step. I heard from Henry Horn. He is getting well fast and will be with us this week. My health is first rate, and I never was in better spirits in the world now that I am hearing from home. I am glad Pers was pleased with my letter. Also that he has got the trains[i] again. Should think he might do well. Tell him to send me a glass of ale.

I learn this morning that one Coyle,[ii] a member of Capt. Stevens Company from Dixon died yesterday in the hospital of fever. I also learn that Maj. Appington[iii] of Polo in Col. Noble's[iv] cavalry was shot day before yesterday and his body had been sent home. I do not know when we may be called into action, but when the call comes most all of our boys will anxiously[v] bounce in. It is reported that Gen. Curtis' division are coming up the river. If so we will soon see the 13th, which will be a pleasure indeed. I will write you often as possible. Give my love to the children and all the family, and my friends who may inquire for me. I learn that business is improving in Dixon and am glad to hear that it is. Good morning, keep the spirits up.

Affectionately your husband,
John T. Cheney

~ ~ ~ ~ ~

Army of the Tenn. in the Field
Near Monterey
May 14th 1862

My dear Wife,

Writing in camp is not attended with all the conveniences that I used to have at home. Still it is a pleasure to sit down on my camp stool and take a company book on my knee, and pen in hand to write to you a few lines. Your letter of 29th ult. was received on the 12th inst. I was very glad to hear that you were well and trying to make yourself as happy as possible. I have nothing specifically new to write you concerning the Army of the Tennessee, except that it is moving along moderately, fortifying as it moves. I trust when the engagement comes off, those who are impatient to hear of a battle at Corinth will see that it

---

[i] Perhaps a reference to Person Cheney getting a concession to supply trains with food
[ii] Pvt. John Coyle of Dixon, IL, Co. H, 46th Illinois Infantry
[iii] Maj. Zenas Applington of Polo, IL, HQ, 7th Illinois Cavalry
[iv] Col. Silas Noble of Dixon, 2nd Illinois Cavalry
[v] For Cheney, "anxiously" means "eagerly" rather than "fearfully"

is all right, and that Gen. Halleck fully realizes the extent of the work he has to accomplish. And has made ample preparations and done it to the active satisfaction of all interested in our prosperity. I have since I came into the field, learned to find no fault with slow movements, though sometimes I wish we could move a little faster, and finish the job at once. Still a safe game is the one to play. We have not removed our camp since I wrote you last, though we keep 3 days rations cooked, and are in readiness to move at a moments notice.

The weather is very fine, only a little too hot. Roads very good again. We expect soon to be able to give you an account of the great battle. The news from Yorktown, Norfolk, Portsmouth, New Orleans etc. has inspired our troops with new courage. Be assured they will fight as never men fought yet, if necessary. When we have beaten them at Corinth it seems as though the game must be nearly, if not quite blocked.

I received a letter from Pers last evening of May 1st. I was glad to hear from him. Tell him to write me often, and consider my letter to you as answers to his, as I cannot write to anyone unless obliged to. We are spending our time drilling and have got so that we can handle a battery quite well; at least we think so. Pers writes me that you stand my absence quite well, but says Lib has no control over her feelings. I have not let you see his letter, but if I could see her, I would give her Jessie.

Lib Vesper you ought to be whipped for fretting as much as you do. You can change nothing. You make yourself miserable. You make those about you uncomfortable. Jim is not terrified; on the contrary, is injured by such giving way to sadness. Finally there is no earthly use in such foolishness. I hope to hear that you have concluded to use a small portion of your common sense, and become a rational woman, practicing the doctrine you believe, making yourself and those in whose society you move, happy. This is plain talk, but is no more than ought to be said. Now Lib you can get mad and say it is none of my business, or you can turn it off with a laugh, in either case it is better than to worry worry worry.

Thursday morning 15th. I was called away from writing last night so thought I would write you a few lines this morning. We go to Pittsburg this afternoon to get some extra ammunition. I doubt not that in a very short time, we will be at work on Corinth. Although it is going to be a good deal of a job to "bring her to Limerick."[i] Still she

---

[i] Bring to Limerick is to do what needs doing

must and will come, and I think with far less loss of life than at Pittsburg.

It is still fine weather, only very hot. The surgeon who attends our battery says we have less sickness than any other in the division. My own health continues first rate. We have lost no men except Murphlett[i] who died at Springfield. Lieuts. Benn and Smyth are both away sick. I learn that Mr. Lanborn and his son have been discharged and gone home. They visited our camp most every day, and did not even come round to inform us that they were going home, after getting a discharge, although they went within two rods[ii] of our camp in going to the river.

Has Royce got well of his cough? Does Gracie croup?[iii] Is Lib crying? Is Marg laughing at her? Does Mother's leg get better?

We expect to be paid again after the fight at Corinth. Give my love to all the friends who may inquire, and expect an early account of the fight from me as soon as it is over, as I will give you all the particulars so far as I can learn them. We have a good surgeon; plenty of bandages. But I don't believe we shall have much use for either in our company, as we will be supported[iv] by 2 of the best regiments of infantry that are in the service.

If you hear from Tom,[v] I wish you would send his letter, as it seems so much better than to just hear a word in your letters from him. I see he has been engaged in a pretty severe fight,[vi] and feel anxious to learn how he likes it so far as he has been. I hope you may all keep in good health and spirits, as I am coming home in that shape, and want to find you the same. Good morning and as Royce used to say, "good yuck."

John

I will write you again next Sunday unless we get marching orders sooner. Isaac Little[vii] is here in our camp today and is well. William

---

[i] Pvt. P. T. Murphlett of Prophetstown, IL, Battery F, 1st Illinois Light Artillery

[ii] Rod is a unit of measure equal to 16 1/2 feet

[iii] Croup is difficult breathing and hoarse cough

[iv] Artillery could not defend itself in an engagement; it was the job of infantry to prevent the artillery from being overrun by the enemy

[v] Lieut. Thomas Cheney of Holderness, NH, Co. A, 6th New Hampshire Infantry, the brother of John Cheney

[vi] Thomas Cheney was part of Burnside's North Carolina Expedition at the Battle of Roanoke Island, February 7-8, 1862

[vii] Musician Isaac Little of Dixon, IL, Co. H, 46th Illinois Infantry

White is also well. If I had a little good butter and some milk for my tea this morning, I should like it, but I don't miss it as much as I did.

John

~ ~ ~ ~ ~

Headquarters Cheney's Battery
Army of the Tenn.
May 18, 1862

My dear Wife,

Your letter of 8th inst. came to hand last night, and as ever, I was very glad to hear from you. Though you were not in quite as good spirits as usual; I suppose because you thought I was not receiving your letters. Well Mary, the letters have all been received, and come along quite regularly now, so that you may not worry about that. Jim has been a little negligent about writing. I gave him a regular blowing up, though it is a good deal of a task to write in camp. He will write today and oftener in future. If I am sick or wounded, you will be informed at once. So you may not expect me to keep anything of the kind from you.

We had heavy skirmishing yesterday and some firing this morning. A general engagement must come very soon; I think about tomorrow. You will undoubtedly hear of the result before you receive this. If I am wounded, a request will be made to have a telegraphic dispatch sent to you at once. I believe that even should I get wounded, it would be better for you to know it at once than to live in suspense.

I have long since learned to take better care of my health than in former years. I now see the benefit of it, and have no fears of sickness. We lose more men from disease than in battle, and I am inclined to think 5 to one. Our surgeon says we have less sickness that any other company, except one. That is Willard's[i] Co. A of Chicago, who have got used to the climate etc. Maj. Willard of Chicago is chief of artillery in our division and we are under his command. I like the Major very well and think we will stand a fair show in his report to General Wallace.

I will continue to write you just as often as possible and hope you may be fortunate enough to receive my letters. I wish I could step in and see you all, and particularly you and the children. They are a treasure under any circumstances, but under present circumstances, what a treasure to you. I am glad to know that Gracie knows me, as it would be too bad to come home and have her afraid of me. I am glad

---

[i] Willard's Battery is Battery A, 1st Illinois Light Artillery, Maj. Charles M. Willard of Chicago, IL

Royce is learning well and hope he may be strong and healthy. If he should not, I would advise that he be taken out of school, though you know what is best about all those matters.

I am glad to hear that you are getting out round to the Post Office, Waverly[i] etc. and would advise that you get out just as much as you can, for it is far better than to sit and watch my photograph. I confidently expect to get home before the snow flies. To get home, and stay at home, as I cannot see how the Rebel army can be kept together long if we whip them at Corinth, which we are bound to do. Then Mary, I think that as highly as I have always appreciated home and family, I will appreciate it still more highly. It would probably be impossible for me to get a furlough, and if I could, I doubt if I would do it. I do not feel as though I would fancy coming home to stay a short time, and then break away again. So you may not expect to see me till we are mustered out of the service.

The weather is still fine and roads good except most awful dusty. My dinner is ready and I will eat and then finish.

I have had some stewed beans, rye bread, fried pork, can lobster (which reminded me of the last one we ate together in Worcester) and pickles.

I have just learned that the firing yesterday was to get possession of a creek that the Rebels had been using to water stock at. It seems they had quite a force there. 75 head of cattle were driven down to water, when a brigade under command of Gen. Smith made a dash at them. After a hard fought battle, the Rebels were repulsed with considerable loss of life, their 75 head of cattle, and also their favorite watering place. The 8th Missouri lost 8 killed and 30 wounded. Have not heard from the other regiment. This afternoon Capt. Cogswell[ii] of Ottawa, Capt. Wallace brother to Gen. Wallace, Lieut. Burton and myself are going to take a ride out to the front. When I come in, I will write more if I see anything of interest.

I have been to Gen. Wallace's headquarters. He refused to give me a pass to go to the front, as he had just let one artillery captain go, and he said if any battery was called for today, mine would go, so you see I am cheated out of my ride. Well I have had a supper of beans, good bread (self raising), maple sugar and a good cup of tea. It is a fine evening. If I could take my family and take a stroll into the woods, it

---

[i] Waverly is the Waverly House hotel in Dixon, IL operated by John's brother Person Cheney

[ii] Capt. William Cogswell of Ottawa, IL, Cogswell's Battery, Independent Illinois Light Artillery

would be a pleasure indeed. But all is well that ends well, so I will not allow myself to think of it more than I can possibly help. When we are reunited we will talk war matters, home matters etc. to our hearts content.

Give my love to every one of our friends and relatives and say to them that the reason I do not write to them personally is not because they are forgotten, but because my first duty is to my family. They must consider each letter to you as for each and every one. Frank is waiting to get the letters to take to the office, so good night and good health and spirits attend you.

Your husband,
John

~ ~ ~ ~ ~

Army of the Tenn. in the Field
May 22, 1862

Dear Mary,

Since I wrote you last, we have moved our camp a little toward the front. Have a beautiful camping ground, and have just got righted up again. So thought I would write you a few lines. We had a very heavy rain Sunday night. Having some fear of an attempt to disturb us, my battery and two others were ordered into position, which was soon done. The men at the guns all night. A picket of infantry were thrown out to give the alarm if necessary. No attack was made and consequently nobody hurt.

Yesterday Gen. Smith and his brigade wanted possession of a hill in our front that the enemy commanded, and moved forward when they were opened upon by a siege battery. They returned and brought up a battery of Parrott[i] guns when the firing was terrific for about 15 minutes. The Rebels thinking discretion the better part of valor, skedaddled,[ii] and our men are fortifying said hill. I have not learned the loss on either side.

Our battery was yesterday visited by Gov. Yates, Sec. Hatch,[iii] and Prof. Pope with several other gentlemen. Had a very pleasant interview. Dick Yates is a true patriot and I feel proud that we have a governor who has so much of the milk of human kindness in him. In these days,

---

[i] Parrott is a cannon designed by Robert Parrott; with a distinctive reinforcing band around the breech
[ii] Skedaddle is to run away; to flee in panic
[iii] Illinois Secretary of State Ozias M. Hatch

when the man, the patriot, become buried and absorbed in the politician, it does seem refreshing to find some who do not lose their manhood by success politically. Such a man is Richard Yates, who is the same as when soliciting our votes for a Republican president, and Governor on the stump.

We know about as little of where we may go, or when we may be moved, as you do. It is for us to be ready to move at a moment's warning, asking no questions. This is a very fine morning. Where we are, we have a fine view of the country for some two miles to the west. We are to be paid tomorrow. I will try and find someone from Springfield to take our money to Springfield and express from there to Dixon. I will be able to send you $200. If you like, you can keep it quiet. Let Jacob Powell have it and take his note for it, after paying 20 to Lynch, the remainder of Jim Ash's, and $15 to Charlie Smith. They all want to be endorsed on notes held by them. Jim Ash's note will be taken up. Use all you want and pray don't go without anything you need.

My own health is first rate. If Pers wants to glean some items from this to publish, wish he would do so. Good morning, love to babies and folks, and good cheer always Mary, for it is far better than to look at the dark side. I am coming out all right. We will spend the mid-day and evening of our days with our children, in a country and under a government that can withstand any shock, and overcome any and all difficulties. This will repay us, won't it?

Jno. T. Cheney

~ ~ ~ ~ ~

Army of the Tenn.
Sunday evening, May 25th 1862

My dear Wife,

Your letter of 17th inst. has just come to hand. I have got a box fixed up to write on, and will try and answer. I have not worked very hard today. Went to the division hospital to see 2 or 3 of our sick boys and found them all improving rapidly. The hospital is some six miles in our rear.

We have not moved since I wrote you last, but I think our stay will be short. It may be possible after all that you may see me before June is past. Still Mary don't expect it quite so soon, as that is not quite probable, though it is all possible. I will be glad to get home if our work is done, but not without, unless on a short furlough after the Corinth fight.

The weather is still fine and roads good. Occasionally a rainy day to settle dust. We know just as much about when the attack will be made as ever, and no more. I received a letter from Henry Horn today and suppose he has left for the Army before this, so will not write him. If the boys have not started, tell them we will be very glad to see them. I miss Henry particularly as he is the only bugler I had, and it makes my work much harder, beside a great inconvenience to the whole company.

We got paid yesterday, and the company sent home over $1500, which we think is pretty good for one company out of two months pay. I sent you $275 and $15 for the Deacon. I have got plenty left to last me 2 months longer. Drew $310.50 for 2 months wages – pretty good. I have forgotten whether I told you to pay Lynch or not. You can pay him $20 or $25 to be endorsed on his note.

I do not expect to always be able to write as often, and as long as I have done the last 6 weeks, but as long as I can get time and facilities, will do the best I can. I watch the mail with a great deal of anxiety. If a letter is received from you, all is right. If not I think, well it will come tomorrow. Remember this and make it all right as often as possible. When I was going to the hospital today, met the mail carrier, and told him I would thrash him if he had no letter in the mail. I got the letter as a matter of course.

I hope before another Sunday, this suspense will be over and the great battle fought. It is a lovely evening and the boys are all in bed. I am at the front of my tent in my shirt-sleeves, boots off and taking the fresh air to my heart's content. It is a beautiful sight to look from the top of the hill upon the surrounding encampments. I wish you could be here to sit by my side and look upon the same grand sight. But as that cannot be, you will imagine you see it all, and I will tell you the rest in June or some other month.

Give my love to all the friends, and particularly our own family. I wish I could see Brother's darling little angel[i] and Brother[ii] too. Well I can look at their pictures, and that only serves to make me want to see them the more. Still it is a pleasure to look at them I assure you. My health is first rate. I believe I am as good for a rough time of it, as anyone in the company. Write often and long letters.

Affectionately your husband,
Jno. T. Cheney

~ ~ ~ ~ ~

---

[i] Grace Cheney
[ii] Royce Cheney

Army of the Tenn. in the Field
May 29, 1862

My dear Wife,

I looked for a letter last night and tonight, but was doomed to disappointment. None came. I thought as I did not get a letter I would write one. Lieut. Burton has received two since I got one, which makes me feel all the worse. But I suppose in a day or two I will get a gust of them all at once. Since I wrote you before, there has been considerable skirmishing. Our whole lines have been advanced a mile, and some shelling done. We, as I told you, are in the army of the reserve. I expect we will move to the extreme right when a general engagement commences. We are in a brigade with the Chicago Light Artillery Co. A and have the 11th, 23rd and 25th Indiana Infantry regiments for supporters, all tried and true. Last night cannonading commenced at 10 o'clock PM and was kept up till 4 o'clock AM this morning. I spent 2 or 3 hours of the time in listening, watching the rockets etc. I hoped a general engagement would commence this morning, but was disappointed.

The weather is quite hot. The health of the boys is quite good, and my own is first rate. While I write - 8:30 PM - one of the boys is playing a flute, and a lot of the boys dancing. We are getting so that we live just as well as men need to, except butter, milk and a few such luxuries. We are getting good fresh beef, salt beef, have good earth ovens. You would be surprised to see the pies and bread the boys bake. It is so nice and so much better than hard bread. I expect we will have to pull up stakes in a day or two. And I hope to soon finish this job so far as Corinth is concerned. The Rebels are undoubtedly short for rations and also for water, drawing water by railroad.

I want so much to see you, but will not allow myself to think of it more than I can possibly help. You must keep good courage and go about with little Gracie and Royce just as much as you can, hoping that ere long we will be together again. I'm well. We drill daily and are kept busy. Give my love to all of the folk and a few thousand kisses for the babies. I can almost see little Gracie and Royce playing together, and the little darling says Pa, almost loud enough for me to hear her. Good night my dear wife. Angels will guard you.

Affectionately yours,
John

Mary will you send me about 30 postage stamps and I will return them again.

Summary

Cheney was a Republican. The Civil War was precipitated because a Republican – Lincoln – had been elected President.

Historically, Southern politicians believed that if slavery was to survive it needed to expand. If all new states admitted to the Union were free, then eventually the South would lack sufficient political power to maintain slavery against Northern opposition. Thus it was vital to the South that about an equal number of slave states and free states be created during the westward expansion of the United States.

The Missouri Compromise of 1820/21 admitted Missouri as a slave state and Maine as free state. The compromise also stipulated that no future states created out of the Louisiana Purchase, and located north of the southern boundary of Missouri, could be slave states.

The Kansas Nebraska Act of 1854 created two territories – Kansas and Nebraska. The Act specified that the residents of the territories could determine whether to be free or slave. The expectation was that Nebraska would be free and Kansas – west of Missouri and north of the southern boundary of Missouri – would be slave. The Kansas Nebraska Act repealed the sections of the Missouri compromise forbidding slavery north of Missouri's southern border.

In 1854 the Republican Party was formed out of Democrats that opposed the Kansas Nebraska Act, and radical parts of the Whig Party, plus the Free Soil Party. The latter party opposed the expansion of slavery into the territories acquired from Mexico. Limiting the expansion of slavery was a core tenant of the new Republican Party.

The election of Republican President Lincoln in 1860 was a serious political loss for slave states. Most of the South rejected the results of the election by seceding.

Chapter 5 - Back to Tennessee

June 5, 1863 to September 6, 1862

Background

The anticipated engagement at Corinth, Mississippi did not occur. *Gen. Beauregard* evacuated his troops and supplies. On May 30, 1862 Maj. Gen. Halleck's forces moved into the abandoned town. Cheney's unit subsequently returned to Tennessee.

Bolivar, Tenn.
June 5th 1862

My dear Wife,

Your kind letter of 25th ult. was received in due season. I was so glad to hear from home again, and know that you were all well. Tell Royce I hope he will not be quite so tired when he writes again, for I am always very glad to receive his letters.

I wish you would write as soon as Gracie gets so as to creep. I do wish I could see her. I was very glad to hear that Mother is better. Hope she may recover entirely. You say that Lieut. Benn called on you, and was to come to us the next week. He has not got here yet. When he comes, I will take the medicine and also the wine. You said that you really hoped there would be no fighting at Corinth, but that we would surround the enemy and force them to surrender. Well instead of forcing them to surrender, we have let them slip through our fingers. Although my opinion is that it is about as well (though evidentially not intentional on the part of Gen. Halleck) as we have taken quite a lot of prisoners. The effect of such a retreat upon the army (Rebel) is disastrous. They are deserting daily, and I have no doubt their army will become decimated more by that skedaddle than it would have been had we fought and driven them. Corinth is evacuated and nobody hurt.

One rather curious incident occurred, which I will relate. In Gen. Pope's division was a battery of 32 pds. Parrott guns that had not been tested. On Friday morning (30th ult.) Col. Dubois (chief of artillery, Gen. Halleck's staff) went out to put them in position, just to test them. He give them a good elevation, directed them toward Corinth, and fired. The distance from Corinth was two miles. The first shot struck a railroad engine, entirely demolishing it, and killing the engineer. I suppose the Corinthians thought the Devil was to pay, if we had guns that would do such execution at such a distance.

On Sunday morning 1st inst, Lieut. Burton and myself mounted our horses and spent the entire day in looking over the town and surroundings of Corinth. The town had been entirely deserted. Not a person (except one Negro woman) nor an article of furniture (of any value) had been left. Some pork, sugar, molasses, camp equipage, corn (which was burning) was left indicting that they left in quite a hurry. Corinth is a young town, said to be four years old. Had contained some 1500 inhabitants, and should think had been quite a place for business. I left the town satisfied that the Rebels had intended to make a strong fight, it having been strongly fortified. They were suffering for the want of water, and believed they could do better by leaving, and drawing us a little more southward. Well we shall see, what we shall see.

Lieut. and I got to camp at about 10 PM, tired and were just getting ready to retire, when orders came to prepare to march (with 3 days cooked rations) at daylight on the morning of the 2nd. We were ready, but did not leave till 12 noon. We took a northwesterly direction, and made through the worst of roads, 5 miles the first half day. At night it rained very hard and we camped under our cannon, wagons etc., not having time to pitch tents. Next morning we were on the move again at about noon (3rd inst.).

Passed through Purdy,[i] a very pretty town on the Mobile and Ohio Railroad. Here the inhabitants were of all shades from fair white complexion to as black a Negro as I ever saw, indicating that the South are really fighting for the liberty or liberties they have so long enjoyed. I can see the point now. The places of business were all closed. Many people standing on the corner of the streets, no demonstration of any kind being made. The truth is there is but little Union feeling or sentiment here. The more we coax and try to persuade the rascals by friendly legislation, the harder they will fight us. I have become no more an admirer of Southern institutions than when in Illinois.

On the night of the 3rd we camped 18 miles east of Bolivar.[ii] On the 4th marched through a rough hilly country to the Hatchie River. Today are in Bolivar in camp, where we will probably remain about 4 days unless disturbed by the enemy, our supply train having returned

---

[i] Purdy, Tennessee is 24 miles north of Corinth, Mississippi
[ii] Bolivar, Tennessee is 66 miles east of Memphis

after forage.[i] The force here consists only of Gen. Wallace's Division. Bolivar is a very pretty town on the Hatchie River, and Mississippi Central Railroad, on high ground. The male inhabitants have generally gone into the Confederate army.

June 7th. Our officers have obtained much valuable information from Negroes. While I write our horses are eating Secesh corn that will not cost the government very much. The railroad company have not tried to run a train over the road, it being in our possession, as is also the telegraph. Gen. Wallace has captured quite a quantity of sugar, corn etc. The inhabitants really believe that they are whipping us at every point. It is surprising how ignorant of the true state of things they are. They concede that the Western boys will fight, but New Englanders they believe to be consummate cowards.

Where we will go from here I do not know, but rather suppose to-ward Memphis. Water very good, and very little sickness in camp. I have been in my saddle since Sunday morning. Feel very tired, but my health was never better. The trip across the country, I consider worth a great deal to me, obtaining a better idea of Southern character than could be obtained in any other way. The inhabitants are not pleased with our remaining here as our pickets surround the town, and their friends in the army find it impossible to come and visit them. We have taken 3 lieutenants prisoners, who were lurking about to learn what they could. The Negroes are very communicative, and in many instances utterly refuse to work, evidently supposing that we have come to liberate them from bondage. I saw a lady slave yesterday, the property of a Secesh colonel who is as white as many of the ladies of Dixon.

We are asked 40 cts. per lb. for lard, $1.00 for butter, which amounts to not selling it to us, as the boys cannot afford it. They mean that we shall have nothing to eat if they can, by high prices preventing our buying. The first day we came, our cook bought butter at $1 per lb. and milk at 5 cts. per qt. They in some instances refuse to sell at any price, asserting that they dare not do it less they be arrested and punished. I have a most excellent cook, who knows how to milk. Thus you will conclude that as often as once a day, I get a nice dish of bread and milk. Our boys have never been so healthy since we left Camp Butler as they are now. I doubt not we will enjoy good health through the summer. We have seen no fighting yet, but are ready.

---

[i] Forage is hay or grain - food for domestic animals

I have just learned that the mail leaves this morning and must close, though there were some other things I wished to say. Give my love to all the friends and direct to "Wallace's Division, Army of the Tenn. in the Field."

Affectionately,
John

~ ~ ~ ~ ~

Union Depot, Tenn.
June 15, 1862

My dear Wife,

Lieut. Benn arrived yesterday. I was very much pleased to see him, and hear directly from one who had been there and seen you. Lieutenant had a hard time getting to us, we being on the move. When he got where we were, we weren't there. He was obliged to sell the medicine, lemons etc. only bringing the letter. I was very sorry about the medicine as I have been having a bilious attack and it would have been just what I want. I am steeping mint and rhubarb and am nearly well again; greatest difficulty being weakness. I have not been badly off, that is I have always been able to go about and am now all over the worst of it. Will be very careful till I get strong again. I have had no doctor and won't have, let what will come, after what I have seen of their practice. Don't worry about my sickness for I have told you just how I am.

I have never received the letter you sent containing the one from Tom and I presume I never shall. I am very sorry to hear that Dixon cannot send but eleven men to Chicago as the troops who are there ought to be sent into the field to take the places of those who have been killed, wounded or rendered unfit for duty by disease etc.

I want you to know Mary that on our marches I often neglected to take physic,[i] which you know I often have to do when at home. Therefore get very bilious but now I shall take a little every other day, even though I am not sick. You must not fear about my health for I fully believe I am just as safe from disease as at home, except getting medicine. I wish you would get some medicine prepared and send in a box to Memphis. I wish Pers to get me a double field glass or in other words an extension opera glass. A good one will cost $16.00. If he has to pay $20 for it, I must have one. If he does not get a chance to send it

---

[i] Physic is medicine, especially a purge

by someone coming down, send it with the medicine. I do not know where we will go from here but presume to Memphis.

Monday June 16th I have written on another sheet that may be published if you think best. I am much better this morning and have no fears of a fall back. The boys are all well and in good spirits. The weather is hot but no worse than in Illinois.

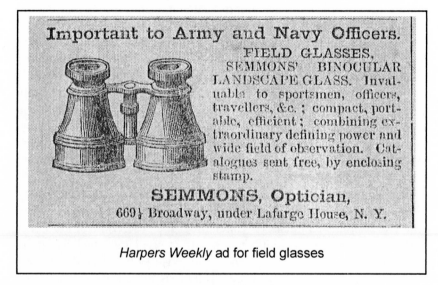

Important to Army and Navy Officers.

FIELD GLASSES, SEMMONS' BINOCULAR LANDSCAPE GLASS. Invaluable to sportsmen, officers, travellers, &c. ; compact, portable, efficient; combining extraordinary defining power and wide field of observation. Catalogues sent free, by enclosing stamp.

SEMMONS, Optician,
669½ Broadway, under Lafarge House, N. Y.

Harpers Weekly ad for field glasses

The above letter just ends there at the bottom of a page; no other sheet; no signature or sign-off. Perhaps there was another page; perhaps it was forwarded to the Dixon newspaper.

Following the Union success in the naval Battle of Memphis on June 6, 1862, control of Memphis, Tennessee passed to the Union army.

~ ~ ~ ~ ~

My dear Wife,

I wrote you on Sunday last and on Sunday night at 12 o'clock we were ordered to be ready to march at 3 o'clock. Men were immediately awakened and at 3 we were marching toward Memphis, where we arrived at about one o'clock PM after one of the most uncomfortable marches we ever had, on account of heat and dust. It is true that I could not see 20 feet to the front half of the time.

Well we are encamped on ground formerly occupied by *Price's* troops (Shelby County Fair Grounds), 1-¼ miles from Memphis. I visited the city on Tuesday and found many of the stores closed, goods having been removed to Grenada.[i] No goods of much value in the city except some few that have come down the river since the taking of the city. On Wednesday went down again and was surprised at the change in this respect. On Thursday went again and Memphis was pretty well stocked with goods of most every variety. The Memphis ladies were buying there quite freely.

When we first came, it was usual to hear the children shout for *Jeff Davis*. They are getting over it, indicating I think that the parents are either becoming Unionists or concluding that discretion is the better part of valor. There is undoubtedly a very strong Union feeling among the middle and lower classes. They only wish to be assured that they will be protected to call them out. Hundreds are taking the oath and many are enlisting in a Tennessee regiment to fight for the Stars and Stripes. This is the bright side of the picture.

There is a large number of businessmen who have and will control the masses unless we control them. They may be seen buttonholing each other on the street corners and look anything but pleasant I assure you. Some of the spouters have been arrested. Many ought to be and sent on a pleasure trip to Camp Douglas or some other Northern camp. It is very mortifying to their chivalry to have us occupying this once beautiful and busy city. Our general and staff are occupying the best hotel in the city. One of the most splendid 5 story hotels has been converted into a hospital. It cannot be excelled in the United States as a military hospital.

It is impossible for us to know anything about where we may go to from here. My own opinion is we will remain here for some little time yet. If we do, I hope I will again receive your letters more regularly. I have not heard from you since Lieut. Benn arrived. You will direct to

---

[i] Grenada, MS is 100 miles south of Memphis, TN

"Memphis, Tenn." My health is still improving. That is I am gaining strength. I feel anxious to get the medicine so I can keep well.

We are getting apples, green pears, milk, butter, cheese, new potatoes, and vegetables of most all kinds, but I tell you we pay for them. Butter 25. Milk 10. Peas 10 ct. qt. in pods. Potatoes $2 bushel. But I will never starve as long as I have a dime. I wish you would send me 1 lb. of black tea with the other things.

Troops are continuously coming down the river. It looks as though this place was going to be a kind of general headquarters for the present. Joseph Brown[i] has been troubled with diarrhea and swelling of feet and went to the hospital yesterday. He is weak and discouraged, and with all homesick. I think he will get able to do duty again in a few days. I will go and see him today. I think of no more at present that will interest you and will wait till I hear from you and then write again.

Weather pleasant and cool. Give my love to all and kiss the children a thousand times for me. It is mail time and I must close. Goodbye and may we soon meet again is my only wish.

Affectionately your husband,
Jno. T. Cheney

~ ~ ~ ~ ~

Memphis, Tenn.
June 23, 1862

My dear Wife

I have just received you kind letter of the 19th and also the one you wrote on the 17th of May with the one from Tom enclosed. Be assured I have had a good treat. Well Mary, I have been gaining in strength since I wrote you last and am about as good as new again. I was as yellow as saffron and went to work and fixed up a medicine of hops, pennyroyal[ii] and rhubarb steeped. I tell you it knocked it higher than a kite. When I wrote you last, it was a letter that was not very well calculated to cheer up a lonesome war widow very much, for I was not feeling as I do tonight.

Since I wrote you last, nothing of very great importance has transpired. Lieut. Burton has gone out about 40 miles, near Grand Junc-

---

[i] Pvt. Joseph Brown of Sterling, IL, Battery F, 1st Illinois Light Artillery; his mother, and probably he, had lived with the John Cheney family – probably at the Waverly House

[ii] Pennyroyal is a species of mint

tion,[i] with one section[ii] of the battery to protect our mechanics while building a bridge. Also one regiment of infantry have gone. Went by railroad so the boys will enjoy it first rate. I went to town today and treated myself to a good dinner of potatoes, roast chicken, beef, radishes, green peas, boiled cabbage, pickled beets etc. Memphis is really a fine city. It looks outrageous that the State of Tennessee has been driven by charade and demagogues into such a ruinous condition. The truth being that almost every laboring man who dares to give expression (even now) to his real sentiments is for the Union. It is a job fixed up by politicians and pushed on by a class of desperadoes who care not what they do. They have some devilish work always on hand.

I could give you many well authenticated instances of the abuse of Union men that would make you shudder. But it is perhaps not best to do so, as I can tell you all when I come home and save writing which is no small item for a lazy man. Suffice it to say that men have been taken from their beds and forced to leave their families and fight against a flag that they loved. Such cases are exceptions it is true. The only difference between the exceptions and the rule is if the men did not go without such treatment they were sure to receive it, so discretion being the better part of valor, in they went. If the men who have forced Tennessee to secede had to suffer alone for their devilish deeds, I could look upon their deserted homes, places of business closed up, exorbitant prices and burning cotton, and any suffering that ingenuity could invent to punish them with, but not with pleasure so. The real patriotic laborer is crushed and my sympathies are strong for them. We hope to be able to send some of their oppressors into the other world from which it will be hard to secede. I claim some little humanity, but the truth is the satans ought to be killed. Then they are certainly incapable of bearing arms or of forcing other to do so.

Wallace is not in command here as reported in the papers, but I wish he was as the "Memphis Avalanche"[iii] would probably fail to discover the gentlemanly, urbane, generous qualities that it was pleased to discover in Col. Fitch. Gen. Lew Wallace has a different mission than acting the bloodhound for Secesh slaveholders, thank God.

We of course do not know how long we may remain here, but no doubt anything that may be sent to us will come to Memphis perhaps during the summer. If our slow couch generals were pushing along as

---

[i] Grand Junction, Tennessee is about 63 miles east of Memphis

[ii] A section is 2 guns, plus their men, caissons and limbers, horses etc. commanded by a lieutenant

[iii] "Memphis Avalanche" was the Memphis newspaper

fast as we think they ought to, we or at least I would be contented, but it does seem as though we were making but slow progress at best.

I have received a letter from Tom today dated June 1st at Roanoke Island.[i] He is well and apparently in good spirits. I was very sorry to learn that Henry Horn was taken sick again. I had been looking for him for two or three days past and was sadly disappointed. I hope Henry may soon recover and return to us. It is now 9 o'clock and the bugs are annoying me most terribly so I will close. I wish you would make me 6 calico[ii] shirts, collars on them, and send down the first opportunity. I would like small figured.[iii]

Remember me to all the friends and particularly to our own household. I wish I could just see our little Gracie. She must be so interesting. She is just the right age for a pet and I am missing it all. I would not object you know to seeing you, Royce and the rest of the folks. If I could see Gracie, I could not help seeing you all. I have received a letter from Pers today; will answer it soon. Good night my dear. May you some time cease to be a war widow and become the same Mrs. Jno. T. Cheney that you used to be. That's what's the matter.

Affectionately your husband,
Jno. T. Cheney

~ ~ ~ ~ ~

Memphis, Tenn.
June 28, 1862

My dear Wife,

Yesterday I was downtown and met Lieut. Smyth on the sidewalk, who had just arrived. The first thing was to ask for my letters, which I knew he had. I was as ever so glad to hear from home. The medicine I was very glad of, although I am much stronger than when I wrote last. I commenced taking it last night and will go through a thorough course, though I hardly know, as I need it now. Still it will do me no harm to take a thorough cleansing.

I went to town yesterday to get a furlough but could not get the promise of one. Still I hope that after the 15th of July if we remain here I may succeed in getting one. I shall be very busy now for some time as we have our payrolls, monthly and quarterly returns to make between

---

[i] 6th New Hampshire Infantry was at Roanoke, North Carolina with Maj. Gen. Burnside

[ii] Calico is cotton cloth printed with a figured pattern

[iii] Small figured would be the calico pattern, not the size of the shirt

this and the 15th of July. Do not place much dependence on my coming home, as by a late general order it is almost impossible for an officer or soldier to get away. Yet I shall make a desperate effort to come, if even for a very short time.

I am sorry to learn that you have such a cold, as it seems to be your luck to be afflicted in that way most always. Be careful and don't try to read or write in the evening. You ask if I will let you come down. Well may you know that it has always been my desire to have you see an army in the field. You also know that I never in my life wanted to see you and our little family as I do now. But it does seem to me that I cannot advise that you come here now. The reasons are that it is very uncertain about our remaining here. Two regiments were ordered to Germantown[i] yesterday. For all we know we may go tomorrow, although we do not expect it. It would be impossible for you and the babies (who would come of course) to be comfortable in camp, as we (the officers) have but one wall tent, and you could take no comfort here. There is no place outside of the lines where you could stop unless at a hotel in town at $2.50 per day for yourself and I don't know how much for the children. Should we be called away and you not find us here it would be rough. So on the whole I think we had better make up our minds that as pleasant as it would be to meet, it is better at present to conclude to wait a little. And trust and hope that ere long something will turn up by which we can spend a few days together.

Lieut. Smyth is quite smart and I think will be better than he has been before. Tell Pers that I was very glad to receive his letter and papers. I will write to him soon, though I wish he would consider my letters to you as answers to his and keep writing. I believe none of the Dixon boys are sick except N. H. Thompson[ii] who is sick with camp fever[iii] at the hospital. Thompson has been very sick but the doctor told me yesterday that he thought he had seen the worst of it. I was down to see him yesterday and thought I could discover a little change for the better. As soon as he gets better, I will make an effort to get a furlough for him to go home.

There is nothing of very much interest transpiring here, only the regular routine of camp life. Lieut. Burton has returned from his expedition that I wrote you of in my last. Nobody hurt. My appetite was very poor for a week but now I can eat my allowance I assure you.

---

[i] Germantown, Tennessee is just east of Memphis

[ii] Pvt. N. H. Thompson of Dixon, IL, Battery F, 1st Illinois Light Artillery

[iii] Camp fever is Typhoid fever; contracted from contaminated drinking water

A train of cars consisting of 4 freight and one passenger car went out on the Memphis and Charleston Road on the 26th and was taken by Secesh cavalry when about 15 miles from here. They took one Col. Kennedy of the 56th Ohio Reg. and several privates prisoners. The engine and train were run into a ditch and burned. So you see the country is not quite cleaned out.

We are having, while I write, fine showers of rain. It is very hot here during the day but the nights are cool and comfortable. I believe on the whole that we have been in no more healthy spot since we left Illinois. I will wait till Frank comes back so as to hear from Thompson.

Sunday Morning 29th. I have just eaten a breakfast of blackberry sauce and good bread and butter. As the mail goes out today, I will close my letter. Frank could not get in to see Thompson yesterday. I will go and see him today and if he gets any worse will write. I am taking my medicine and getting along first rate. Remember me to all the friends and to our own household in particular. Good morning Mary.

Your affectionate husband,
Jno. T. Cheney

~ ~ ~ ~ ~

Monday evening, July 1, 1862

My dear Wife,

I have today received a letter from you written on the 15th of June. So you see there is no such thing as getting letters regularly. Lieut. Burton has just received a letter from home dated June 17th saying that you have not heard from me in two weeks. Well I have never let a week pass without writing once and hardly ever less than twice. I know from letters that Lib writes that some of your letters have never reached me as some news that she wrote, you would be sure to write.

Brown expects to get a furlough in a day or two. He is homesick and I am glad he is going home as he would never get well here as long as he is so homesick. Thompson is very sick, but I hope he has seen the worst of it. We have done all that could be done for him had he been at home. As soon as he gets well enough, I will try and get a furlough for him to go home.

Since I wrote you before, we have moved down the river about 4 miles. Are now some two miles from town. How long we will remain I do not know. There is considerable damage being done all about as in the way of cotton burning etc. I only wish our generals would let a few regiments and batteries loose and left to use their own discretion for a few days. There would be a few gentlemen suspended for a short time, and cotton burning would be stopped. The fact is we are trying to be too gentlemanly. The result is we are only taken for cowardly mudsills[i] who are here courting Southern favor. I get almost discouraged sometimes at the slow pace at which we move. Would be glad if we could only be allowed to subsist ourselves on the property of traitors and hang every guerrilla we could find to the nearest tree. Then they would feel a little differently and be compelled to submit or die. I believe it has got to come to that yet, and how long it will take to get up to the scratch is more than I can tell.

I have helped hide away a smart Mulatto slave tonight and by God I will try and find some way to get him north. He is smart. Is owned only 5 miles out of town. This I would be liable to be punished for, was it known, but if I … [missing pages] …

You ought to be as cheerful and happy as I am at least. My health is very good. I take my medicine every night. The bugs are tormenting me dreadfully and I will close, only adding my love to all and specially our own. Write me often and I will do the answering. Good night and may you all at home live cheerfully and pleasantly hoping for that good time coming when this accursed treason shall have been punished and our country united, free and prosperous. We again seated around the family board, united by bonds made stronger (if possible) by our long separation and happy reunion. This is my only wish, desire and hope and we will see it.

Affectionately,
John

~ ~ ~ ~ ~

Memphis, Tenn.
Thursday morning, July 6th 1862

My dear Wife,

I received you kind letter of 28th ultimo on the evening of 3rd inst. and was delighted to hear again from home. You say you are feeling quite anxious about my health. Well Mary I am just as well as I was before my sickness, only that I am not quite as strong. I have taken my medicine regularly and it is almost gone. I wish I had some more. Tell Pers I have got a splendid glass. Found it in Memphis and paid $20 for it.

---

[i] Mudsills are people from the lowest level of society

You speak of my coming home. I think it will be impossible for me to get a furlough this summer. I do want to see you all and will look about and see if there is any place you can be made comfortable at an expense within our reach. If so, will send for you to come down. If you come, Lib will come as a matter of course. I could not think of having the children (either of them) left at home. I would advise that you be in readiness to come, so that if we can get a place, you can come at once.

Be careful of your eyes and if a doctor tells you what to do for them, wish you to do as he tells you to! This may be an unnecessary request but if it is, you have changed since I left home haven't you? I am sorry to hear that Mother is suffering so much with her leg. Do hope she may get relief. Thompson's fever has turned and he is better. Has been very sick but I have no doubt he will recover though it will be some time before he will be able to do duty. I will try hard to get a furlough for him to go home on. I have tried to get a furlough for Joseph and have not succeeded. He is better and will be able to return to duty soon. He is weak and has been homesick as he could be, but now that he finds he cannot get home I think he will recover rapidly. I dislike to write thus, but believe it to be true. I would have written you a little oftener but have been very busy making up reports, returns etc. and have not got quite through yet.

On the 4th the battery was called out for drill and the firing of a national salute of 34 guns. We done it in good shape. Returned to camp and found a Secesh major and captain (or rather have been and got out of service) both Irishmen. They both addressed the company and were followed by myself. Opened and drank half barrel ale. Had dance and a good social. Orderly time generally, without drunkenness or disorder. Thus passed the anniversary of our national independence.

I flattered myself that as the writing was mostly done, the 4th passed, that I would have a good time to take notice of passing events and write home often and long letters covering what I might find to interest you. But received notice of my appointment to sit on a court-martial the next day at 10 o'clock. Well I was there. We were all day in disposing of one case. I judge we have at least 50 cases and it would not be surprising if we were to sit two weeks. I will have this advantage and an opportunity to get a pretty good knowledge of military discipline. Though it is not pleasant to sit all day these hot days.

Lieut. Burton is assisting Col. J. B. Webster in engineering, surveying etc, for entrenchments, so you see they are calling pretty heavily on our company, evidentially not intending that we shall be long idle. Col. Webster is one of the best men that lives, forgetting his elevated position, and coming right down to the common affairs of life, treating every man as his equal.

Gen. Halleck has ordered entrenchments here and also ordered that contrabands build them. Last evening some 100 of them came in with our cavalry, who had been out in the country for the purpose of getting them. So it seems that the Negro is really to be allowed inside our lines, now that there is work to be done. Well I hope there will be some way for them to be freed after they have worked on government works.

I have just been out to see them and found each one with a piece of bacon and hands full of hard bread, apparently delighted with the idea of working for the Yankees. At least they seemed to relish Yankee bacon and bread. I wish you was here to go out and see them with me, as you can have but little conception of their real condition. You could easily tell what kind of a man owned each one by his looks and dress. The slaves in the country are not all black by any means. Some black, some Mulattos, and many Quadroons nearly as white, and occasionally one as white, as his owner. I hate slavery and shall be glad if there can be some way provided by which it can be entirely abolished without doing injustice to some Union men.

Monday Morning. Thompson is still gaining and Joseph has got his furlough. I expect Joseph will start for home today or tomorrow. Wish him a pleasant journey and don't care whether he comes back or not. Last evening I went to a Negro prayer meeting just a few rods from my own tent. I tell you if they don't pray with an earnestness and faith unknown to many white Christians, I am mistaken. There is some 300 of them in now and constantly coming in.

I looked for a place yesterday but could find none that would answer. Board is $1.00 per day for each person at the cheapest place and so on up to $2.50. Rooms are worth about $8.00 per month each. I will keep on eye open for some place and if we can get 2 rooms, or 3 would be better, will go to house keeping on a small scale. It is mail time and I must close. Will write in a day or two.

Your husband,
John T. Cheney

~ ~ ~ ~ ~

Memphis, Tenn.
July 10, 1862

My dear Wife,

I looked anxiously for a letter tonight, but was disappointed so thought I would write you a few lines. I am enjoying most excellent health. Never since I have been in the service have I been better. I am still on that court-martial and from present appearances will be for 2 weeks to come. I have been out nights after adjournment to see what I could do about getting a place for you and Lib. Have some prospect of getting the house of a lawyer whose wife talks of going East to spend some 3 months time. Could tell you about it, but in a few days will know.

There is a rumor that General Wallace's division is going to Virginia, but I do not believe we shall go. Will know certain about it next week. Then if we stay here, I will come home or send for you immediately. I feel disappointed about Richmond,[i] but still hope it may be taken. Then it will look a little like coming home soon to stay.

Thompson is getting better and is considered out of danger. Lieut. Burton has charge of the fortifications under Col. J. B. Webster. I wish I could step in and see you this evening, but as I can't do so will make the best of it. Hope to see you soon. I suppose you have seen Joseph. He went before I could get a chance to see him. Therefore I could send no particular word.

There is very little excitement here now. Some skirmishing between the pickets. It would not be very strange to me if we would be attacked here as we have not a very strong force, and the desire to burn the city by the Rebels may induce them to try us on.

I do not suffer from heat anymore here than in Illinois. The nights are quite cool. It is very dry and dusty. Give my love to all the folks and the children in particular. The boys are all very anxious to have you come down. If Royce comes, he will fare first rate as the boys think a great deal of him. Be patient a few days (as I am trying to be) and I believe we will meet somewhere either here or at home.

We have some 400 Negroes at work on the fortifications. A merry set they are, dancing and praying till midnight every night. I wish you could see them. Some of them are very intelligent and many very eloquent in prayer. Much useful information is obtained from them.

It is getting dark and as I light no candles on account of the bugs (which are awful) I will close. Good night and may you and the babies be cheerful and happy. Kiss Gracie and Royce (if he will let you) 1000 times for me and give my love to Mother, Lib, Marg, Tate, Jed, Pers and all both great and small.

Affectionately your husband,
Jno. T. Cheney

---

[i] McClellan's Spring/Summer 1862 Peninsula Campaign aimed at Richmond was unsuccessful

~ ~ ~ ~ ~

Memphis, Tenn.
July 16, 1862

My dear Wife,

Henry Horn arrived here about one hour since. Be assured I was pleased to hear from you. Gracie's picture is worth a great deal to me and I am very glad you were so thoughtful as to send it. Grace is really a very pretty girl.

July 17th

The flies and bugs bothered me so last night and I was forced to quit. As I have just returned from the court-martial; will try again. The shirts are just the thing. I have one of them on now and it is very comfortable. Since I wrote you before, there has been some considerable fear of an attack. I have thought best to wait a little before sending for you. Just as soon as I dare to send I shall do so, and I wish you to make all necessary preparations to come. If you do not come, there will be no harm done.

Tell Lib I am very much obliged to her for the wine, and as often as I partake, it will be in remembrance of her. I hope to see her here soon. My health never was better than now. My medicine is most all taken and I wish I had another bottle. Our court-martial has now sat two weeks, but I hope it will close in two or three days, as I have enough to do without sitting on it.

I hope Gracie may not have a serious time while cutting her teeth. I know it must be an awful job taking care of her. As she has always had so much attention given to her when she is well, she will expect still more when sick. I have no fear about her, as I know you, Lib and the doctor will bring her out all right. You need not make any more shirts as I had bought two before these came, and I have as many as I want.

I will do all I can for Henry Horn. He seems quite smart and if I can only prevail upon him to take care of himself, I doubt not he will soon be well as ever. We have got rid of pretty much all of the babies in our company, and now are all right, only wanting a few more good men to fill up the ranks. I care but little whether Brown comes back or not. I can see just how Royce looked when he came home with the drum. I am glad he has got it. Although I hear any amount of drumming, if I could only hear him drum, it would be worth more than all the bands in the army.

Saturday morning 19th

I received your kind letter of 13th last night while at supper, and I was as ever pleased to hear again from you. While reading the letter it grew dark and I had to stop writing, and strange as it may seem, it is 4 o'clock AM and I am up writing to you. Verily you will exclaim, what may not occur during this war. We have commenced to drill in the morning at 4 o'clock finding it much more comfortable than in the heat of the day.

We have made some considerable progress on the fortifications and our battery have removed inside of them. My tent, in which I now sit, is within a rod of the bank of the Mississippi on a bluff and in a very cool pleasant place. I do wish you was here to take a stroll with me this morning. I must have you come when the fortifications are completed. We anticipate an attack here most any time as we suppose they will try us on while we are weak, but even now they would find a warm meal at any hour.

I will write to Royce and send him in this. Lieut. Benn has resigned and his resignation will undoubtedly be accepted.[i] What the reason is I do not know. He assigns all kinds of reasons and I would be glad if you can learn what reasons he assigns up home. The real disease is very similar to Brown's. Well God damn such babies to hell is the mildest language I can use. Write often. Good-bye, I remain the same John T. Cheney (only get up earlier mornings).

[Letter to son Royce inserted as part of this letter to Mary]

Memphis, Tenn.
July 19, 1862

My dear Son,

Your letter of July 13th was received on the 17th inst. I was very glad to hear that you are studying Geography and Arithmetic, and hope you may make good progress. It seems that you still have a company at Dixon. Well you ought to agree in your own company, but if you are called a traitor, I suppose you are just fine in resenting it. I will take time and write you again soon, but will close this now, as my sheet is full. Give my love to all the folks.

Affectionately your father,
John T. Cheney

~ ~ ~ ~ ~

---

[i] Benn's resignation official September 2, 1862

Memphis, Tenn.
July 25, 1862

My dear Wife,

As Lieut. Benn is going home, thought I would take a little time and write you a few lines. I am very busy and will write you more at length very soon. I have not drawn my pay for the last two months as I consider it as safe in the hands of the government as anywhere else. I know of no particular use that we have for it. I can borrow what I want for the next two months.

I have just received your letter of 20th inst. and have read it hurriedly over. Am glad to hear that you are well. Am glad to be able to say that there is some prospect of my being detached for recruiting purposes. I will know about it in about a week. If I recruit, will be in Dixon and Lee County most of the time. If I do not do that, will send for you.

Thompson is some better but I cannot get a furlough for him. I think it cruel, but there is no possibility of getting one. My health is most excellent. I hope and believe that the time will soon come when I can meet my dear family. Give my love to all friends.

Affectionately your husband,
Jno. T. Cheney

~ ~ ~ ~ ~

Memphis, Tenn.
July 31, 1862

My dear Wife,

I believe I wrote you that for two Saturdays in succession we had been called out in line of battle. Well sure enough last Saturday we were called out in the morning instead of the evening. The cause of the alarm was a company of cavalry went to the front to discharge their carbines, and the signals came back long roll.

I have not yet heard from Gen. Grant's headquarters, and cannot tell whether I can go home on recruiting service or not. But one thing is certain; if I can't I will have you come down. If we move, will do the best we can under the circumstances. It seems as though I could not wait much longer to see my wife and children.

Last Sunday morning I learned that Lieut. Henry Dement[i] was in town. Lieut. Burton and myself went up to see him, and learned that he had left for home. I suppose he did not know that we were here or he

[i] Lieut. Henry D. Dement of Dixon, IL, Co. A, 13th Illinois Infantry

would have called to see us. I felt disappointed and hope on his return he will call on us if we are here. We met Capt. Bushnell[i], Lieut. Brown,[ii] Lieuts. Patterson[iii] and Henderson[iv] of the 13th Regiment all from Sterling[v]. Also Sergt. Adams[vi] who lives near Jacob's.

Gen. Lew Wallace has not returned yet but will probably be here by the 4th of August and then we hope to know whether we remain here all summer or not. The infantry of our division have all gone down to Helena[vii]. I would not be surprised if the artillery went as soon as Gen. Wallace returns, in which case we would be with the 13th.

We are (while I write) having a fine storm and as it has been very dusty, it seems refreshing. Capt. Hughes,[viii] Lieuts. Bullock and Snyder[ix] and Capt. Marble[x] have just been in to see us. They are all well. The 46th are encamped about one and ½ miles from us. Lieut. Burton and myself visited them last Sabbath, and attended religious services with their regiment in the evening. It being very dark and in the timber, we stayed all night. The Dixon boys in their regiment are all well, but would be glad to come into our company. They now see the difference between artillery and infantry, and believe what I used to tell them in Dixon.

My health is first rate and I now have no fears about health. It is true that almost every man has to go through a regular course of sprouts.[xi] If he remains here and gets well, he is all right. Whereas if he goes home and recovers, he is very likely to travel the same route over again. Such is my observation. Thompson is improving but not very rapidly. Lieut. Burton has had the jaundice,[xii] just as I had, but is all

---

[i] Capt. (later Maj.) Douglas R. Bushnell of Sterling, IL, Co. B, 13th Illinois Infantry

[ii] Lieut. (later Capt.) George P. Brown of Fulton, IL, Co. B, 13th Illinois Infantry

[iii] Lieut. Jasper M. Patterson of Sterling, IL,Co. B, 13th Illinois Infantry

[iv] Quartermaster William C.Henderson of Sterling, IL, HQ, 13th Illinois Infantry

[v] Sterling, Illinois is 13 miles west of Dixon, IL

[vi] Sergt. Matthew R. Adams of Sterling, IL, Co. B, 13th Illinois Infantry

[vii] Helena, Arkansas is on the Mississippi River, 71 miles south of Memphis

[viii] Capt. John A. Hughes of Lane, IL, Co. A, 46th Illinois Infantry

[ix] Lieut. Edward A. Snyder of Dixon, IL, Co. H, 46th Illinois Infantry

[x] Capt. John M. Marble of Bloomington, IL, Co. E, 46th Illinois Infantry

[xi] 'Course of sprouts' is instruction marked by corporal punishment, rigorous discipline or difficulty

[xii] Jaundice is yellowish color to the skin, often associated with liver dysfunction

right again. I guess he has done as I did, not write much about it till he got better. He has taken Lib's medicine; prepared from her recipe.

Yesterday morning a colored man (as I discovered through my glass) was on the Arkansas side of the river, motioning for someone to come and take him over. I took two of the boys down the river about a mile. We got a skiff and went over and got him. He had traveled 15 miles. He is smart and is in our lines. Will either go to driving our mules or the fortifications. There is some eight hundred Negroes here at work now.

What do you think about Farragut and Davis letting the *Ark*[i] run through to Vicksburg? We don't think it very smart down here, but it compares very favorably with a great many little operations in the army, though is rather stranger in the naval department. Jim is well. He wants very much to go home but it will be impossible for him to do so. As you see, I have tried hard to get a furlough for Thompson and couldn't even do that.

Give my love to all the friends and look forward to the good time coming when we may be reunited. I hope and pray to never again be separated while life shall last. I used to think no man living appreciated home more than I did, but now I know how to appreciate it, I tell you. Not that I am sorry I left, for if I was not in the army I would never rest a moment till I was enlisted. I hope some of the Dixon boys will come with me if I come up, as they will certainly fare as well with us as in a new company that have everything to learn. I could interest you with a thousand little and large incidents that occur here, but want of time and fear of having nothing to tell when I get home prevents. I hope to get a letter today.

Affectionately yours,
Jno. T. Cheney

~ ~ ~ ~ ~

Memphis, Tenn.
Aug 6, 1862

My dear Wife,

Your letters of 27 and 30 ult. have been received. I have delayed writing, waiting for the return of Gen. Wallace, hoping to get leave of absence. He has not come yet. I cannot tell what the prospect is, though I think you will see me within two weeks. Capt. Noble has been up here on business and stopped with us 2 days. He is in excellent health and

---

[i] Confederate Ram *Arkansas*

fine spirits. Henry Snyder, who used to board with us, has also been here.

The weather is very warm but not any hotter than in Illinois. I think our men stand it just as well as they would in Illinois. There is nothing of interest transpiring here except the work on the fortifications being done by 1057 Negroes. Tell Jacob I will see to everything connected with Joseph's[i] affairs so far as it can be done at present. Mrs. Brown[ii] cannot claim his pay of any paymaster till he is reported to the adjutant general and an order issued for his payment. When I come up, will see to it, and will bring up all the effects he left here. I am very anxious to get home, as I need a little rest very much. Be sure and write very often. I will write you again as soon as Gen. Wallace returns. My love to all the friends

Affectionately your husband,
Jno. T. Cheney

~ ~ ~ ~ ~

Memphis, Tenn.
Aug. 12, 1862

My dear Wife,

Mrs. Brown arrived here on Sunday evening. She stayed at the Gayoso House[iii] Sunday night and came to camp yesterday. She is stopping in the tent with Burton. Had I only have known soon enough to have had you come with her, should have done so by all means. I wish you had come. I hardly see how you kept from coming with her.

I have had a pretty hard week of it. Have been sick with a kind of bone fever, I call it. I got better so that I went to town Sunday and Monday morning to see Mrs. Brown. I was taken sick again and came to camp, and what do you suppose came next? Well first a shake, then the fever; in short I have got fever and ague.[iv] I believe I can break it up in a few days. Mrs. Burton kept me as comfortable as possible yesterday; waiting upon and taking care of me.

A messenger goes to Corinth this morning to get out papers for recruiting for the batteries. I expect that by Sunday I will be on the way home. If it were not for that, I should send for you at once. I feel quite smart this morning and have taken my medicine. Will follow it up

---

[i] Pvt. Joseph Brown, of Battery F died July 24, 1862 at home in Sterling, IL

[ii] The mother of Pvt. Joseph Brown

[iii] Gayoso House in Memphis was a first rate hotel built in 1844

[iv] Ague is chills, i.e., shaking and shivering

closely; don't worry about me as I am now doing well. But for the absence of Gen. Wallace, I would have been at home a week since. Gen. Wallace has not yet returned and God only knows when he will, so we send directly to Gen. Grant.

Tell Pers to get his men on the roll and if he prefers and can get transportation, to come down, or wait till I come. If I come home, I shall stay till I get thoroughly recruited. Now be patient yet a few days Mary and all will be well.

I can account for your feelings on Wednesday last. It was the hardest day I ever put in. Keep good grit yet a little while, and have no fear about me as I am doing well now. Jim is well and has been very kind to me. Give my love to all the friends and write just the same as though you did not expect me home, for if anything should happen to prevent my coming, want my letters. Good morning.

Affectionately your husband,
Jno. T. Cheney

~ ~ ~ ~ ~

Memphis
16 Aug. 1862

My dear Wife,

I received yours of 11th yesterday and have time to write a few line before the postmaster goes. I am having the ague yet, but it is getting a little better every day and so am I. I expect to start for home the 1st of next week. You must accept a short letter and expect to see the writer. Love to all.

Affectionately your husband,
Jno. T. Cheney

Cheney returned to Dixon on recruiting service. He was very sick during his time at home. He wrote the following letter to his commander.

Dixon, Ill.
Sept. 6th 1862

Col. Adams,

Your favor of 1st inst. came to hand last eve and it is with much difficulty that I answer you. I have now been 2 weeks confined to the house with sickness, hoping to be able to report to you, but I see no prospect of being able to do so at present. I wish Lieut. Whaley[i] would come to Dixon and make some arrangement to get my men clothed and transportation for them. I will make all right with him. If he will come, I wish him to telegraph me and I will have someone to meet him. I have 22 musters in.

Lieut. Col. C. H. Adams   Yours faithfully,
Comdg. 1st Reg. Ill. Artillery   Jno. T. Cheney
Springfield, Ill.   Capt. Etc.

Summary

While at Memphis Cheney expressed his view that the rebellion was the work of the Southern elite. He saw the middle and lower classes as victims of a Southern upper class that wanted to protect its privileges. One of those privileges was white Southerners impregnating their slaves. Cheney expressed moral indignation when he observed the wide range of shades of color in the slave population.

During the Civil War, sickness took a larger toll of soldiers than did battle injuries. Cheney's health had now failed him. He was "bilious" and "yellow as saffron" in June. That may have been a viral liver disease and probably not life threatening. He recovered by July, but was sick again in August. In late August while at home on recruiting service he was bedridden. His August and September 1862 illness was gastrointestinal and much more serious. Cheney could no longer count on strength and good health as he did his patriotic duty.

---

[i] Following the resignation of Lieut. Benn, Jefferson F. Whaley of Brooklyn, IL, was promoted to lieutenant, Battery F, 1st Illinois Light Artillery

Chapter 6 - Grant's Central Mississippi Campaign

November 26, 1862 to December 20, 1862

Background

On November 2, 1862 Maj. Gen. Grant began his Central Mississippi Campaign aimed at Vicksburg, Mississippi. He moved troops out of Memphis and Corinth into the Grand Junction, Tennessee area, (west of Memphis) then south into Mississippi along the line of the Mississippi Central Railroad. Later Grant decided to split his forces and sent Sherman down the Mississippi River to Vicksburg. Grant hoped to use his overland army to draw Confederate troops into northern Mississippi while Sherman operated against Vicksburg.

John Cheney returned to Battery F in November 1862. His wife and children accompanied him as far as Memphis. Cheney's unit was part of Maj. Gen. Sherman's District of Memphis, Army of the Tennessee. Cheney began keeping a diary.

Memphis, Tenn.
Wednesday, Nov. 26th 1862

Left my wife and children on the steamer Von Phul homeward bound, and left Memphis for Mississippi. Made 14 miles. A pleasant day and stood the march well. Nothing of particular interest transpired. Boys in high glee with the prospect of a march on the enemy.

Thursday, Nov. 27th 1862

Moved at 8 o'clock. Passed through a good country. The Rebels had burned several bridges, but we got along well and went into camp at Cold Water, Miss. A fine day. The boys have destroyed considerable property notwithstanding orders to the contrary.

Cold Water, Miss.
Friday, 28th November 1862

Started at 8 AM. Passed Byhalia, Miss., found the town deserted. Went into camp at Pigeon Roost Creek. Were joined by Smith's and Denver's divisions. Maj. Gen. Sherman and staff came up. Don't like Gen. Sherman. Do like Gen. Lauman for the reason that I believe that Gen. Lauman's heart is in the work, and Gen. Sherman is in for Gen. Sherman every time.

Pigeon Roost Creek, Miss.
Saturday, Nov. 29th 1862

Spent the day at Pigeon Roost Creek. Don't see any reason why we should not advance, but suppose the powers that be understand the lay of the ground and will bring the thing out all right. Hope so. Nothing of interest has transpired.

Pigeon Roost Creek
Sunday, Nov. 30 1862

Were ordered to march at 7 o'clock AM. Marched at 11 AM. We have been unaccustomed to start 4 hours later than ordered, and regret that we are not under command of Gen. Lew Wallace who means 7 o'clock when he says it. Rainy day. Went into camp at Chulahoma, Miss. Had a strong wind in the evening which blew our tents down. Got well wet.

Learned that Gen. Grant's cavalry had fought the enemy near Holly Springs. Heard some firing of cannon. Enemy skedaddled as usual.

Chulahoma, Miss.
Monday, Dec. 1, 1862

Got up wet, but concluded that it only added to the romance of war. Good prospect for a fight on the Tallahatchie. Received orders to march at 7 o'clock tomorrow without tents or baggage. Boys all right and well.

Chulahoma, Miss.

Tuesday, Dec. 2, 1862

Left Chulahoma at 7 o'clock. Rainy day, bad roads. Bridges burned. Trees fallen across the road. A hard march to Wyatte on the Tallahatchie. At night a building (in which were some 100 soldiers) fell, fatally injuring one and seriously two. Strange that more lives were not lost. Wyatte is a God forsaken town. No bridge across the river. The enterprising inhabitants here used a ferry boat, but that had been destroyed. The river has to be bridged.

Wyatte, Miss.

Wednesday, Dec. 3, 1862

Our cavalry have taken 250 prisoners and are chasing the enemy south of Oxford (distance to Oxford 14 miles). Bridge being built across the river.

Wyatte, Miss.

Thursday, Dec. 4th 1862

Bridge not completed. Rainy day, and muddy roads horrid. From our camp to water, one and one half miles. Two miles to forage. Men on ¾ rations, but I suspect the other ¼ they get except bread, which can neither be bought or stolen.

*** *** *** *** *** *** *** ***

Wyatte, Miss. on the Tallahatchie
Dec. 4th 1862

My dear Wife,

Well here we are waiting for a bridge to be built across the Talla- hatchie. I thought I would improve the little time I have in writing to you. First then my health and strength have been very much improved since I left you. You would be surprised to see me, for I eat my rations and feel well except my rheumatism. And that is better although we have had very wet weather and horrid roads. The Rebels had burned bridges, felled trees across the roads etc. etc.

We are but about 5 miles from Grant's army. Day before yesterday (Dec. 2nd) Gen. Grant's advance cavalry drove the enemy from a fort about 3 miles from here, and took 250 prisoners. The cavalry are now in pursuit of the devils and when last heard from were beyond Oxford some 16 miles from here. I feel a little fearful that we will not get at

82

them for some time yet. Perhaps not till we have driven them to Jackson.[i]

It is reported and believed that Gen. Steele has come over from Helena and cut the railroad near Grenada. The health of the boys is generally good. Mr. Hetler[ii] has got the measles, is doing well. Charlie Kennedy[iii] has a cold but is doing well. Yates[iv] got his foot injured by being run over by a piece, but will be at his post in two or three days. We have seen no paymaster yet. Should we be paid here I don't know how we could with safety send it home, although a little would be very convenient here.

We get plenty of pork, beef, chickens, geese, some sweet potatoes, honey etc. Our boys are good foragers. I have no fault as long as they will keep out of the General's sight and avoid arrest. We have had 7 under arrest but I have begged them off. This is a God forsaken country, towns deserted, and got up for a race just such as inhabit it; ignorant and a century behind the age.

I had no doubt when I left you that I would see you and our dear children again to say good-bye, but when I overtook the column it was 5 miles out and on the move. We camped 14 miles out that night and I could not come back. I hope you got home all right. I will wait patiently to hear all the particulars. Are you all well? Tell Mother, Lib, Marg, Pers, Mr. Merrill's and Jacob's folks, that I will never forget the kind attention that I received from them while I was sick. The neighbors generally and say to Jed and Tate, they are not forgotten. I am better off by far than I could have been had I stayed at home. I need not say to you and Royce that your sleepless nights and weary days and Royce's running for papers is not forgotten. I have a very nice saddle for Royce. If I can ever get it home, I will do so. I don't know as I think of more to write. I hope you will not be modest enough to fail to ask Pers for a little money as I don't know how you can well get along without it.

Snyder[v] is much better than when he left home and eats his rations well. Mr. Hollister[vi] has been sick, but is now well again. It is well

---

[i] Jackson, Mississippi – the state capital
[ii] Pvt. Hiram Hetler of Dixon, IL, Battery F, 1st Illinois Light Artillery
[iii] Pvt. (later Sergt.) Charles Y. Kennedy of Dixon, IL, Battery F, 1st Illinois Light Artillery; "Mrs. Kennedy" is his mother
[iv] Sergt. (later Lieut.) John Q. Yates of Dixon, IL, Battery F, 1st Illinois Light Artillery
[v] Pvt. William C. Snyder of Dixon, IL, Battery F, 1st Illinois Light Artillery
[vi] Pvt. Justin Hollister of Dixon, IL, Battery F, 1st Illinois Light Artillery

Royce did not come as he would have had a hard time of it. Don't fret about me for I am all right and have enough of everything. The boys are very kind to me. This country will be pretty effectively cleaned out by the time our army has passed through. I will put this into an envelope and write again before sending it.

Dec 5th 8 o'clock PM

I learn that the division train goes to Holly Springs[i] tomorrow, so I thought I would write you a few lines. Last night it rained and some snow fell, but this morning it cleared up, although the roads are horrid. Our provision train has been detained and today we have had neither bread nor flour to make it of. We are on ¾ rations but if you could see the mutton, beef, chickens and pork come in you would give the boys credit for being good foragers.

I have been out with the carpenter to put into a wagon, a pole that was broken some 3 miles out. (Don't make this read that the pole was 3 miles long). Borrowed a box of hard bread from the Deacon who kept tally for us the night we played old sledge,[ii] so the boys will have bread for breakfast. We will have bread tomorrow. We move again tomorrow to Hurricane Creek some nine miles from here, where we hope not to have to carry water a mile and one half. Charlie Kennedy is much better tonight and his mother need not worry about him. Jim Vesper is healthy as a buck and would write, but I tell you it is winter, we have no fires except outside and my fingers are cold. The boys do no grumbling and make themselves quite comfortable.

I send you a specimen of Southern love letters. Hope it will prove entertaining and it certainly would prove instructive to lovers. I am all right to what I was, and have no fear of sickness as I am determined to be careful. You can direct to "Cheney's Battery, Right Wing, Army of the Tenn., Gen. Lauman's Division, In the Field."

I can just imagine you sitting by the fire, Mother dodging round and wondering where poor John and James are. Well Mother we are all right and wish to God we had some of your corn bread. Have you weaned Gracie? How did she stand it? I will bid you good night and as often as I can get a chance to send you a letter I will do so. I want you to write me often as I don't expect to get more than half of your letters.

Affectionately your husband,

Jno. T. Cheney

----

[i] Holly Springs, Mississippi was used as a Union supply depot

[ii] Old sledge is a card game also known as 'all fours' or 'seven-up'

*** *** *** *** *** *** *** ***

Wyatte, Miss.
Friday, Dec. 5th 1862
    Received orders to march on the morrow at 7 o'clock. Went out foraging, good success. Wrote to wife.

Wyatte
Saturday, Dec. 6th 1862
    Pleasant day. Learned that on account of our supply train not coming up, we would not move today. Went out with Division Quartermaster Burr after horses and mules. Got 5 mules and 3 horses. Were 10 miles out. Had a good dinner at a planter's. Found one Negro who rode one of the mules into our lines - another man free. Ordered to move at 8 AM tomorrow.

Wyatte, Miss.
Sunday, Dec. 7, 1862
    Left Wyatte at 8 AM. Fine day, bad roads. Passed through the enemy's fort on the south side of the Tallahatchie. They would have been easily taken had the enemy made a stand there. Arrived at Hurricane Creek at 3 PM. The boys have struck a load and are coming into camp laden with pork, dried apple, molasses, sugar, and potatoes. A restful night, a little sick. One and one half miles to water.

Hurricane Creek
Monday, Dec. 8th 1862
    Went one and a half miles to the creek. Had a good wash all over. Feel better. Fine day. Capt. Waterhouse[i] and Surgeon Pratt dined with us. Grant's cavalry reported to be advancing on the enemy and sending back prisoners. Why don't we move? Why should we be so long in coming from Memphis?

---

[i] Capt. Allen C. Waterhouse of Chicago, Battery E, 1st Illinois Light Artillery; later a major and a lieut. colonel

Hurricane Creek, Miss
Tuesday, Dec. 9, 1862

Were ordered to be ready for review at 3:30 PM. Maj. Gen. Sherman came and surprised us by announcing that he, with Gen. Smith's division, were to go back to Memphis and with other troops to go by water to Vicksburg. Our battery was highly complimented. Gen. Sherman said in substance, I go by water to Vicksburg, you go by land, we hope to meet again there. We have achieved a great victory, without the loss of a life. The enemy have been driven from their strongholds, simply by an effort of mind, or in other words strategy.

I confess that I am too dull of compression to see the point as it seems to me we ought to have come through in 4 days from Memphis and crossed the Tallahatchie at Wyatte, and flanked the enemy at Abbeville and cut their army entirely to pieces.

Hurricane Creek, Miss.
Wednesday, Dec. 10, 1862

Read the President's message,[i] like it. Seemed good to get the "Chicago Tribune" of the 5th as we had not seen one of later date than Nov 22 till today. Wrote to my wife. Lieut. Snyder and I. Little of the 46th Illinois came to visit us. Went out and confiscated a company desk. Don't know who is going to command us.

*** *** *** *** *** *** *** ***

Hurricane Creek, Miss.
December 10th 1862

My dear Wife,

I wrote you on the 5th inst. that we were at Wyatte and would leave on the 6th. But owing to our supply train's not coming up, we did not leave. I went out some two miles with the quartermaster after horses and mules. We got 5 mules and 3 horses. It looks a little rough to enter a man's yard and take his teams, harness etc, and then go into the house

---

[i] In Lincoln's annual message to Congress, among other things, he asked for a Constitutional amendment providing compensation to all states, i.e., Maryland, Delaware, Kentucky and Missouri, that voluntarily abolished slavery before 1900. This was separate from Lincoln's September 22, 1863 Emancipation Proclamation to take effect January 1, 1863, freeing slaves in states in rebellion (except parts of rebelling states under northern control).

and order a dinner, but that is what we done. We got a good dinner of boiled turnip, potatoes, corn bread, milk, canned beef etc.

On the morning of the 7th we were off . Crossed the Tallahatchie; about 2 miles from which we passed the Rebel fortifications. I was lead to exclaim as did Romulus[i] "call you these the walls of a city" as he leaped over them. They are the poorest apologies for fortifications that I ever saw.

On the morning of the 9th were ordered to be ready for review by Maj. Gen. Sherman at 3:30 o'clock PM. We were much surprised on review to learn that Gen. Sherman had been ordered to move with Gen. Smith's division to Memphis, and from thence to Vicksburg by water. I have since learned that Gen. Lauman's division is to be broken up and the 5th Brigade, Col. Buckland in which we are, are to go to Abbeville – next station south of Waterford.[ii] And the 6th Brigade to Waterford. We hope not to be kept long there, but to be assigned to somebody's division and go south. I wish Gen. Wallace could only be our commander.

10th. It is a lovely day and we expect to leave here tomorrow. As Lieut. Snyder is here from the 46th I will close my letter and send by him. I feel anxious to hear from you as I have not heard a word since I left you on the boat. I think you will be much more likely to get my letters than I will be to get yours. I will write you as often as possible and know you will do the same by me.

My health is quite good, considering all things. I am not what I used to be, but get along very well being careful. I was weighed today and weigh 125 lbs. My rheumatism is not yet well and I am not entirely free from pain in the bowels. But should I at any time get sick I will be right in the line of the railroad and will certainly come home, so you need not fear for me. I believe I will be entirely well in a month. I promised to write you just how I am and I do so. You know the worst.

Gen. Sherman complimented us very highly yesterday and said if he had a command where we were, he should certainly apply for Cheney's Battery. The discipline and drill of the battery, he particularly mentioned. I wish I could know that you were all well at home. But I

---

[i] Romulus was the mythical founder of Rome. The historian Livy wrote – Remus, by way of jeering his brother, jumped over the half-built walls of the new settlement, whereupon Romulus killed him in a fit of rage, adding the threat, "So perish whoever shall leap over my battlements." Perhaps the quote Cheney gives is better attributed to Remus.

[ii] Waterford, MS

have learned to do the best I can under such circumstances as we are placed, and hope for better days. Give my love to all the friends and keep the same stone heart that you have always had under all circumstances and we will be well. Kiss the children for me and write often. Good-bye and angels bless you.

Yours truly,
John

*** *** *** *** *** *** *** ***

Hurricane Creek, Miss.
Thursday, Dec. 11, 1862

Received an order at 9 o'clock AM assigning our battery to Gen. Denver's division, which is in camp at College Hill some 4 miles in advance. Reported to Gen. Denver at once and found his division in columns ready to move. Gen. Denver said he supposed I had been notified to report with my battery the night before, and asked me how long it would take me to get my battery. I told him three hours, but in 2 1/2 hours we were in column ready to march. We had not even time to bid good-bye to Gen. Sherman or his staff for whom we had formed a strong attachment. We were assigned to Col. McDowell's brigade. Marched 10 miles to Clear Creek. Good supper of boiled chicken, fish, potatoes, coffee, corn bread etc. Fine day.

Clear Creek, Miss.
Friday, Dec. 12, 1862

Left Clear Creek, marched over horrid roads 15 miles to the Yocknapatalfa River. Now in the advance; Right Wing. Rebels said to be in force at Grenada. Good supper of mutton, liver and fixtures. Rainy, windy night. Boys well. We are in line of battle on the hill, north side of the river. On our left and rear are Gens. Lauman's and Logan's divisions.

Yocknapatalfa
Saturday, Dec. 13, 1862

Wrote to my wife. Rumored that Gen. Burnside is superseded; don't believe it. Hear that a brigade consisting of 3 regiments of infantry, 1 battery artillery and a squadron of cavalry under command of Col. Moore of Illinois had been gobbled up by *Morgan's* cavalry without the firing of a gun.

Yocknapatalfa
Sunday, Dec. 14, 1862

Went to the river and had a wash. Rumored that Burnside is whipped,[i] don't believe it. 46th only 4 miles from us. Division train gone to Holly Springs for provision. When shall we move? A bad road across the bottom on the south side of the river is being corduroyed[ii] for one and one half miles.

Yocknapatalfa, Miss.
Monday, Dec. 15, 1862

Visited the 46th Illinois. Rains tremendously. Got my feet well soaked up and Lieut. Bullock furnished me with a pair of dry socks. Lieut. Bullock came home with me and we sat up till 12 o'clock at night talking. Received an order from Gen. McPherson to be ready for inspection at 10 o'clock AM tomorrow.

Yocknapatalfa
Tuesday, Dec. 16, 1862

Were inspected by Capt. A. Hickenlooper,[iii] chief of artillery for Gen. McPherson. Were complimented and made a very credible appearance. In company with Capt. Hickenlooper and Capt. Cogswell went to front to examine roads, which we found bad. A regiment was detailed to repair them.

Yocknapatalfa
Wednesday, Dec. 17, 1862

Appointed Lewis Bymaster,[iv] sergeant. Appointed George Goodwin,[v] corporal. S. E. Parker[vi] resigned as sergeant, resignation accepted.

---

[i] Burnside commanded the Army of the Potomac (having replaced McClellan in Nov 1862) at the bloody Union defeat at Fredericksburg, VA Dec 11-15, 1862

[ii] Corduroy is to build a road with logs laid side by side; used in swampy places

[iii] Capt. Andrew Hickenlooper, 5th Ohio Light Artillery

[iv] Sergt. Lewis Bymaster of Grand Detour, IL, Battery F, 1st Illinois Light Artillery

[v] Corp. George W. Goodwin of Dixon, IL, Battery F, 1st Illinois Light Artillery

[vi] Sergt. S. E. Parker of Brooklyn, IL, Battery F, 1st Illinois Light Artillery

Fine day, anxious for an advance. All kinds of rumors about the Army of the Potomac, guess there has been a fight.

Yocknapatalfa
Thursday, Dec. 18th 1862

Fine day, nothing important. Wrote my wife. Anxious to hear from home, as we have had no mail since we started.

Yocknapatalfa
Friday, Dec. 19th 1862

Another fine day and no sign of moving. Got a Cincinnati paper of the 15th. Learn that Gen. Burnside tried the enemy on the 13th but no definitive results given. Hope he has used them up. God help the Army of the Potomac.

Yocknapatalfa
Saturday, Dec. 20th 1862

Beautiful weather. Nice beds of Secesh cotton, plenty to eat, but we want marching orders as we came to move upon the enemy's works not to gormandize[i] on their pork and poultry. The brigade quartermaster, who went out with a forage train today, told an old Secesh that the South were a hospitable people. He would if he was taken sick go to some plantation in preference to going to any Federal hospital and doubted not he would be well cared for. Also said the South if they would only hold out a little longer would get a compromise on good terms. Would not suffer a man to buy (not to say confiscate) a particle of provision lest the natives should get some bad money. Damn such officers. It is such men that are keeping us here today.

Summary

At this point in the war the official policy was to respect the property of Southern civilians. Cheney exercised his belief that hardship in the civilian population led to a lessened abil-

---

[i] Gormandize is to eat greedily

ity of the Confederacy to fight. He encouraged his men to forage the countryside. That included more that just taking food. In Cheney's Dec. 4, 1862 letter to his wife he included some "Southern love letters." It was a common practice for Union soldiers to enter Southern homes and take letters that Confederate soldiers had written to their wives.

John Cheney had three brothers in the Union army. Lieut. Thomas Cheney of the 6th New Hampshire received a disability discharge November 25, 1862. Sergt. Samuel Cheney[i] and Lieut. Daniel Cheney,[ii] both of the 12th New Hampshire, were part of the Army of the Potomac and had fought at the December 1862 Battle of Fredericksburg without injury.

John Cheney's health, while not robust, was okay. What he called rheumatism was sciatica. His symptoms were pain in the back radiating into the buttocks and down along the back of the leg. As well as being painful, it made him lame such that he sometimes used a crutch to get around.

His more serious illness that developed in June-August 1862 (dysentery or something similar) was hinted at again in his December 10, 1862 reference to being "not entirely free from pain in the bowels."

---

[i] Sergt. (later Lieut.) Samuel Cheney of Holderness, New Hampshire, 12th N. H. Infantry, brother of John Cheney

[ii] Lieut. Daniel Cheney of Holderness, New Hampshire, 12th N. H. Infantry, brother of John Cheney

Chapter 7 - Backtracking out of Mississippi

December 21, 1862 to January 9, 1863

Background

On December 20, 1862, *Maj. Gen. Van Horn* captured the Union supply base at Holly Springs, Mississippi. The surrender of the Union garrison by Col. Murphy of the 8th Wisconsin was considered a disgrace. The loss of the Holly Springs supply base caused Maj. Gen. Grant to abandon the overland march to Vicksburg. Grant's army returned to the area around La Grange and Grand Junction, Tennessee.

Yocknapatalfa
Sunday, Dec. 21, 1862
    Received information that some Rebel cavalry had made a raid on Holly Springs; captured some 500 prisoners, a million dollars worth of provisions and clothing. Gen. Denver[i] is notified by Gen. Grant to be ready for an attack at any moment. Was ordered by chief of artillery to go to the front and select positions for batteries in case we were attacked, and made an advance. In company with Capts. Cogswell and Mueller, Lieuts. Etting and Burton went and visited the tops of several peaks to which we gave appropriate names.
    In the evening were ordered to be ready to march for Wyatte on the Tallahatchie at 7 o'clock AM tomorrow morning. Rather humiliating to take the back track but such is strategy.

Yocknapatalfa
Monday, Dec. 22, 1862
    At 7 o'clock promptly we marched to the time of Get Out of the Wilderness.[ii] Made 19 miles to a beautiful creek 2 miles southeast of College Hill.

---

[i] Battery F is in Gen. Denver's division
[ii] The song "Ain'tl Glad to Get Out of the Wilderness"

During the day Capt. Cogswell and ye commissary's clerk rode up and ordered an action rear. I looked up and found a gun with a bore of about one inch[i] which I soon silenced and nobody hurt. The key that will unlock this mystery is <u>Whis Key</u>.

Tuesday, Dec. 23rd 1862

On our way at 7 o'clock. Learned that the Rebels had destroyed the bridge at Wyatte and we went to Abbeville. From there across the Tallahatchie through the enemy's fort and went into camp about one mile from the river. Gen. Quincy's division passed us this evening. Gens. Logan's and Lauman's divisions were most of the night in getting up. Will not soon forget this day.

Wednesday, Dec. 24th 1862

It is one of the most magnificent sights I ever beheld to look over our army this morning. Visited the 46th about ½ mile from us. Washed in the Tallahatchie. Received the following order from ye commissary's clerk.

> Commissary's Department
> December 24, 1862
> Tallahatchie River near Abbeville
>
> Captain
>
> Ye humble commissary's clerk desires to remind ye captain of ye bloody battery that tomorrow is Christmas and if ye bully captain will send his vessel, ye commissary's clerk will pour into it such spirits as ye captain delightith in.
>
> From ye humble commissary's clerk
> With respect
> Signed Brisbin

In compliance with the forgoing order ye captain sent his vessel, and ye commissary's clerk did fill it. Ye captain was delighted so much so that he went in person to ye commissary's clerk and expressed his gratitude. Ye captain was reminded that ye men of ye bully battery would be delighted with a drop of the same fluid, and proceeded to secure 3 gallons of said fluid. An invitation was immediately sent to

---

[i] A jug or canteen

93

Lieut. Col. Jones, Maj. McCracken,[i] Adjt. Woodbury,[ii] Lieut. Bullock and Capt. Cogswell to visit us. It is perhaps necessary to say that they came on double quick. A large fire was built in front of headquarters and the evening was spent in liberty and glee. Songs were sung. Speeches were made. Ye fluid was disposed of and Christmas was ushered in with a will. May we all be at home with our families and friends next Christmas and the rebellion crushed out, the cause of it removed or in course of everlasting extinction, is ye wish of ye captain and ye officers and men of ye bully battery.

Abbeville
Thursday, December 25th 1862, Christmas

All hands feeling first rate after a merry Christmas Eve. Gens. Quinby's, Lauman's, Logan's and Denver's divisions are here this morning. Found Capts. Bolton,[iii] Spears, Burnap, Rodgers[iv] and many acquaintances that I had been long separated from. Gen. Quinby's division go to Memphis as a guard for our train, who go after provisions.

PM. Gen. Logan's and Gen. Lauman's divisions have gone on about 3 miles.

Forage is getting scarce and we must scatter some or go short. Horses in good condition. Men in good health. We are all anxious to get a paper or letters from home. Every movement for the last 20 days has been in other departments. All that is contemplated in our own are studiously kept from us. I have wondered how the friends at home have spent Christmas. My own health is quite good. We have but little doubt that we will remain here till our train comes back from Memphis.

Wonder if the little folks at home have found anything in their stockings this morning.

---

[i] Maj. John M. McCracken of Freeport, IL, HQ, 46th Illinois Infantry
[ii] Adjt. Henry H. Woodbury of Amboy, IL, HQ, 46th Illinois Infantry
[iii] Capt. William H. Bolton of Chicago, IL, Battery L, 2nd Illinois Light Artillery
[iv] Capt. Benjamin F. Rodgers of Jacksonville, IL, Battery K, 2nd Illinois Light Artillery

Abbeville

Friday, December 26th 1862

It is raining quite hard and every thing indicates a long storm. It is dull indeed to lie round camp in a storm, but we can't have all sunshine. Maj. Gen. McPherson sent out 15 teams for forage with 30 infantry as a guard. 38 mounted guerrillas[i] attacked them, took 4 teams, 2 teamsters, and 3 soldiers. No news and there is a strong suspicion that our mails are being suppressed. Why can't we get a paper; none since the 15th.

10 PM, still raining.

Saturday, December 27th 1862

Met Maj. Rogers, who has been commissioned by Gov. Yates to obtain a correct history of all the regiments and batteries in this department from Illinois. Still raining. Boys on half rations. Our camp is now well policed and looks fine.

Abbeville

Sunday, December 28th 1862

Commenced on our muster and payrolls. Got two of them completed. Received orders to march tomorrow morning at daylight. We are reputed to be going to Lafayette, Tenn.[ii] It is reputed that Vicksburg and Richmond are ours,[iii] but we don't know what to believe. Have been down to look over the Rebel fortifications. They are well planned and but for Gen. Sherman's divisions advancing south of them at Wyatte for the purpose of flanking them, we would have had some work to do to cross at Abbeville. It has been a fine day, but the roads are bad. We have a hard march for tomorrow. I am very anxious about home, but all communications by mail is cut off, and I can neither get a letter from home, or send one home. Such is war, may it soon be closed, but not till it is closed effectively.

---

[i] Guerrillas are irregular military groups that operate independently

[ii] The village of Lafayette, TN was about 10 miles from Moscow, TN, near Memphis, not to be confused with the town of Lafayette in northern Tennessee

[iii] Neither Richmond nor Vicksburg had been captured by the Union army

Abbeville
Monday, Dec. 29th 1862

Got a good start soon as daylight. Fine day. Passed Waterford at 12 M, arrived at Holly Springs at 3 PM. Column remained in the streets about 2 hours and then learned that our division would remain in Holly Springs for the present. Went into camp on the south side of the town. First as we were pitching our tents, Sergeant Raub[i] came in with a package of mail and it was soon distributed. What was our disappointment was that it was old, none of it written later than November. I received one letter from Brother Pers dated Nov. 26, 1862, same day we left Memphis. No word from my family.

Poor camping ground. Water for animals scarce and poor. We have passed 15 sets of chimneys today, all ready to build houses to. The houses that they were built for have been burned by our troops, some burning as we passed. Passed 10 dead horses.

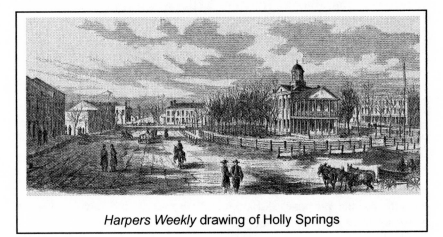

Harpers Weekly drawing of Holly Springs

Holly Springs
Dec. 30th 1862

Moved our camp to a better position for the battery, on the left of the division. For the first time came into battery fronting the north. Finished our muster and payrolls, and are ready for muster tomorrow. It is said that on the evening of the 19th inst. *Gen. Van Dorn* came into town in disguise, visited a sutler, bought a box of cigars, asked the sutler if he would be here tomorrow, was answered yes and he said he

---

[i] Sergt. (later Lieut.) Theodore W. Raub of Dixon, IL, Battery F, 1st Illinois Light Artillery

would see him again. On the 20th (date of the disgraceful surrender of this town) *Gen. Van Dorn* did come in and made himself known to the sutler.

Everything indicates that there was treachery on the part of Col. Murphy of the 8th Wisconsin Infantry who was in command of the post. Two roads were not guarded. It is estimated that 1 ½ millions of government property was taken away or burned. It is also reported that 13 millions of green backs were burned by the paymaster to prevent it from falling into the hands of the Rebels.

The troops at the post were the 101st Illinois, 6 companies of whom got away. 8th Wisconsin all taken, and the 2nd Illinois Cavalry of whom about 75 were taken, 7 killed and several wounded. The 109th Illinois who kept a respectful distance and hurt nobody, neither were they harmed. It is believed that the prisoners taken were generally willing captives. The 2nd Illinois Cavalry and 101st Illinois Infantry did themselves much credit. Maj. Gen. Grant feels very much mortified.

Holly Springs
Wednesday, December 31, 1862

Were mustered for pay this morning by Capt. Cogswell, chief of artillery, 1st Division. Fine day. Coming to the conclusion that we are destined to garrison this town this winter. In the evening a large hotel has burned. We all came out and admired the fire, magnificent truly. We wish the last dime's worth of Rebel property in Holly Springs was burned and we ordered to the front or rear. Masterly inactivity.

Holly Springs, Miss.
Thursday, January 1st 1863

A fine day and as happy a new year as can be expected among a lot of patriotic soldiers who have left home and friends to fight for the very existence of their government, and believe they are held in check, when action would soon finish the war, and let them return to their homes and friends. It is also believed that our mail matter has been kept away from us, as there is no possible way by which we could be without mail for 30 days unless by intervention from some source.

Soldiers in the ranks are possessed of good common sense. I think they should at least not be deprived of newspapers – let them contain whatever news they may. They cannot harm our soldiery, who will only fight the harder if we have met with reverses. If Gen. Burnside has been successful or Vicksburg has been taken or Gen. Rosecrans has wiped out *Bragg*, the private in the ranks is entitled to a knowledge of it, that he may rejoice. Such are the soldiers conjectures in camp at Holly Springs, Miss. Shut out from the world and the rest of mankind.

It is reputed that the 109th Illinois Infantry have thrown down their arms,[i] assigning as a reason that they cannot live on half rations. The real reason appears to be, they wished for a chance to be taken prisoners on the 20th inst, but did not succeed. Blank paroles were found on the officers. The lieut. col. commanding has been heard to say he would rather be a private in the Confederate, than a colonel in the Federal service. The 109th have been relieved of their arms and are now being guarded by the 99th Indiana. Shame for Illinois who has done so nobly in the present contest, but Illinois is not free from traitors.

It is a beautiful evening. Gen. Grant is sending up a few rockets. Some would think this in bad taste so soon after so disgraceful a surrender. But whistle to keep the courage up. No news from home. I wish you all a happy New Year and speak for a roast turkey and some butter next New Year's. Have had no butter (save once) since we left Memphis.

Holly Springs, Miss.
Friday, January 2nd 1863

Spent the day in filing away papers and writing generally. Wind from the south and some rain. Looks like a storm. It makes but little difference to us rain or shine so long as we must remain in camp. A Negro reports that we are to be attacked here tonight. It is all a mistake I suppose. Should it be true, Gen. Denver's division will give them the best they have in their cartridge boxes, and the batteries will surrender if they can't help it. The train has just returned and it is rumored or rather reported that Burnside is whipped. We will know the truth probably tomorrow. I hope we will get some papers and letters now, but have been disappointed so often that it is all right with me whether school keeps[ii] or not.

Holly Springs
Saturday January 3rd 1863

Received no letters by the train. Did get a "Memphis Bulletin" of the 31st ult., but it contained no news from the Potomac. Gen. Sherman

---

[i] Officially, the 109th Illinois Infantry objected to having inferior/unfit arms.
[ii] A common expression at the time

is reported as going up the Yazoo to St. Charles, Miss., only 6 miles from Vicksburg by land. Vicksburg has not been taken it seems. Gen. Burnside has not crossed the Rappahannock. Have we got to take Vicksburg and then go and help the Army of the Potomac take Richmond?

Have been at work on a history of the battery by request of Gov. Yates to be kept with the archives of the State of Illinois.[i] It has rained hard all day and is still (9 PM) raining. Have been successful in getting a stove today, and have set it up and running in good order. A train of cars has arrived this evening said to be direct from Memphis.

*** *** *** *** *** *** *** ***

Holly Springs, Miss.
January 3, 1863

My dear Wife,

I wrote you last from Abbeville on Sunday the 28th of December and don't know that it has gone outside of our lines yet, as there is no mail coming into the division.

My health is first rate. I have worked hard for the past few days and stand it well. We arrived here the same day we left Abbeville. Suppose we will remain here perhaps all winter. I hope we will go either north or south as I dislike very much to lie idle in camp, though I am not idle much of the time. Holly Springs is quite a pretty town and in time of peace has been quite a smart town, larger than Dixon. Our guns point toward the north and it looks curious to see them in battery. This retreat is a bitter pill for us, but we sugar coat it and down she goes.

I am writing a diary dedicated to you. In about another week will complete the first volume and send to you the first opportunity. If my letters are short, be assured you will get all the news on the reception of the diary.

We mustered for pay on the 31st inst. and hope to get paid sometime but don't know when. If a paymaster comes into our division, I will be after him with a sharp stick. I have been fortunate enough to get all the money I needed so far and will explain. Two captains came into my tent and made a bet of $5 and deposited $10 with me. I used the $10 as the bet cannot be decided under two months. I will be all ready for them. I expect some other way will be open about the time this is gone.

---

[i] I can't locate a detailed history of Battery F; existing ones are just brief summaries

I still have $1.50, which is plenty so long as it lasts. Kiss the babies, love to the folks, and myself for you when the war is over.

Affectionately yours,
John

*** *** *** *** *** *** *** ***

Holly Springs, Miss.
Sunday, January 4th 1863

Was ordered with 30 men to go in pursuit of beef. Took 15 of Capt. Cogswell's and 15 of my own men. Procured arms[i] of the 99th Indiana and went 10 miles across the Chewalla. Procured 32 head of cattle, several chickens, geese, dried peaches etc. Got very tired. Got back at 10 PM. Found many widows as usual. As disconsolate as they were, they had beef and though reluctantly, they parted with it. Fine day but bad roads.

Holly Springs, Miss.
January 5th 1863

A cloudy morning, appearances of rain. At 1 o'clock PM the advance of Gen. Lauman's division came up. I started for the rear thinking the division would go beyond us, and we could give some of the 46th Illinois a cup of coffee. Found Col. Jones, Capt. Hughes, Lieuts. Bullock and Woodbury who came forward and dined with us. The division went into camp here and the above named came and spent the evening with us and Col. Jones all night. At 10 PM got orders to move at daylight tomorrow morning. We march east and only know that we have to go not knowing where. Gen. Logan's division have come up and gone into camp here.

On the march
Tuesday, January 6th 1863

Stormy and cold but we got an early start. Cleared up before noon and quite pleasant. Marched east on the Salem road. At noon we stopped at Chewalla Creek where the boys found some flour in a mill which they took possession of. I wanted some graham[ii] flour and went in and ordered the miller to grind for me while we remained. He

---

[i] Artillery batteries didn't have muskets; they borrowed them for such duty
[ii] Graham is whole wheat flour

declined, but on being told that the mill must grind he preferred to run it himself and we have a sack of good graham, all of which was well. Arrived at Salem Miss. at 4 o'clock PM, distance from Holly Springs, Miss. 17 miles. Plenty of forage.

On the march
Wednesday, January 7th 1863
Started at 8 AM. Fine morning. Marched through a fine country, passed Spring Hill to the valley of the Wolf River. Bad bottom, very muddy, were detained two hours to repair roads. Crossed the Wolf and went into camp about one mile from the river near Smith's Mill. Distance marched 10 miles. We are 6 miles southeast of La Grange, Tenn. Learn tonight that there has been a terrible fight at Vicksburg.[i] That Col. John B. Wyman[ii] of the old 13th was killed and that the 8th Missouri went in with 600 men and came out with 134 men only. Very anxious to hear particulars concerning the 13th. I know that they have done themselves and Illinois and Lee County and Dixon honor.

Smith's Mills, Miss.
Thursday, January 8, 1863
Wrote my wife and sent to Memphis by Dr. Shaw[iii] of the 6th Iowa. Rainy and muddy, cold and gloomy. Started out visiting batteries, regiments and Gen. Denver's headquarters. At Gen. Denver's found a "Memphis Bulletin" of this morning from which learn that Gen. Rosecrans has attacked *Gen. Bragg* at Murfreesboro. Although it has cost us many valuable lives, Murfreesboro is ours and *Bragg* retreating. This helps cheer up the soldier a little. Rain, mud, half rations, away from civilization and impatient to get a chance to whip or be whipped.

*** *** *** *** *** *** *** ***

---

[i] The flotilla with Sherman's army arrived at the Yazoo River in the Walnut Hills area just north of Vicksburg on Dec 26/27, 1862. Sherman unsuccess-fully attacked the Confederate defenses in Battle of Chickasaw Bayou.
[ii] Col. John B. Wyman of Amboy, IL, HQ, 13th Illinois Infantry
[iii] Surgeon Albert T. Shaw of Fort Madison, IA, 6th Iowa Infantry

Wolf River 4 miles east of La Grange
January 8, 1863

My dear Wife,

I have just been to headquarters. Found I could send a letter by Dr. Shaw direct to Memphis, and have hastened back to write you a few lines. We left Holly Springs on the morning of the 6th and arrived here last evening. The reason of our being sent here was *Van Dorn* was reputed to be in this vicinity with some 8,000 cavalry. We were wanted within a short distance of any point he would be likely to attack. Last evening when our advance came in here there was quite a force of guerrillas. A bugler in the 6th Iowa was shot through the head and killed. His regiment immediately proceeded to burn a nice house and buildings near the spot where he was shot.

The 46th were at Holly Springs when we left. They were all well. Don't know where they will go to. Give my love to all the friends and to the little folks in particular. I wish I could have slipped something into the stockings of the little ones on Christmas Eve. I am as usual willing to remain as long as may be necessary, but wish we could move a little faster. The many friends who advised and urged me to resign[i] ought to see me now. Their advice was well intended but I did well to do as I did. I believe you never asked me to do it and the reason I know well. Good-bye and God bless you.

Affectionately yours,
John

Summary

The war was not going well for the Union. In the East, Burnside had been soundly defeated at the Battle of Fredericksburg in Virginia. In the West, Vicksburg remained a Confederate stronghold. Cheney was marching north not south. Cheney blamed the loss of the Holly Springs supply depot on the poor leadership and cowardice of Col. Murphy of the 8th Wisconsin. Cheney had yet to engage in combat and was frustrated by the inability to take decisive action.

---

[i] Friends suggesting resignation, underscores how sick Cheney was back at Dixon in August and September 1862

Chapter 8 - Guarding the Railroad at Davis Mill, Mississippi

January 10, 1863 to January 20, 1863

Background

Battery F (in Brig. Gen. Denver's division) did duty for the rest of January 1863 protecting the Mississippi Central Railroad at Davis Mill, Mississippi (present day Michigan City). That railroad continued through Grand Junction, Tennessee 6 miles to the northeast. Davis Mill had been the site of a December 21, 1862 skirmish.

Drawing of Davis Mill, MS in *Harpers Weekly*

Davis Mill, Miss.
Friday, January 9th 1863

At one o'clock AM get orders to march at 8 o'clock AM. Rainy morning but cleared up at about 9 o'clock. We marched with the 40th

Illinois to Davis Mill, on the south side of Wolf River, 6 miles from Grand Junction.

We learn that *Van Dorn's* cavalry made an attack upon this post on the 22nd ultimo, on their return from Holly Springs, but were repulsed with a loss of 18 killed and many mortally wounded. The post was commanded by Col. Morgan of the 25th Indiana Infantry. He had but 250 men. He had notice of the approach of the enemy and immediately threw up fortifications around a little mound (supposed to have been the work of Indians) and put one company into a log house. He then had them where it was impossible to cross the bridge to get into the town. Col. Morgan did himself much honor. Had Col. Murphy done as well at Holly Springs, we would undoubtedly not have been retreating today.

The remainder of our division went to La Grange and Grand Junction. When or where we will come together, we don't know. It has been rainy this afternoon and the roads horrid. Col. Hicks[i] of the 40th Illinois assumes command of this post.

Davis Mill, Miss.
Saturday, Jany. 10, 1863

Have had a rainy night, but slept very comfortably on a good mattress given to me by Capt. De Collier 8th Michigan Artillery, who left as soon as we came in. This morning the sun is shining brightly. Train after train of cars are passing to and from Holly Springs which place is being evacuated by our forces. Gen. Grant's headquarters are now at La Grange.

Holly Springs has suffered severely by a fire which consumed a large portion of the best part of the town. It is currently reported that the smallpox had been there. Our troops knowing it to be a very contagious disease, they concluded to stop it effectively, and burned the buildings. Not being certain what building it had been in, concluded to make a sure thing of it, and so (notwithstanding a whole division were ordered to prevent it) they fired every one that they could get fired. I think the soldiers showed their good sense as smallpox is terrible, particularly in a large army.

A train has just passed with the arms of the 109th Illinois. Lieut. Burton with 16 men has gone out after forage. Hope he will be successful as we are still on half rations and a few luxuries will go very well. We get no mail yet and have no hope of getting any till the division is

---

[i] Col. Stephen G. Hicks of Salem, IL, HQ, 40th Illinois Infantry

again united. It is supposed by some that we remain here a long time as this is a good point for wood and water for the railroad – there being no water at La Grange or Grand Junction. Uncle Sam has a steam engine here for sawing wood and raising water. It seems a little like civilization to be where we can see a railroad train passing every few minutes. Learn that Gen. Lauman's division leave Holly Springs today, and move in the direction of Memphis.

The Mr. Davis who owns the mill here is a large man. Has been an officer in the Confederate service, but has come in and surrendered himself, taken the oath of allegiance. I predict that oath won't save him, as the boys know him and when we get through with his mill (for fear that the Rebels get it to do their grinding in) it will share the same fate of Holly Springs. A clear case of military necessity.

3 PM, very latest from Holly Springs. William Witt has just returned by the train and is entirely reliable, says Gen. Grant's late headquarters is burned and almost the whole city burned. Hundreds of Negroes are waiting for transportation north. The train on which Witt came had at least 200 Negroes with all kinds of baggage presenting a curious appearance.

6 PM, another train and on the tops, sides and ends of the cars are Negroes; women and children. Where they will go to, or what may be their fate nobody knows or apparently cares. Unfortunate beings, I hope there may be a better future for them than has been the past or is present. I have been down to see the building in which was a company of the 25th Indiana during the late fight. It is or was a sawmill and Col. Morgan had put up a breastwork of green planks leaving a space 2 inches wide for his men to shoot through. The thing was admirably planned and well carried out. The skirmishers[i] of the enemy were dressed in United States clothing. After a volley had been fired, an order was given to cease firing fearing we were firing on our own men. After the enemy had been repulsed 3 times, *Gen. Van Dorn* rode onto the bridge under a flag of truce. Col. Morgan rode up to the bridge and ordered *Gen. Van Dorn* to halt, which he did. Col. Morgan asked *Gen. Van Dorn* what he would have and was asked by *Gen. V. D.* if he was ready to surrender. Col. Morgan answered when I am whipped I will.

Just at that time one 6 pound gun had arrived from La Grange and was put in position. Two shells were thrown into their lines and away went *Gen. Van Dorn* with his indomitable cavalry. Thus ended one of the most brilliant little fights that has occurred during the war. Less

---

[i] Skirmishers are small groups set out from the main body of troops to probe the location of the enemy

than 200 able men put some 3000 Rebels to flight. Bully for ye 25th Indiana and Col. Morgan.

Lieut. Burton has returned. A beef, some Negroes, fodder and corn were the fruits of the expedition. Sergt. Richey[i] has been to La Grange for 5 days rations. We are on full rations except sugar and coffee. Capt. Cogswell and Lt. Woodworth have come from Grand Junction and La Grange. Report that Gen. Grant has been called upon for 25,000 men and it is possible we may get a chance in. We can only say we are ready, willing and anxious to go. Capt. Cogswell says he has orders to visit me and if he thinks best to leave one section here and remove our headquarters to La Grange or Grand Junction. Capt. Cogswell accedes to my wishes and we will not be separated. Capt. Cogswell has gone to La Grange and Lt. Woodworth stays all night. I go to La Grange with him in the morning. Gen. Grant and Gen. McPherson meet at Memphis tonight where a council of war will be held. I predict that in two or three days we will be on the road to Vicksburg.

Well we have been up the hill and come down again. Many cotton speculators have made fortunes and our trains are moving it to Memphis now. Not a bale is marked U.S. and rumor says much of it should be marked U.S.A. Our advance was slow but we soldiers were enthusiastic hoping to overtake and rout the enemy. They were not allowed to advance. Our retreat has been in haste, and well conducted but the enthusiasm of the soldiers is gone. They are all willing to go north but not till the enemy are used up.

*** *** *** *** *** *** *** ***

Davis Mill, Miss.
Jany. 10, 1863

My dear Wife,

It is now 10 o'clock PM. I have just finished up Volume 1 of my diary. Thought I would send it to you and write a few lines. I have not heard a word from you since you left Memphis and as you are well aware I am very anxious about you. Still I feel assured that you are all right. When I do get a letter it will be such a treat, as I have never had before, if you are all well. My health is good. You will see by the diary that I send you, that I have written you often. I hope you have had better luck than I have and received them all. But it would be strange if you have.

---

[i] Sergt. (later Lieut) Robert Richey of Brooklyn, IL, Battery F, 1st Illinois Light Artillery

Seth Thomas[i] has been quite unwell for a week past. I have sent a good faithful man to go with him, and 4 others that you don't know, to Memphis by railroad to get into the hospital. Seth will come out all right. Jacob Hoffman[ii] from Palmyra is one of the 5 who went to the hospital. You will recollect we called on his wife on our return from Henry Smith's.

My opinion is we will go to Vicksburg by water. If we do I will write you at Memphis. We have not received our boxes yet as we have not been in one place long enough to dare to send for them. I expect we will go back to Memphis and get them. Mr. Leach[iii] has gone to Memphis hoping to get a job where he can get better pay.[iv] All the Dixon boys well.

Tell Royce I will try and get his saddle through for him. If my horse Tip lives through the war, he will have a nice rig. If I get home by next Christmas, I will put them in his stocking. I hope his health is better than when he left Memphis. I have been trying to think what Gracie could be afflicted with this winter. Don't know unless mumps or smallpox. I don't need to say I want to see you, but get along as happily as possible. And all will be well. Give my love to all of the family and friends.

I wish we had 20 more men. I think there ought to be about that number in and about Dixon who ought to come. We have the fullest battery in the division but there is no danger of having too many. We can take 175 if we wish. Good night Mary

Affectionately your husband,
John

*** *** *** *** *** *** *** ***

Davis Mill, Miss.
Sunday, January 11th 1863

Lovely morning. In company with Dr. Woodworth[v] (assistant surgeon in our regiment) and Lieut. Whaley, went to La Grange. Were delighted by the singing of woodcock and robins and the skipping of squirrels. Green hollies beautiful and many pine and beech trees which reminded me of a May morning in New England. We went expecting to

---

[i] Pvt. Seth Thomas of Sterling, IL, Battery F, 1st Illinois Light Artillery
[ii] Pvt. Jacob Hoffman of Palmyra, IL, Battery F, 1st Illinois Light Artillery
[iii] Pvt. Leander L. Leach of Dixon, IL, Battery F, 1st Illinois Light Artillery
[iv] This is a sarcastic reference to Leach's discharge
[v] Surgeon John M. Woodworth, HQ, 1st Illinois Light Artillery

find some mail and learned that the battery mail had been forwarded the evening previous by the 40th Illinois postmaster.

Returned as soon as possible and learned the postmaster went up on the train. As no train has come down today, our mail has not come. I had got a good ready to devour the contents of my letters. Have had my dinner and will wait patiently for the return of said postmaster. If I don't get a letter, will be led to exclaim with another disappointed man, on a certain occasion, "If a man thinks he is, he ain't also, more'n (more than) like Hell by a damned sight."

Gen. McPherson's headquarters are now up at La Grange. Everything indicates that we remain here for a time; long or short do not attempt to predict which. Gen. Sherman has been repulsed at Vicksburg and is waiting for reinforcements. He has got where it requires more than simply an effort of mind to whip the enemy. *Price* is reported at Vicksburg and I believe there is not earthly reason why we should not have followed him closely, save one and that is the disgraceful surrender of Holly Springs by Col. Murphy. And that is not sufficient reason as we could have lived off the country and no soldier would have complained, as never will complain, so long as we are crowding the enemy.

Our whole movement since we have left Memphis has been a succession of blunders. Too late to remedy now, but the same should not be allowed the second time by the same men. Gen. Grant's trying Col. Murphy, the second time,[i] caused the surrender of Holly Spring. The question is, is not Gen. Grant directly responsible for entrusting the command of so important a post to a man who had proved himself unworthy of any command at Iuka? Thus we reason but it is all of no avail. The administration have put too many of its enemies in important commands and today such men as Cassius M. Clay, John C. Freemont, Lew Wallace and other who are fighting men, and whose hearts are in the right place are left in the cold to make room for political demigods and men who never had nor can have a higher motive than personal aggrandizement or the money that cotton will bring. Patriotism is so near played out that true patriots almost despair of ever accomplishing what should have been done a long time ago.

Ye 40th Illinois postmaster has come. I have two letters from my wife; one of the 14th and one of the 19th ultimo. I am delighted to hear from home as it is the first letter I have had since the 26th of

---

[i] Col. R. C. Murphy, 8th Wisconsin had evacuated Iuka, MS upon approach of Rebel forces two months previous to Holly Springs

November. 45 days[i] and not a word from home. I shall never forget the good nature produced through the company on the receipt of the mail today.

The train went to Lamar 7 miles south of us and has just gone up laden with cotton. Negroes and soldiers having burned the depot buildings, Holly Springs is entirely evacuated by our troops (Gen. Lauman's division having gone to La Grange) and is once more in the possession of the Rebels. That is the ground on which Holly Springs was.

We are now in the rear, the 40th Illinois and 200 men of the 25th Indiana only being with us, and no other troops nearer than La Grange (6 miles). We some expect to be annoyed by Secesh cavalry, but will give them the best that the town affords, if they attempt to come in.

*** *** *** *** *** *** *** ***

Davis Mill, Miss.
January 11th 1863

My dear Wife,

I have just received two letters from you. One of the 14th and one of the 19th ult. Although I have felt confident you were all right, still I was not certain and the assurance by letter has made me feel good.

It is reported that we have scarcely made out to get food enough to sustain life. Now I don't know who the grumbler is. I do know that we have been compelled to take half rations from the commissary and have for a day or two had but one cracker a day. But we never were out of meat and have almost always had corn meal and good bake kettles to cook it in. One night when we had no bread to issue I went and borrowed a box of hard bread of the 99th Indiana. We have tonight more meat than we know what to do with. I know I have faced as hard for provisions as any man in the battery and have never seen cause to complain although we have not had all that heart could wish. You can give the lie to any such stories. If I have a man who complains after knowing (as they all do) the circumstances, all I have to say is he is unworthily of a place in the battery and I sincerely hope he may never fare worse. One thing is certain, while there is corn in Egypt,[ii] or food

---

[i] John had last seen Mary and his children on November 26, 1862 when they departed Memphis to return to Dixon after accompanying him back to the front

[ii] Now when Jacob saw that there was corn in Egypt, Jacob said unto his sons, Why do ye look one upon another? And he said, Behold, I have heard that

in the Southern Confederacy, no man in Cheney's Battery shall go hungry, orders or no orders. It touches my pride a little to have it said that we have scarcely enough to sustain life, when it is known that there is plenty in the country to eat. We draw 1 lb of meat per day for each man, and have never drawn less of meat. In addition to that, day before yesterday we foraged one beef and two hogs. Today we have dressed one beef and one hog. Understand this is against orders and in addition to our 1 lb per day. Think you we have scarcely enough to sustain life?

It is true we have not been able at all times to get coffee, but we have been furnished with rye.[i] I have drunk that at home and expect to again. We have always had sugar. There occasionally gets into the army a gingerbread man who expects to sail pleasantly through a civil war and never want for anything that his appetite craves without getting it. There is another class who make the best of everything, are not heard to complain, come with the expectation of privations and hardships. Of the latter class are the men of my battery generally. The sick child who writes that he has scarcely enough to sustain life is fooling away his time in writing. I hope it is not true that such a letter has been written. I am inclined to believe that someone has written that we were on half rations (which is true) and someone has drawn the inference that we were starving, and thus the report. We are not starving nor do we intend to.

My health is good. I will continue to keep a diary and if my letters are short you will get a full account of our doings about once in 15 days. I will continue to write you often.

Give my love to all the friends. Good night Mary and be assured that your prayers and desires are all right, and so am I. Grace must be a little duck of a girl. Oh how I wish I could hear her say "air" and "paper", but I'll not whine while I can hear from home once in 45 days and get enough to sustain life. I expect you will be highly entertained by reading my diary, but you will recollect it is unlike sitting down in the parlor at home to write.

Lieuts. Burton and Whaley have gone to bed and Lieut. Smyth is reading from a New Church paper. A theological discussion is going on.

---

there is corn in Egypt: get you down thither, and buy for us from thence; that we may live, and not die. Genesis 42:1,2.
[i] Roasted rye was used as a coffee substitute

I will once more bid you good night. God bless you. No paymaster. Still have $1.50, a piece of tobacco about the size of a piece of chalk, or large enough to sustain life.

Affectionately your husband,
John T. Cheney

*** *** *** *** *** *** *** ***

Davis Mill, Miss.
Monday, January 12, 1863
Lovely morning. Ordered to accompany Col. Hicks of the 40th Illinois (commandant of the post) to go round the camp and examine the outposts. Did so and find that we can easily fortify here with cotton bales, so that we can hold the post against a greatly superior force.

Afternoon took 30 of my men, and took out a bridge and prepared another so that it can be destroyed in 5 minutes time, leaving it so that we can cross it to go for forage. Lieut. Burton went to La Grange this morning. I have just learned that he obtained leave of absence for three days and has gone to Memphis.

5 PM received an order from Gen. Denver notifying us that there is in the neighborhood 6,000 Rebel cavalry and we must be on the lookout. Col. Hicks mustered 100 men and all his trains to go to getting cotton for us to build breastworks about our guns. We have built two forts commanding the only two roads leading into the place and have Section No. 1 inside one under command of Lieut. Whaley, and No 2 in the other under Lieut. Smyth. Horses harnessed and the boys eager for a fray.

I have been waiting to get sleepy for a long time but 12 o'clock and not sleepy. At 1 o'clock went to bed and rested well. Nobody hurt.

Davis Mill, Miss.
Tuesday, January 13, 1863
Another fine day. Went out to see what kind of forts we had built the night before and found we had done well and that was all we did do. Teams started for forage and found that some officer had misunderstood the order the night before, and the bridge we had prepared to take out the night previous, had been taken out. We had made use of the same strategy that Orpheus C Kerr[i] speaks of on the Potomac when his regiment pursued the enemy across a stream and took up the bridge

---

[i] Orpheus C. Kerr is the penname for author Robert C. Newell.

after them, leaving themselves on the wrong side of the stream. I went with the boys, with their prolonges,[i] axes etc. In one hour the teams with a guard of 50 infantry were across.

We learn today that the Democrats of Illinois have after so long a time shown their hands. They condemn the President's message and declare their intention to do nothing for the suppression of the Rebellion. Well it is very easy for political wine drinkers to remain quietly at home, find fault with the administration, and try and clog the wheels that thousands of patriots, i.e., Democrats and Republicans, have indirectly put their shoulders to. Gentleman you work with a zeal worthy of a better cause, but you can't win.

Fort Lafayette[ii] is a very strong one and ought to afford a home for you.

Davis Mill, Miss.
Wednesday, January 14th 1863

Commenced raining before daylight and looks as though we were to have a long storm. A contraband has come in and informs us that the Rebels intended to attack us, but found the road blocked up. The roads both commanded by our artillery, they were compelled to give it up. We expect and are ready for an attack.

Learn that Gen. Sherman has been compelled to retreat from Vicksburg. That Springfield, Mo. has been retaken by the Rebels. That Gen. Rosecrans has whipped *Bragg* out handsomely, taking 7,000 prisoners.

It has rained hard all day and getting quite cold. We have no stoves for the tents. It is far from being comfortable. Still the boys keep quite good natured.

Davis Mill, Miss.
Thursday, January 15th 1863

Rain and snow has been falling all night. This morning the ground is white with snow. If this is the sunny South, give me the severe North. Our horses are without shelter and only corn to eat. Today is

---

[i] Prolonge is a rope with a hook on the end, used to move the gun when positioning it or attaching it to the limber
[ii] Fort Lafayette was a Union prisoner of war camp on an island between Staten Island and Long Island, NY

ration day but not a team can get to La Grange on account of the flood. See sketch of position.

Our position is impregnable. Indeed we cannot be taken, as no man or set of men can get at us on account of water on all sides through which few could swim. In fact we cannot get out after rations by walking to La Grange. We can only get our rations by railroad. We are in no particular danger of being driven out of this unless drowned or starved out.

Snowed all day. No dry wood. It has been the hardest day we have ever seen since we have been in the service. What we are kept here for is beyond our comprehension. Lieut. Burton has not yet returned. We hope that he will bring us some news.

Sergeant O'Brien[i] had just presented us with a side of fat mutton and 4 snow birds. I have dressed the birds and prepare to have them for breakfast.

---

[i] Sergt. Edward O'Brien of Dixon, Battery F, 1st Illinois Light Artillery

Davis Mill, Miss.

Friday, January 16th 1863

Cold stormy morning. Had a breakfast of the birds dressed the night before. With Lieut. Whaley, Corporal Christiance[i] and James Ball,[ii] started for Grand Junction to see what could be done about rations and forage. Found nothing and started for La Grange where we made known our condition. Learned from quartermaster that there was only two hundred sacks of corn in La Grange for the whole division. Gen. Denver ordered that we have 50 sacks. After much running about for teams, got it on to a car; also 5 days rations for the men. All this was accomplished in one day. Night had come, but no engine to run it to Davis Island (formerly Davis Mill). Gen. Denver ordered 40 men detailed from the 70th Regiment Ohio Infantry to run the car to Grand Junction. Col. McDowell was to furnish a detail at Grand Junction to relieve them and run us through to Davis Mill.

Cold. The detail came swearing about artillery etc. Mr. Perkins who has charge of the railroad station said we could have an engine to run us through in the morning. I released the detail and they did not damn the artillery so much as they had. Now we were all right. The only trouble was to fret about our poor men on the island without rations and the horses without shelter or food and a chance to sleep. We had 4 men from the 40th Illinois who were among strangers. Got them in with the 70th Ohio. Christiance and Ball went to the hospital where we have some sick boys. Lieut. Whaley and myself went to Capt. Bouton's some ¾ of a mile distant.

I had been on the tramp[iii] since morning and it being cold and slippery was completely used up; more so that at any other time of my life. Felt well except the lameness of the legs. Lieut. Whaley was not better off than myself and that was some satisfaction. We coughed at each other and had it been daylight anyone would have sworn we were wounded officers well whisked up. Capt. Bouton ordered a supper for us of which we ate largely of. Went into his tent, lighted pipes and drew boots. We were getting ready to lay our bones out to rest from our labors, but "when a man thinks he is, he ain't also."

In comes a soldier and asks "is Capt. Cheney here?" Being answered affirmatively, he said you can have an engine to run your car to Davis Mill tonight. We reluctantly put on our boots, proceeded to the

---

[i] Corp. (later Sergt.) Cornelius Christiance of Brooklyn, IL, Battery F, 1st Illinois Light Artillery

[ii] Pvt. James Ball of Dixon, IL, Battery F, 1st Illinois Light Artillery

[iii] Tramp is to travel on foot

hospital and also to the 70th Ohio and got our men together ready for a start.

We were informed that one engine was off the track, another out of water and a third must take the 2nd to get water. Tomorrow morning an extra freight would pass which should take our car to Davis Mill. We each went our way, some to the aforesaid hospital and 70th Ohio, some into a car, and Lieut. Whaley and myself went to Gen. Denver's room. Found him sleeping and an unoccupied bed in his room, which we proceeded to occupy without disturbing anybody. This has been the day of the war with me. Cold, tired and rather disgusted with soldiering generally and the Quartermaster's Department particularly. It is all for the Star Spangled Banner though and we are content as it is useless to feel differently.

We have heard of the taking of Arkansas Post[i] by Gen. Sherman and a confirmation of the report of Gen. Rosecrans victory over *Bragg*. Gens. Grant and McPherson go down the Mississippi River and Gen. Hamilton takes command of this Army Corps.

La Grange, Tenn.
Saturday, January 17th 1863
Awoke this morning and found Gen. Denver very quietly looking over his unexpected, but not unwelcome guests. We were cordially received and partook of a good breakfast of ham and eggs, hot corn bread, good butter etc., etc.

Mercury stood this morning at 8 above zero, but it seems as cold to us as zero ever did at home. I had supposed that the winter of -/62 and -/63 would pass and we never realize that we had had a winter, but this is winter with a vengeance. We feel better this morning. All ready to take a quick trip to Davis Mill after visiting the boys at the hospital. We found the boys doing very well except McCoy[ii] who I fear will die. Again we go to the depot to be ready for the extra freight whose engine is to take us to Davis Mill. We learn that said extra freight did not leave Memphis at the time promised, but would follow the regular mail train which is due at 10:45 AM.

At 12 noon, regular mail passed. Soon after the long looked and wished for extra freight came rambling into town. "Now we are right

---

[i] Confederate *Fort Hindman* at Arkansas Post, AK was captured January 9-11, 1863
[ii] Pvt. Martin McCoy of Springfield, IL, Battery F, 1st Illinois Light Artillery, he recovered and continued to serve at least until March 1865

and the boys and horses will soon be relieved and perhaps saved from starvation" – this we cogitate. The extra freight proves to be the regular freight but we are assured that the extra freight is hard on the regular freight. We must transfer our freight to another car. The one in which it is, being off the track, and in a difficult place for the extra freight to get at her. Several Negroes soon did this, and we were ready for the aforesaid extra freight.

We are informed that there will be no extra freight in consequence of no water in Memphis. It is now night. Boy's rations ran out two days since. Horses nothing to eat and almost frozen, and we without steam of any kind to run the car to Davis Mill. Our case is submitted to Gen. Denver and he orders a detail from 70th Ohio to run us to Grand Junction.

Procured ropes. I took the break. Out we went kiting.[i] At Grand Junction obtained another detail from 46th Ohio and 6th Iowa and went to Davis Mill. We arrived at midnight; hungry and cold, expecting to be met by the nearly famished boys eager to smash open a barrel of hard bread. But the boys had slaughtered several hogs. Got plenty of corn meal. The 25th Indiana had marched for Memphis and left plenty of corn for our horses. On the whole there had been no suffering. On the contrary they had lived as usual quite well, and rather supposed that we had been gobbled up by the enemy's cavalry.

Gen. Denver is a thoughtful general. Loves his men and interests himself very much in making his men comfortable. He is deservedly popular. Very free and social and a gentleman every inch. Loves good order and discipline, but will allow no soldier to go hungry as long as there is food to be had.

Davis Mill, Miss.
Sunday, January 18th 1863

The only way that a man knows that it is Sunday is the almanac says so. It is not quite as cold as yesterday and begins to look like another storm. The whole division was notified last night to expect an attack at any moment, but we are all right yet. Feel rather worse for wear, but quite well considering the labor I have performed in the last two days. The boys are rejoicing over their full rations again. Lieut. Burton has not yet returned. Wrote to my wife. The 25th Indiana left yesterday for Memphis. We are now left with the 40th Illinois. Why we should be here is more than I can understand.

---

[i] Kiting is to go in a rapid carefree manner

Davis Mill, Miss.

Monday, January 19th 1863

Cold rainy day. Busied myself in writing the morning. In the afternoon Lieut. Burton arrived from Memphis. For the want of transportation Lieut. Burton could not get my boxes so that after all our expectations we are doomed to disappointment.

Our muster and payrolls for July and August have come and are signed. Expect the paymaster in a day or two. Spent the evening with Col. Hicks at his quarters. Pleasant time. Rains like the duce.

Davis Mill, Miss.

Friday, January 20th 1863

It has been a very rainy night. This morning I started for La Grange to visit the sick men at the hospital to obtain their signatures to the payrolls. Saw Maj. Atkinson (the paymaster). Have the promise of pay this week. Tried to get some tents, but did not succeed. Have the promise of some hay tomorrow.

Our horses have had no hay since the 26th of November and I expect the greatest horselaugh when it comes that I ever listened to. I have not mentioned the matter of hay to the horses and dare not till the hay comes for fear that it will not come, for it is or may be true that "when a horse thinks he is, he ain't also."

The boys have commenced on stables for horses. We have two very respectable houses put up for the men. I rode across the bottom this morning on horseback. Water up to my boot tops when on my horse and bottom 150 yards across. The water is getting higher and our island getting smaller.

I have received two letters tonight from my wife, one of January 11th and one of January 15th. A letter from home only 5 days after it is written and all well, marks an epoch in our campaign down South such as not before has been marked. Who says this is not an age of progress.

I have been made glad by the reception of good news from home. I have also received a letter from Brother Pers informing me of the discharge of Brother Tom, who resigned on account of disability. Also a letter from Brother Sam who with Brother Daniel was in the late battle at Fredericksburg. Neither of them were injured. So much good news in one short hour serves to make me feel that the fortunes of war after all are not so very severe.

It will be a happy day, when the war is over, to return and meet the many friends who are in other departments and divisions of the army and perhaps fight our battles over again. That we may live to meet under the roof of the old brick house with Father, Mother, Sisters and Brother Pers (who would have been in the army had his health permitted) and all our families, is my hope. Such a meeting is perhaps possible. If all feel as I do, such a meeting will be had as soon as we are honorably discharged from the service of the government we have volunteered to support.

*** *** *** *** *** *** *** ***

Davis Mill, Miss.
January 20th 1863[i]

My dear Wife,

It is now 10 o'clock PM. After finishing up my diary thought I would write you a few lines. You will see by the diary that I have received two letters from you and be assured I have been rejoiced. Tell Royce that I expect to come out all right. I hardly know what to say to Grace that she can appreciate more than kiss her for me.

I will get 4 months pay and will send the money to you by express. You can make such disposition of it as you think best, after paying Pers and the rent on the house. The boys get two months pay for the months of July and August. I will write you again soon. I am well.

Affectionately your husband,
John

Summary

Cheney was annoyed. Other troops had departed the area but Battery F remained. He wanted to be part of the Vicksburg Campaign, not guard the railroad in the rear. His annoyance was furthered by the presence of Northern civilians buying and transporting cotton under the protection of the army. Cheney was not moving against the enemy and the railroad he was protecting was used by cotton speculators to prosper as a consequence of the war.

John Cheney's three New Hampshire brothers had experienced combat. John had not yet done so.

---

[i] This letter is on the last page of his diary; that is he sent his diary home when full and used the last page of it for a letter.

Chapter 9 - Former Slave in the Battery

Davis Mill, MS
January 21, 1863 to January 30, 1863

Background

While Battery F continued to guard the railroad at Davis Mill, Mississippi, an event from the previous summer lead to controversy in the battery.

In the summer of 1862 thousands of run-away slaves made their way to the Union army at Memphis. Their status (prior to the Emancipation Proclamation taking effect January 1863) was contraband of war. The slave Richard Petty living at Senatobia, Mississippi 40 miles south of Memphis, TN was one who took advantage of the closeness of the Union lines and ran away from his master.

Richard Petty wasn't like other contrabands. Richard Petty was white. That is he was a light-skinned, straight haired, blue-eyed, European featured man who had been born into slavery. Under chattel slavery, a person whose mother was a slave, was born a slave. Over several generations of white men impregnating slave women, a wide range of physical appearances occurred in the slave population, including slaves who were completely white European in appearance.

Petty doubtless knew he could "pass for white," but prior to the Union army's occupation of Memphis in June 1862, that reality did him little good. In the rural areas and small towns of Mississippi where he lived, the local people would know his status as a slave regardless of his appearance. His speech and accent would also likely mark him as a slave. In July 1862 Richard Petty came under the protection of the Union army and he had a new option that he exercised – be a white person.

In the year and a half since Battery F had been formed, it had lost men due to disease and hardship. Those soldiers had not been completely replaced. John Cheney was prepared to enlist a man from Tennessee or Mississippi who swore loyalty to the Union – and was white. At that time the army had no Colored Troops and army regiments were strictly white. For example, blacks living in Illinois could not join a unit such as Battery F.

Richard Petty did not disguise his status as a former slave. Still John Cheney felt very strongly that Petty's status as a slave was not to be held against him. Cheney considered Petty to be white by looking at him. As such Petty qualified to be in a white regiment.

On August 1, 1862 Capt. John Cheney enlisted Richard Petty of Mississippi as a private in Battery F. Cheney's action was not technically legal as Petty's official status at the time was contraband of war.

Davis Mill, Miss.
Wednesday January 21, 1863
    With 25 men drew a car to Grand Junction (7 miles) after hay and oats. We were gratified to learn that we could have 7 bales of hay, 18 sacks of oats and 20 sacks of corn; and a locomotive to run it down to Davis Mill.
    Memorandum. In August last I enrolled as a soldier, a young man named Richard Pattee.[i] It was said and undoubtedly true that he was a fugitive slave and had escaped from slavery and came into our lines. Pattee is as white as I am. His hair is very light colored. His eyes are blue. He is a faithful soldier. Has never been on extra duty, nor has there ever been a complaint against him. He is neat and tidy. But unfortunately he has been a slave. Some of my men are so much afraid that they will be considered no better than a Nigger as they term him, have become uneasy. They have been induced by several gentlemen, whose superior qualifications for offices in the Battery have not been appreciated by the majority of the Battery, to sign a petition to Gen. Denver to investigate the conduct of officers of Cheney's Battery. On my return from Grand Junction today the following petition was

---

[i] Cheney wrote the name Pattee – perhaps because he had a great uncle who spelled it that way – while official records usually spell it Petty

handed to me by Henry Horn who is now under arrest for straggling from camp and staying 24 hours. But to the petition.

> In Camp at Davis Mill, Miss. Railroad
> January 21, 1863
>
> Maj. General Denver
>
> Sir – We the undersigned privates and non-commissioned officers of Company F (Cheney's Battery) 1st Reg. Light Artillery, Ill. Vol. have had our feeling outraged on several occasions by our officers. We respectfully appeal to you for an investigation.
>
> Specification 1st
> In that Capt. John T. Cheney has enrolled Richard Petty a Negro and formerly a slave a private in said Company and mustered for pay on three separate occasions. Said Petty was a slave at Senatobia on the Tenn. and Miss. Railroad in this state previous to the breaking out of the Rebellion.
>
> Specification 2nd
> In that Lieut. S. S. Smyth of said Company has declared that a Negro was as good as an Irishman or any other foreigner or white man of any nationality. This has caused great dissatisfaction in our Company and is likely to continue unless an investigation is granted in order that we may ascertain if such conduct is tolerated in the Army.
>
> Signed
>
> | | |
> |---|---|
> | James Thompson | Peter Gleason |
> | H. A. Horn | Charles Horen |
> | W. O. Loveland | Edward Martin |
> | John W. Graves | George P. Lane |
> | Reuben Booth | John Minter |
> | Henry Menchin | M. McManas |
> | E. A. O'Brien | Lawrence Snyder |
> | Max Lentz | John Reardon |
> | Ezra Risley | Henry O'Conner |
> | George Conrad | Joseph Losee |
> | John H. Lyle | John H. Singleton |
> | L. A. Sewell | John Ford |
> | E. F. Braley | Jeremiah Lennihan |

James Vance	George Gatenley
Thomas Mitts	James Marks
John Mann	William Phillips
Michael Kearns	George Clark
Elijah P. Vance	William Blair
George W. Beardsley	Matthew Callahan
J. W. Bossack	Thomas Shelly
E. N. Haight	J. E. Thornsbury
Lloyd Berninger	Peter Renland
Nathan G. Eades	James Taylor
F. Rheam	Philip Otto
C. N. Moon	H. Overcutter
Joseph Tober	E. L. Loveless
W. M. Kempe	Henry Wittee
Albert Zorings	Fred Holden
C. E. Christiance	Charles Hough
John J Cox	Addison Wagner
John Guyler	George Carey
John Haynes	Rush Shick
James Lahey	Frank Reubendall
Augustus Baker	Walter Little
Edward Murat	

45 of the above named have been punished at different times, two have been court-martialed and 6 were and are under arrest, and will be court-martialed. Henry Horn, Corporal Luman A. Sewell, Corporal James Thompson and Privates George P. Lane, Charles Hough, James Lakey are the ones under arrest. I asked Mr. Horn what he wished me to do with the petition and was informed that I was requested to forward it to Gen. Denver. They having presented it to Col. Hicks of the 40th Illinois and he respectfully referred them to me. I informed him that they could select a man from the petitioners to accompany me to Gen. Denver's headquarters to see that they had fair play. He said they did not wish to send anyone but I insisted. Michael McManas was the one selected.

After looking over the petition I found the signatures were all in one handwriting. I informed the men that I must have the genuine signatures or else no notice would be taken of the petition. I respect-fully requested them to call at my quarters and sign the document with their own hands. In a very few minutes I was furnished with the original document and found that it read as follows. The signatures appended by Corporal Luman A. Sewell under arrest.

Davis Mill, Miss Railroad
Jany. 12, 1863

Maj. Gen. Denver

Sir

We the undersigned privates and non-commissioned officers of Company F (Cheney's Battery) 1st Reg. of Light Artillery, Ill. Vol. having had our feelings outraged on several occasions by our officers we respectfully appeal to you for satisfaction.

Specification 1st
In that they enrolled Richard Petty a Negro (and formerly a slave) a private in said Company F and mustered him for pay on three separate occasions. Said Petty was a slave in Senatobia on the Tenn. Railroad in this state, previous to the breaking out of the rebellion.

Specification 2nd
In that some (if not all) our officers have frequently and also recently declared that a Negro is as good as an Irishman or any other foreigner or Whiteman of any nationality and we respectfully appeal to you for an investigation into this matter as it is the cause of much dissatisfaction in the Company.

The foregoing was signed on the 12th. After certain gentleman were under arrest, it was remodeled to suit the taste of the scribe who copied it.

Davis Mill, Miss.
Thursday, January 22, 1863
This morning the signers of the declaration of independence (as some of the boys call it) were called up to learn from them which petition they wanted to go in. Some wanted one and some another and some neither. They all acknowledge that Pattee (his real name) was as good a soldier as we had, declared there was not a man in the battery who wished to censure me. One said he meant Lieut. Burton as he had written to the "Republican and Telegraph," that his Nigger Tom was highly intellectual and had he had an education would have been superior to ¾ of the white men.

I concluded that the petitions should both go. Accordingly McManus and I mounted our horses and started for La Grange. Gen. Denver had gone to Ohio. Col. McDowell in command of this division, the matter was submitted to him, and at my request a court of inquiry was ordered. Col. McDowell informed Mr. McManus what the consequence would be if it should appear that the charges were malicious. After visiting Grand Junction, we returned to our camp well satisfied that small fires sometimes create a vast amount of smoke. "When a man thinks he is, he ain't."

I do not know when the court will sit or what its decision may be in the case of Richard Pattee, but here is my record. A man is a man who behaves himself properly. Let his nationality be what it may. Let him be slave or free. If a slave so much more sympathy for him. If I am to be punished for any crime I prefer that it be for trying to build up and encourage than to crush any one of God's creatures in His own image. I say also that if Richard Pattee is forced to leave the service of the United States, I will also leave the service if I can honorably get out.

I would like to open a battery on the so called Democratic politicians of Illinois who have caused all such prejudices as now exist among the members of the army, who are ready to sign such petitions as the ones referred to. Six months since we hardly knew that we had ever been Republicans or Democrats, but now how different.

Davis Mill, Miss.
Friday, January 23, 1863

A wet, muddy, rainy time. Stables not completed on account of not being able to get boards to cover it. Sent to Grand Junction 3 teams after hay and corn. Got 18 bales hay and 20 sacks corn. Our horses are enjoying their feed. Considering the weather and feed they have had in the last 3 weeks, they look very well. Have not lost a horse since we left Memphis. That can be said of no other battery who left with us. Not much chance for a fight as we are surrounded by water and no pickets are needed.

Lieuts. Burton, Smyth and Whaley and Sergt. Raub are in my tent. It is 10 o'clock PM. After a very exciting game at pitch[i] in which thousands have been won and lost with nary red in the mess, we are trying to get the origin of each other. The decision is that we are all sons of Adam, but instead of being of the dust of the Earth we are of and in the mud of Mississippi without much probability of getting out.

---

[i] Pitch is a card game

I will lay aside my pen and play 3 games of pitch for $15.00, best two in three. Sergeant Raub is my competitor.

Sergeant T. W. Raub is defeated and I am well satisfied with my evening's work, having taken an order on Siegel for the amount.

Davis Mill, Miss.
Saturday, January 24, 1863

This morning I was sent for by Col. Hicks and presented with the following document.

Special Orders No. 4   Headquarters, 2nd Brigade
1st Division, Grand Junction, Tenn.
January 23, 1863

A commission is hereby convened to investigate certain charges against the officers of Cheney's Battery. Detail for the commission
     Capt. D. M. Whin
     Capt. H. W. Hall
     Lieut. T. F. Galvin

The commission will meet immediately at Davis Mill, sit without regard to hours, and report the proceedings to these headquarters. The quartermaster of Cheney's Battery will furnish the Commission with suitable quarters.

By order of C. C. Walcutt[i]
Cmdg.
B. H. Coles
Acting Asst. Adj. General

11 o'clock AM. The court is now organized and ready to proceed to business. We are notified that the enemy were within 15 miles of us last night and moving toward us. We are ordered to be ready at any moment for an attack. It is a very wet day, rain falling in torrents. We have a large number of men throwing up fortifications for our guns.

But to the court of inquiry. Michael McManus was sworn. In answer to questions said substantially that he did not know that Pattee ever was a slave. Could not tell that there was a drop of Negro blood in

---

[i] Col. Charles C. Walcutt, 46th Ohio Infantry

his veins. Knew that Pattee had been mustered for pay by Majors Taylor, Willard and Capt. Cogswell and never by Capt. Cheney. Luman A. Sewell testified to the same and also that he wrote the petition and was under arrest at the same time. Concerning Lieut. Smyth, having ever said that a Nigger was as good as a White man, neither knew anything except by hearsay. Court adjourned to 2 o'clock PM.

Met at 2 PM and adjourned to Monday 26 January

*** *** *** *** *** *** *** ***

Davis Mill, Miss.
January 24, 1863

My dear Wife,

It is Saturday afternoon and a very rainy day. We just begin to know what the rainy season is in the South. You can hardly conceive how unpleasant it is to wade through the mud. For be assured that as bad as Illinois is in a muddy time, she don't begin to compare with Mississippi. We are now having full rations, and hay and oats for our horses. But no shelter for horses yet, although we have the frame up for stables. We are getting a steam saw mill in order to cut out some boards to cover it. My horse Bird is quite sick and I am afraid I will lose him.

I think I wrote you that Seth Thomas was sick in the hospital at La Grange. He is still there and considerably better than when he went there. However I am of the opinion that he will be unfit for the service for some time. I shall do my best to obtain his discharge. I wrote you on the 18th instant and sent you Volume 2 of my diary, which I hope you have received. It is almost impossible for me to give you much of an idea of how things move as my whole attention and time is required to keep all things properly moving. All of my own writing is done at night. Yet I presume it will be a source of much gratification to you to read almost anything that I may write, although it might not pay anyone else to peruse the documents.

I am very glad to learn that you are having a mild winter. Am glad to learn that Mr. Leach is at home. Give my best regards and wishes to Edson[i] and Burkett[ii] (if you see them). Tell them I am very sorry that it became necessary for them to be discharged. I hope they may fully recover and at some future time if necessary rally to the call of this

---

[i] Corp. Eliphalet Edson of Dixon, IL, Battery F, 1st Illinois Light artillery discharged Dec 24, 1862
[ii] Pvt. Calvin Burkett of Dixon, IL, Battery F, 1st Illinois Light Artillery

country. I hope the Deacon is again able to walk, as it will be hard for him to be idle. Give him my respects and best wishes.

The course that Illinois Democrats have recently taken with regard to the President's message, and particularly the "Chicago Times," is having its effect upon the army. Many who have nearly forgotten that they had ever been Democrats or Republicans, begin to discuss political matters very freely and often bitterly. It extends to my battery to some extent. Out of the Springfield recruits many are intensely Democratic. I believe the "Chicago Times" should be suppressed. You will know that I have often predicted serious troubles at home. Well I am still fearful but sufficient unto the day are the evils thereof.[i] Therefore I will do the best I can in the field in which I am called upon to labor and believe that all will be well in the end. I was glad to learn that Sam and Daniel come out all right at Fredericksburg as I was very anxious about them.

You ask me if I sing any. Well I sang on Christmas Eve and have not sung since. The book I gave to Ed Parker as I had not time to learn to sing new pieces. We received an order from headquarters this morning stating that the enemy was within 15 miles of us last night and moving toward us. And would probably attack us today. It is now 5 o'clock PM and has rained for the last 24 hours. It is still raining so I think there is no danger of an attack. But if they come, we are ready to receive them very warmly.

The health of the men is generally good and my own is good. Indeed I would not have believed that I could have endured so much. The paymaster has not yet visited us probably on account of the storm. I have been fortunate enough to borrow $5 of Capt. Bouton of Bouton's Battery and am all right now till I get paid.

Monday Morning January 26th.

I thought I would write you a few lines this morning before the mail leaves. Yesterday we were at work throwing up fortifications. By tonight we will be in shape to do good fighting, if we have any to do. Have very good protection for our men. It rains most all of the time and is terrible muddy. We continue well generally. We are making ourselves as comfortable as possible though it is far from being pleasant to wallow through the mud. We expect the paymaster today. If possible I will get leave of absence to go to Memphis to send our money home

---

[i] Take therefore no thought for the morrow: for the morrow shall take thought for the things of itself. Sufficient unto the day is the evil thereof. - Matthew 6:34

and get those boxes for the boys. Give my love to all the friends. Fret not about us as we are all right.

Affectionately your husband,
John T. Cheney

Bird[i] is all right.

*** *** *** *** *** *** *** ***

Davis Mill, Miss.
Sunday, January 25, 1863

We have been notified every day for the last week to be ready for attack and are so notified again this morning. Around the Indian mound (before mentioned in my diary)[ii] is thrown up infantry breast works. The circumference of the works is 155 yards. The mound is about 30 feet high. I went this morning to Col. Hicks and asked the privilege of making an excavation in the top of the mound and mounting one of my guns there. He consented and with 25 men went at it. Notwithstanding it has been a very rainy day, we have made considerable progress.

Found some relics among which are one tooth, apparently a horse's tooth, one human tooth and an arm bone. These were about 5 feet below the surface.

The 40th Illinois are working 75 men throwing up rifle pits. Lieut. Burton has been to Grand Junction and reports the paymaster to be coming tomorrow.

Davis Mill, Miss.
Monday, January 26, 1863

Rains yet and we can do but little on our fort. Still we have done something and will get a gun mounted tomorrow if the Rebs will give us another day's time.

The military commission do not sit today on account of the sickness of the president of the court (Capt. Hall).

One of the most uncomfortable days we have had. Cannot keep a fire in our tent on account of smoke. Another scare today. Pickets reported driven in near La Grange. All the officers got letters except me.

---

[i] "Bird" is John Cheney's horse
[ii] January 9, 1863 entry

Davis Mill, Miss.

Tuesday, January 27, 1863

Col. Hicks is again notified that this post must be held and he may expect an attack at any moment. This order comes from Maj. Gen. Grant. It seems to us that we ought at least to have one more regiment of infantry, but the Col. thinks we can whip one hundred thousand men. At least one would suppose so to hear him talk. The fortifications are not in accordance with my notions but since getting the fort on the mound out of him I feel as though we would stand some chance to hurt somebody considerably before defeat.

For the first day in many we have had no rain. It has been cold. We have our gun mounted inside of Fort Cheney as the boys have named it. In the fort are three embrasures[i]. The fort is in the form of a circle, the diameter of which is 27 feet; height 6 feet. If we can have another day to put the other guns in shape then we are all right; if allowed to use our own discretion in arranging them.

Lieut. Burton has gone to La Grange after tents, nails, grain sacks (for our embrasures) etc. Col. Hicks has visited the fort and says it is all right. We will injure the intestines of some of the Rebs if they come in or attempt to.

Davis Mill, Miss.

Wednesday, January 28, 1863

All hands have been turned in and done good work on the fortifications. We are making good progress. Rainy unpleasant weather.

We have been made glad today by getting two months pay.

Davis Mill, Miss.

Thursday, January 29, 1863

We have been successful in obtaining 7 hospital tents. Getting them up in good order, and very comfortably situated for winter quarters. Learn that Gen. Burnside has been superseded by Gen. Joe Hooker. Owing to late storms and bad state of the roads, all is quiet on the Potomac. All quiet at Davis Mill.

---

[i] Embrasure is a flared opening for a gun in a wall or parapet

Davis Mill Miss.

Friday, January 30, 1863

Went to La Grange after gunnies[i] for embrasures and after finding them thought the last obstacle in the way of finishing up our fortifications to our liking had been overcome. But "when a man thinks he is, he ain't also." I received orders to move with the battery to Grand Junction, Tenn. Learned that we would be relieved by one section of Dupree's Battery. I returned to the never to be forgotten Davis Mill. On informing the boys of the orders received, they expressed their regret that they must leave before getting a chance to use the fort against the enemy. Such is war. It is hard to tell whether we are fortifying for our own or the enemy's benefit. We leave rather reluctantly but will have the advantage of better mail communications with home.

The long roll calls us to our guns but someone has been shooting hogs. No fight.

Summary

The existence of a white slave with no African features such as Richard Petty is a surprise to some. The relative commonness of such slaves was noted by the 19th century writer and landscape architect Frederick Law Olmsted. He traveled extensively though the South prior to the war and reported his accounts in newspaper articles and books. His accounts include the following (*Cotton Kingdom* page 458f):

> Riding through a large gang of hoers, with two overseers, I observed that a large proportion of them appeared to be thoroughbred Africans. Both of them thought that the "real black niggers" were about three-fourths of the whole number, and that this would hold as an average on Mississippi and Louisiana plantations. One of them pointed out a girl – "That one is pure white; you see her hair? (It was straight and sandy.) "She is the only one we have got." It was not uncommon, he said, to see slaves so white that they could not be easily distinguished from pure-blooded whites. He had never been on a plantation

---

[i] Gunnies are grain sacks make out of burlap

before, that had not more than one on it. "Now," said I, "if that girl should dress herself well, and run away, would she be suspected of being a slave?" (I could see nothing myself by which to distinguish her, as she passed, from an ordinary poor white girl.)

"Oh, yes; you might not know her if she got to the North, but any of us would know her."

"How?"

"By her language and manner."

"But if she had been brought up as house-servant?"

"Perhaps not in that case."

Further contemporary information on Richard Petty is contained in a letter that Lieut. Samuel Smyth wrote to his father on February 10, 1863 (in the Davidson Library, Univ. of Calif., Santa Barbara):

... Now the facts of case are as follows: While we were at Memphis a young man came to us and wanted to enlist. The Captain of course enlisted him for at that time were in need of men. To all appearances was as white as any man, but it seems that he had been at some time held as a slave. The men say that he acknowledges that he was, but he also says that so far as he could ever trace his lineage, his ancestors were white. However that amounts to nothing. He is a white a man to all intents and purposes. His skin is as white as most men, brown straight hair, and he exhibits none of the characteristics of the Negro ...

What is surprising about the Richard Petty case is not that white slaves existed and not that Petty was one. Rather what is surprising is that a company commander such as Cheney would admit a contraband into his unit. But Cheney did and felt very strongly that it was the right thing to do.

Chapter 10 - Guarding the Railroad at Grand Junction, TN

January 31, 1863 to April 6, 1863

Background

Battery F continued duty protecting the railroad as part of Brig. Gen. Denver's 1st Division, 16th Army Corps. Grand Junction was the crossroads of the Memphis and Charleston Railroad with the Mississippi Central Railroad.

In this chapter and the next only diary entries are included. Seventeen letters from John Cheney to his wife covering this period survive but they do not add much to the diary content.

Saturday, January 31, 1863

Left Davis Mill and went by way of La Grange to Grand Junction. Roads bad and as usual when we march a rain has come on. We are in camp about one half mile northwest of town on a hill commanding the whole country. A beautiful spot, but rather airy.

Sunday, February 1, 1863

Last night was a very stormy one, but this morning the sun shines beautifully. There is some expectation that this point will be attacked, and for that reason we have been sent here. Nine Rebs have been captured and brought in today by our cavalry.

Grand Junction, Tenn.

Monday, February 2nd 1863

Went to La Grange to obtain leave of absence for Sergeant Vesper to go home for twenty days. I succeeded in getting the approval of Col. McDowell and a leave to go to Memphis to see if Gen. Hamilton would approve of it.

Grand Junction, Tenn.

Tuesday, Feby. 3rd 1863

With Sergeant Vesper went to Memphis by railroad. Cars crowded with cotton buyers, speculators and soldiers. Seats occupied by citizens. I stood up all the way in. Went down to Mrs. Wayman's and can board with her while I remain in Memphis.

Tired tonight.

Memphis, Tenn.

Wednesday, Feby. 4th 1863

Went this morning to see Gen. Hamilton concerning Vesper's leave of absence and was told that a furlough could only be obtained from the Secretary of War. Gen. Hamilton would approve of it, but it was doubtful about obtaining it. Gave the thing up in disgust. Run all over the city to learn if clothing could be obtained for the boys. Found that we could get it when our turn came. Learned that the 10th Missouri Cavalry[i] were in town and soon were in their camp where we found Capts. A. P. Curry,[ii] M. H. Williams,[iii] Lieut. John Dysart,[iv] Dr. Auld[v] and Sergeant William Dickson, all from Dixon.

We spent the evening very pleasantly at Capt. William's tent and went back to Mother Wayman's tired and sleepy.

Memphis, Tenn.

Thursday, Feby. 5th 1863

Still find plenty to do to get together articles for the boys from express office etc. A perfect rush at quartermasters for clothing. Have the promise of goods tomorrow. Heavy snow and very cold. Another evening with the 10th Missouri.

---

[i] 10th Missouri Cavalry included Dixon, IL men. Illinois State Archives records indicate that 5,610 Illinois residents served in Union Missouri regiments.

[ii] Capt. Amos P. Curry of Dixon, IL, Co. B, 10th Missouri Cavalry

[iii] Capt. Martin H. Williams of Dixon, IL, Co. D, 10th Missouri Cavalry

[iv] Lieut. John Dysart of Lee County, IL, Co. D, 10th Missouri Cavalry

[v] Lieut. Martin C. Auld of Dixon, IL, Co. B & I, 10th Missouri Cavalry

Memphis, Tenn.

Friday, Feby. 6th 1863

Have got my goods shipped and will go home tomorrow. Evening spent with 10th Missouri who go to Corinth tomorrow. Fine day. The 4 inches of snow that fell last night most all gone.

Memphis, Tenn.

Saturday, Feby. 7th 1863

Took my leave of Capts. Curry and Williams, visited Dr. Howe and went to the depot. Seated myself on a bale of hay and rode to Grand Junction where we arrived at 8 PM. Was rejoiced at the reception of two letters from my wife and one from Pers.

Grand Junction, Tenn.

Sunday, Feby. 8, 1863

Walked to La Grange after my goods. Two mule teams went to draw them. Got back at night tired and hungry. Lost one box for Burr[i] and Snyder that I got at the express office in Memphis. Boys glad to know that they are to have some clothing in the morning. Mud! Mud! Mud!

Grand Junction, Tenn.

Monday, Feby. 9th 1863

Issued clothing to the boys. Walked about the outpost. Received another letter from my wife. Spent the evening in writing to my wife.

I learn that the military commission appointed to investigate charges against officers of Cheney's Battery have concluded not to meet again. They will report that the charges if proven were not military offenses. The whole thing is too foolish to receive the attention of any military commission. So much for the commission. It only arose from a few disaffected ones who were either under arrest or uneasy, sick of soldiering when the rough part of it came, and were anxious to join hands with the traitors at home and create as much disaffection as possible.

The boys are sick of it but I am sorry that the court did not follow the thing and make all out of it possible. The members of the commission were all Democrats and one an Irishman. If there had been

---

[i] Pvt. Benjamin Burr of Dixon, IL, Battery F, 1st Illinois Light Artillery

anything wrong in the matter, they would have been likely to have discovered it. The importance of the case scarcely demands a place in my diary. It will be a source of amusement in after time, to call to mind the many influences that have been brought to bear to cripple our government during this unholy rebellion. All is well that ends well and the end of this will be all right or else we have no government.

Grand Junction, Tenn.

Tuesday, Feby. 10/63

Where we are now is J. W. Denver's division (1st Div. 16th Army Corps, Army of the Tenn.) Col. McDowell's Brigade, in the mud and in the belief that we are making slow progress (if any) in crushing the Rebellion. We are out of patience, out of fresh meat, outside of civiliza-tion, out of fence rails for fire, out of hell and on praying ground. We manage to keep in pretty good spirits. These are a part of our ins and outs.

Rain is falling in torrents. We are assured by the oldest inhabitant that it is almost spring and that by the 10th of March all planting is ordinarily done. It looks as though it would not be this year, for there is not a fence for miles from camp, neither is there a horse or mule or ox to plow with or a Negro who could be induced to plant cotton. Verily the way of the transgressor is hard.[i]

Grand Junction, Tenn.

Wednesday, Feby. 11/63

This is a fine morning. The sun shines brightly. Col. Cocksell of the 70th Ohio, Walcutt of the 46th Ohio called and gave me an invitation to ride with them round the outposts. Went with them. Had a pleasant ride and find that our position is being made a very strong one. Learn that Gens. Hamilton and Hurlbut have issued an order prohibiting the circulation of the "Chicago Times"[ii] in this army corps. It is an order that should have been issued long since but better late than never. It will make some Copperheads[iii] sore but the real patriots will rejoice.

---

[i] Proverbs 13:15

[ii] The "Chicago Times" newspaper had a Copperhead bent

[iii] Copperheads were Northern Peace Democrats. The name Copperhead may have come from the wearing of copper coins as badges. Copperheads were depicted in political cartoons as the snake of the same name. The position expressed by some Copperheads was that secession of the Southern states was

Grand Junction, Tenn.

Thursday, Feby. 12/63

Have been favored with a heavy rain and strong wind during the night, but pleasant this morning. Spent the entire day in making final statements etc. Have spent part of the evening in playing muggins,[i] a new game that serves to pass off time quite pleasantly. Wrote to my wife. Father is 63 yrs. old today.

Grand Junction, Tenn.

Friday, Feby. 13th 1863

Another fine day. Walked about for an hour with Lieut. Smyth. Made the acquaintance of several officers of the 12th Indiana Infantry, and like the regiment very much. In the evening was quietly seated at the table writing when I was startled by the sound of a band of music at my tent door. Went to the door and found the 12th Indiana Silver Band accompanied by Capt. Nelson and Lieut. Godwin. Listened to Yankee Doodle, Ben Bolt[ii] and other favorite airs. Invited them in. We partook of refreshments and spent the evening in conviviality. A complete surprise, enjoyed very much by me and apparently by the members of the band and officers. Long life the 12th Indiana. It is easy to become attached to Indiana troops after serving with the 11th Indiana and under command of Maj. Gen. Lew Wallace.

Grand Junction, Tenn.

Saturday, Feby. 14, 1863

We are again enjoying ourselves as well as men can while shut up in a tent and listening to the continual patter, patter on the roof of the falling rain. It is said that the rainy season has commenced and we think it is true. I am reminded that Mother is 63 years old today. Wish I could fly to the old homestead and spend the evening with the old folks at home. May she live to enjoy many anniversaries of her birthday is my wish. Saint Valentine's day but few valentines in the army. We have had a thunder shower this evening that lasted a full hour and a half, and eclipses any one that I ever witnessed in Illinois. We learn this evening that Gen. Denver has returned to his command, and is now in

---

a legal action. As such, Lincoln's waging war to deny secession was an illegal act.

[i] Muggins is a domino game

[ii] "Ben Bolt" was a 1848 song based on an 1842 poem

La Grange. Thrice welcome Gen. Denver say I, and hope we will now be put in motion.

Wrote to Father and Mother.

My wife is 33 years old today Feby. 14, 1863. No birthday's presents today, 'twere useless to say more. May she live to see many such anniversaries and I be with her.

Grand Junction, Tenn.
Sunday, Feby. 15, 1863

The almanac says it is Sunday and although that is the only evidence that we have of it, we admit it to be true and worship just as much as any other day. War is a great leveler, makes all days alike. Levels many houses, many fences, much timber. Brings many up and many down to their proper level. Many, too many, cannot always say truly that their heads are level. May our army be successful in leveling the Rebels and all mankind be level with each other so far as the enjoyment of natural rights are concerned. Thus endeth my Sunday worship.

Have been to La Grange today to visit the boys at the hospital. Found them improving and very well supplied with everything to make them comfortable. The day has been very pleasant and but for bad roads would be very pleasant riding. Wrote to my wife.

Grand Junction, Tenn.
Monday, February 16, 1863

On account of work to be done inside the fort, it becomes necessary for us to move our headquarters outside. We got moved just in time to prevent getting wet, for another rain storm has commenced. Much rain has fallen during the day and while I write (10 o'clock PM) is falling in torrents. Frogs are singing. Verily this is the rainy season. Nothing particularly worthy of note today. Wrote to Reuben Eastwood.

Grand Junction, Tenn.
February 17th 1863

Rain has been falling most of the day. In the tent in which I sit writing, the mud is soft and deep. My chair (for I have one that the boys confiscated) sinks in the mud so that it often has to be moved. I slept very little last night on account of sickness, but feel much better tonight. Received a letter from my wife today, dated 11th inst. Pleased to hear that family and friends are well. Learn that the Illinois Legislature has adjourned to meet again in June. Hope we may achieve some decided victories before they come together again, as it must have some influence upon their action.

Grand Junction, Tenn.
Wednesday, Feby. 18, 1863

Went to La Grange today to make arrangements for clothing and other supplies. Visited the hospital and found the sick boys all improving. Went to the depot at 7 o'clock and learned that the train had not yet passed Germantown and concluded to stop for the night with Maj. Wm. Price, formerly of the "Chicago Times." It has rained today just as copiously as though no rain had fallen for three months. Every soldier in Tennessee would certify that we have had some rain and do not need any more at present. La Grange is some on muddy streets. Mud. Mud.

Grand Junction, Tenn.
Thursday, Feby. 19th 1863

Left La Grange at 11 o'clock AM. Got back all right. The sun rose beautifully. Strong winds from the south, no settled weather yet. It is a relief to be able to go out of the tent without getting wet. Notwithstanding the wind has blown our stove pipe away several times, and we are enveloped in smoke. We have had a supper of fried oysters, good butter, fresh bread, picnic crackers etc. Who wouldn't be a soldier?

The order of Gens. Hamilton and Hulbert suppressing the "Chicago Times" has been revoked by order of Maj. Gen. Ulysses S. Grant. That infamous sheet is allowed to circulate again among its secret admirers.

Grand Junction, Tenn.
Friday, Feby. 20th 1863

A lovely morning. In company with Capt. Cogswell, Lieuts. Burton and Godown,[i] went to La Grange. Bought a horse, made arrangements for some camp and garrison equipage. Returned to camp and found Lieut. Bullock of the 46th Illinois, who had come to visit us. Spent the evening in playing muggins, eating fresh oysters, fried, and raw. Who wouldn't be a soldier? The sun set beautifully tonight. It was

---

[i] Lieut. John M. Godown, Co. F, 12th Indiana Infantry

a common remark "a fine day tomorrow and about Monday we will go to drilling again."

Grand Junction, Tenn.
Feby, 21st 1863

Last evening we all flattered ourselves that the rainy season was over and we were again to be favored with good weather. But during the night a terrible wind and rain came upon us. Thunder and lightening took a hand in the game. On the whole we are anchored out of sunlight. It is a gloomy day indeed. I have received a letter from my wife making the day pass a little more pleasantly than it otherwise would. Lieut. Bullock is with us. Our old tent is leaky making it muddy and uncomfortable.

Lieuts. Burton, Whaley and Bullock have taken refuge in the boys tents. I am stuck in the mud writing up my diary and writing to my wife. Our tent is christened Floating Palace. Our boys are very fortunate in having good tents and are very comfortable considering all the circumstances. We begin to believe that they do really have a rainy season down South and that is not all fiction, but stubborn fact.

Grand Junction, Tenn.
Feby. 22, 1863

February 22nd [i] has come and finds one section of our country arrayed against the other. Finds us engaged in civil war on a scale the grandest and most terrible that the world has ever witnessed. Little did George Washington, the father of his and our country suppose during the days of the American Revolution, that in less than one short century an attempt would be made to destroy the work so nobly done by the fathers of the Revolution. Would to God that the spirit of Washington (known as such by every American) could today speak to us and give us such council and advice as we need. It would seem as the mention of the name of Washington, ought to awaken old recollections. And palsy the arm of every man whose arm is raised against a government for which died and suffered so many. Who shall be the Washington of today? Is Joe Hooker the man? Or has he yet to make his appearance, perhaps from the humblest walks of life? These are questions not easily answered in times when men are made and unmade almost every day. Every emergency brings with it its man for that emergency. God grant

---

[i] February 22 is Washington's Birthday

that we may soon be delivered from our troubles, and again North, South, East and West unite in celebrating the birthday's anniversary of Washington. Honesty, integrity, patriotism and military skill are united in some man. Who is he?

Went to Lafayette with Lieut. Bullock. Witnessed some target practice by Capt. Burnap's 9th Ohio Battery. Found the 46th Illinois well.

Monday, Feby. 23, 1863

Still at Lafayette. Spent the day with Lieut. Col. Jones riding about the country. Have had a pleasant visit and will go back in the morning.

Grand Junction, Tenn.
Tuesday, Feby. 24, 1863

Left Lafayette this morning and learning that Capt. Rodgers of 2nd Illinois Artillery was at Moscow, concluded to stop over one train and visit him. Found the captain and with him visited Gen. Lauman in whose division I once was. Also met Quartermaster Burr of whom I obtained my horse Bird. Capt. Rodgers concluded to come to Grand Junction with me and we arrived safely at 8 o'clock PM. Found a letter from my wife. Little Gracie is sick.

Grand Junction, Tenn.
Feby. 25th 1863

One year ago today my battery was mustered into the service of the US. One year ago today I was commissioned as captain of the battery. 33 years ago today I was born. I had sent for a flag to present to the battery. For some reason it has not arrived, though I am assured it was started on the 18th inst. by express.

It was a rainy uncomfortable day and our celebration will have to be postponed to a more convenient season. One year has passed since our labors commenced and although we have not accomplished as much as we often think we ought to, still we have done much. We hope that on the next anniversary of our muster, we may be at home.

Grand Junction, Tenn.

Thursday, February 26th 1863

A very rainy day. Went to La Grange in company with Capts. Cogswell and Rodgers and Lieut. Burton. Called on Capts. Bouton and Mueller.[i] Considering that it has been a terrible day, have passed time rather pleasantly. Capt. Rodgers went home by railroad.

Grand Junction, Tenn.

February 27th 1863

Tomorrow will be the day for mustering for pay. Our rolls have been made and we are ready. Rain.

Grand Junction, Tenn.

February 28th 1863

A fine morning. Went to La Grange to muster the boys in the hospital. Returned and were mustered for pay by Capt. Cogswell, chief of artillery, 1st Division.

Grand Junction, Tenn.

Sunday, March 1st 1863

Spring has come and a beautiful day is the 1st day of March. Improved it in riding to La Grange in company with Capt. Nelson, Lieut. Godown of the 12th Indiana, and Lieut. Burton. Made the acquaintance of Col. Stoughton of the 100th Indiana and spent an hour pleasantly at his quarters. Wrote to my wife.

Grand Junction, Tenn.

Monday, March 2nd 1863

Another fine day. The 40th Illinois now stationed at Davis Mill have taken a stationary engine formerly used for sawing wood and mounted it on a platform car. By attaching a pulley to the axel and running a taut line from the pulley on the engine, have a locomotive. This morning they ran the machine to Grand Junction. Several officers went with it to La Grange were we took on board Gen. Denver and rode to Davis Mill and return. Can Yankee ingenuity do more? Old Davis

---

[i] Capt. Michael Mueller of Evansville, IN, 6th Indiana Light Battery

thinks there is nothing that Yankees cannot do. Learn that the Ram Queen of the West[i] has been captured up Red River by the Rebels.

Grand Junction, Tenn.
Tuesday, March 3rd 1863

Cold windy day. Went to La Grange to see a paymaster. On account of leaving our payrolls with Maj. Terrill last fall, who promised us he was coming along with us, we have to make new rolls for Sept and Oct. We get but two months pay this time. Last night at 12 o'clock we were notified from headquarters that the enemy's cavalry were hovering about us and we must be ready. We are ready. Wrote to my wife.

Grand Junction, Tenn.
Wednesday, March 4th

A fine day. It has been improved by drilling the battery for the first time since we left Memphis.

Grand Junction, Tenn.
Thursday, March 5th 1863

Cold, windy, dry, but we have been out and had a lively drill. Received a letter from Brother Pers informing me that Brother Sam is quite sick on the Potomac. Learn that the Conscription Bill has passed both houses of Congress and no doubt will receive the President's signature and become law. We are glad to know that our ranks, that are being thinned by sickness and death, will be filled. Good for conscription.

Grand Junction, Tenn.
Friday, March 6th 1863

It is rather a foggy day and looks as though we would have a bad time for a review.

The review by Gen. Denver came off at 3 PM. Rained some and some injury was done to white gloves and other fine trappings. The review was very creditable to our troops and also to the general and his staff. Ye captain of ye battery was complimented by Gen. Denver on

---

[i] US Ram Queen of the West ran aground and was captured by Rebels Feb. 14, 1862. She became the Confederate Ram *Queen of the West*

the good appearance of men and horses. Altogether the review has been a success and all feel pleased.

Grand Junction, Tenn.
Saturday, March 7th, 1863

I was about starting for La Grange to visit the boys at the hospital, when I was informed that John W. Graves,[i] who had been sick some three weeks, had died last night at La Grange hospital. I concluded to bury him here as there were so many buried at La Grange that it would be almost impossible for the friends of the deceased to ever find his remains, should they wish at any time to obtain them. Selected a good spot. Rode to La Grange and got permission to return with the body and bury at Grand Junction.

At 2 o'clock PM the mortal remains of John W. Graves were buried by the battery with the honors due a deceased soldier. In the absence of our chaplain, a few remarks were made by the captain of the battery. John W. Graves was a good soldier, a worthy and trustworthy man. Leaves a widowed mother in New York. Died in the service of his country. John W. Graves has fallen, another victim to the insatiable ambition of politicians. Another sacrifice on the altar of his country.

This evening we hear the report of musketry and expect a fight is going on at La Grange. Battery being harnessed and regiments falling into line preparatory to an engagement. I receive a letter from my wife. Stop to read it and wonder if it is the last one I will receive. Can't help it, here goes. Boys hitch up. All hands ready. Anxious for a hand in. Firing lasts about an hour. Orderlies flying in all directions.

Grand finale – the 6th Illinois Cavalry permitted to discharge their carbines and also to have a little target practice. Nobody hurt.

Grand Junction, Tenn.
Sunday, March 8th 1863

A rainy day has been spent in writing and reading. Nothing of interest has transpired. We learn that another brigade has been organized in our division to be commanded by Col. Loomis of the 26th Illinois Infantry. The 100th Indiana have gone to Collierville. 46th Ohio gone to La Grange. Cogswell's Battery have gone to La Grange. Leaving the

---

[i] Pvt. John Graves of Jacksonville, IL, Battery F, 1st Illinois Light Artillery

12th Indiana, the 15th Michigan, one section of Dresser's Battery[i] and our battery here.

Learn that the 15th Michigan is to leave us tomorrow. Only 6 guns and one regiment left to take care of Grand Junction. Learn that the 4th Division (Gen. Lauman, in which is the 46th Illinois) are going to Vicksburg. Gen. Denver's division have the railroad to guard from Davis Mill to Memphis.

Grand Junction, Tenn.
Monday, March 9th, 1863

I am afflicted with rheumatism and move about but little. Looks lonely to look out upon the vacated camps so recently occupied by regiments of our brigade. Nothing specifically interesting today.

Grand Junction, Tenn.
Tuesday, March 10th 1863

A terrible stormy day. Most of it I have kept in the tent applying hot bricks for rheumatism. Various rumors concerning the evacuation of the railroad from here to Columbus. Already have the troops from along the line of the road commenced going through toward Memphis. 48th, 49th and 103rd Illinois have gone to La Grange.

Grand Junction, Tenn.
Wednesday, March 11th 1863

Went to La Grange today. Learn that the 6th Iowa are ordered back to this place. The 12th Indiana ordered to Germantown. Spent the evening with officers of the 12th Indiana, as they leave us tomorrow. Will long remember the 12th and hope we may again come together.

Grand Junction, Tenn.
Thursday, March 12th, 1863

Rode to La Grange this morning. Received orders to leave the fort and fall back about one half mile near the 6th Iowa. The 6th Iowa are back and the 12th Indiana have gone. It seems that the railroad north from us is being evacuated as train after train is passing laden with

---

[i] Dresser's Battery was Battery D, 2nd Illinois Light Artillery

soldiers. Have received a dispatch saying that there is fighting near Germantown. Wrote to my wife.

Grand Junction, Tenn.
Friday, March 13, 1863

A fine day. We have moved to our new camping ground. Have a very pleasant camp and have taken some pains to get in good shape. Have been considerably annoyed today by rheumatism.

Grand Junction, Tenn.
Saturday, March 14th 1863

Took a squad of men to build a bridge across a ravine between us and La Grange. Fine day and got a good start toward having a bridge to retreat across if compelled to retreat. After the labor of the day, came back to camp and was pleased to receive a letter from my wife. All well at home.

Grand Junction, Tenn.
Sunday, March 15th 1863

Rather a dull day with some rain. Went out to work on the bridges, as we concluded to build two. Were driven back by the rain. Wrote to my wife. Suffering from rheumatism.

Grand Junction, Tenn.
Monday, March 16th 1863

Went out in the morning and completed the two bridges giving us a good chance to retreat in a hurry if necessary. Rheumatism better. Our flag has come tonight. Tomorrow at 3 o'clock PM is the time fixed upon for the presentation. Received a letter from Brother Pers saying my little Gracie is very sick.

Grand Junction, Tenn.

Tuesday, March 17, 1863

A fine morning. Walter Little[i] has been designated as the color bearer. S. E. Parker[ii] has been designated as the one to make the reply to the presentation remarks that the Captain may make.

At 3 PM the battery mounted, were drawn up in line, and the flag presented by Capt. Cheney with a few remarks, which were eloquently responded to by S. E. Parker on behalf of the battery. Capt. Cogswell being present was called upon and very beautifully and eloquently paid a just tribute to the American flag. After a short drill all came back to camp apparently well pleased with the exercises.

Grand Junction, Tenn.

Wednesday, March 18, 1863

Another fine day, which has been spent partially in drilling and partially in getting from the paymaster, two months pay. Nothing of special importance has transpired.

Grand Junction, Tenn.

Thursday, March 19, 1863

Still pleasant weather. Afflicted with rheumatism yet. Have had a ride in company with Lieut. Whaley outside the pickets. Found beautiful fields of wheat, peach trees in full bloom, and a fine country really.

Grand Junction, Tenn.

Friday, March 20, 1863

Went to La Grange this morning and consulted with Dr. Shaw, medical director in our division. He calls my disease neuralgic rheumatism and has prescribed for me; promising to cure me in ten days. Hope he may succeed. Lieut. Smyth has leave of absence to go to Memphis for 3 days. Rumors of an attack on us very soon. Received a letter from my wife and am happy to learn that Gracie is much better. Have just had a good bath and written up my diary.

---

[i] Pvt. Walter Little of Malugins Grove, IL, Battery F, 1st Illinois Light Artillery
[ii] Pvt. S. E. Parker of Brooklyn, IL, Battery F, 1st Illinois Light Artillery

Grand Junction, Tenn.

Saturday, March 21, 1863

A fine morning. Getting ready for a drill when up comes the commander of the post and orders us to hitch up and take our position on the hill near the fort. Two thousand Rebel cavalry reported within two miles of us. A wood train reported captured and the cars burned. Took our position and remained in line of battle till 3 o'clock PM, when we returned to camp.

The train was captured also the conductor and engineer. The engine was retaken. The cars were burned, tracks torn up some and all done by about 30 guerrillas. A regiment of cavalry (the 6th Illinois) have gone out in pursuit of the enemy. We moved today with our flag at the head of our column. The boys say, "will rally round the flag."

Grand Junction, Tenn.

Sunday, March 22, 1863

Rather a dull foggy day. Rumored that Brig. Gen. Denver has resigned, that his resignation has been accepted, and that Brig. Gen. Smith succeeds him. Who Brig. Gen. Smith is we do not know, but suppose that he belongs to the family of Smiths.

Later received an order from Brig. Gen. W. S. Smith, commanding 1st Division 16th Army Corps saying that the enemy's cavalry are at Senatobia.[i] We are ordered to be in line of battle at day break till further notice.

Capt. Sprouse[ii] of the 40th Illinois visited us and stopped all night.

Grand Junction, Tenn.

Monday, March 23rd 1863

It is a very unpleasant day. Rain is falling quite profusely. Rather hard on rheumatism, but on the whole I am better than when I commenced taking medicine provided by Dr. Shaw.

Grand Junction, Tenn.

Tuesday, March 24, 1863

Rainy day. Suffered terribly with rheumatism. Nothing of interest has transpired today.

---

[i] Senatobia, MS is 40 miles south of Memphis, TN

[ii] Capt. William T. Sprouse of Kinmundy, IL, Co. B, 40th Illinois Infantry

Grand Junction, Tenn.
Wednesday, March 25, 1863

Went to La Grange. Applied to Dr. Shaw for a certificate on which to make an application for a leave of absence to go home. Obtained it and visited Gen. Smith to get his approval. Gen. Smith approved. Like Gen. Smith very much. Met him for the first time today.

Below is the application for leave of absence due to sickness

---

Grand Junction, Tenn.
Mch. 25, 1863

Gen.

I respectfully request that a leave of absence be granted me for 20 days, dating from April 1st 1863. The cause for such application may be found in Division Surgeon's Certificate accompanying this application. I have the honor to be General

Very respectfully your obedient servant,

Brig. Gen. W. S. Smith   John T. Cheney, Capt. Comdg.
Comdg. 1st Division   Bat. F, 1st Reg. Ill. Lt. Artillery
16th Army Corps

Attachment

Capt. John T. Cheney having applied for a certificate on which to grant an application, I hereby certify that Capt. Cheney has been under my immediate care for the last ten days in consequence of the command being so extensive that Ast. Surg. Woodworth could not attend upon him. And I believe that his ailments are such that he cannot recover without a change of climate for the next twenty days, in as much as he is afflicted with sciatica which in all probability will not be relieved without a change of climate and mode of life which is impossible in the present condition of Capt. Cheney.

A. T. Shaw
Surg. 6th Iowa Infty.
Headquarters, 1st Div. 16th Army Corps

*** *** *** *** *** *** *** ***

Grand Junction, Tenn.

Thursday, March 26th 1863

Left today for Memphis where I arrived safely at 12 o'clock noon. Went to the Gayoso House.

Memphis, Tenn.

Friday, March 27, 1863

A luxury to sleep on a good spring bed. Visited the 46th Illinois Infantry who are encamped about one and one half miles from the Gayoso. Col. Jones of the 46th has presented my application for leave of absence to Gen. Hurlbut. I am to have a leave, but must take my turn and will probably be detained a day or two before getting my papers.

Memphis, Tenn.

Monday, March 28, 1863

Pleasant day. Have been trying to get my papers through, but must wait.

Memphis, Tenn.

Sunday, March 29, 1863

Cold rainy day. Had a fire in my room. Lieut. Snyder of Gen. Grant's engineer corps called upon me and stayed all night.

Memphis, Tenn.

Monday, March 30th 1863

Am informed this morning that I must be examined by Maj. Campbell, medical director of the 16th Army Corps before getting leave of absence. Visited Maj. Campbell and my leave ordered. Have the promise of papers tonight.

Memphis, Tenn.

Tuesday, March 31, 1863

Visited the 46th Illinois Infantry. Found Lieut. Bullock sick with ague. Promised papers in the morning.

Memphis, Tenn.
Wednesday, April 1st, 1863

April fool. No papers today. Wait and hope. Capt. Marble and his wife arrived today.

Memphis, Tenn.
Thursday, April 2nd 1863

Went out to see the review of the 4th Division by Maj. Gen. S. A. Hurlbut. Spirited division. No leave of absence.

Memphis, Tenn.
Friday, April 3rd, 1863

Politely informed that on account of informality in surgeon's certificate, my papers must be sent back. Red Tape.

Memphis, Tenn.
Saturday, April 4th 1863

Am informed that I will certainly get leave of absence tomorrow. Met F. A. Moore of La Crosse, Wis. an old school mate whom I had not seen for 17 years. Visited Capt. Rodgers and spent the night.

Memphis, Tenn.
Sunday, April 5th 1863

Spent the day and night in company with F. A. Moore at Gayoso House.

Memphis, Tenn.
Monday, April 6th 1863

Received a leave of absence for 20 days. Took passage on the Champion for Cairo.[i] When arrived safely on the 7th, found Brother Pers and Richard Roberts watching for me having started in pursuit of me fearing that I was sick in some hospital. Left on the same evening and arrived safely at home on the morning of the 9th of April 1863.

---

[i] Cairo, IL, at the southern tip of the state is on the Mississippi River. Cairo was connected to Dixon, IL by the Illinois Central Railroad

Summary

John Cheney was growing tired of the war. In the year since his battery was mustered into service, they had not participated in a battle. Cheney was enduring the hardships of soldiering but didn't feel he was accomplishing much. Guarding the railroad at Davis Mill or Grand Junction did not seem to him to be very fruitful.

Cheney was now laid up due to sciatica – what he called rheumatism. Added to his debilitating gastro-intestinal illness of August/September 1862, John Cheney now had a history of two ailments capable of rendering him unfit for duty.

Chapter 11 - Siege of Vicksburg

June 1, 1863 to July 19, 1863

Background

In May 1863, *Lieut. Gen. John Pemberton's* army had been forced by Grant's army to move into the city of Vicksburg, Mississippi. *Pemberton* took up a defensive position and Grant began the Siege of Vicksburg. In June 1863 *Gen. Joseph Johnston* concentrated his troops in the Jackson, Mississippi area east of Vicksburg.

When John Cheney returned to Memphis from his medical leave of absence, Battery F was about to depart by boat for Vicksburg. At Vicksburg they would serve under Capt. William Cogswell, chief of artillery in Brig. Gen. William Sooy Smith's 1st Division, Maj. Gen. Cadwallader Washburn's 16th Army Corps (Detachment) in Maj. Gen. Grant's Army of the Tennessee.

Battery F now had a high probability to "see the elephant."

June 1st 1863

Left Dixon for Dixie at 11:40 AM. Arrived at Decatur[i] at 6 PM.

June 2nd 1863

Left Decatur at 1:50 AM after a rich entertainment while listening to a conversation (in a low tone) between two Copperheads. Arrived at Springfield at 4 o'clock AM. Finished my business and after forwarding a few keepsakes to my family, left for the field at 11:40 PM.

*** *** *** *** *** *** *** ***

---

[i] The Illinois Central Railroad running north–south in Illinois went through Decatur, IL not Springfield 40 miles to the west

Springfield, Ill.
June 2, 1863

Dear Wife,

I have succeeded in getting my recruiting account and sent to you $200. I start for the battery tonight. Am feeling quite well. Will write you as soon as I get through. Remember me to all the friends and particularly to the children. Don't fret about me as I am all right and am coming out all right. Write me often. I was with you last night when you went to bed with the little one. Good courage wife. I have no more time.

Affectionately yours,
John T. Cheney

*** *** *** *** *** *** *** ***

June 3rd 1863

Arrived at Decatur at 2 o'clock and at 5:30 AM took the Illinois Central for Cairo where we arrived at 4:30 PM. Took passage on the City of Alton, a fine boat laden with sanitary stores and chartered by Gov. Yates to take them to our sick and wounded soldiers at Vicksburg.

June 4th 1863

Left Cairo at 5:30 AM. Learn that several banished ladies and gents are aboard among whom are the wife and two daughters of *Lieut. Trustin Polk* of Missouri, and in the Rebel army. Many ladies and gentlemen from Illinois are on their way to administer to the wants of our wounded soldiers. On account of fog lay up for the night throwing out pickets.

June 5th

Start again at 5 AM. Pleasant day. Arrived at Memphis, Tenn. at 5:30 PM. Stayed the night at the Gayoso House.

June 6th 1863

Reported to Maj. Gen. Hurlbut. Learn that the 1st Division, 16th Army Corps are on the way from the line of the Memphis and Charleston Railroad to go to Vicksburg. Our battery will be here in a day or two. I remain here till they arrive. We go to Vicksburg just in time.

Memphis, Tenn.

June 7, 1863

Battery arrived at 12 o'clock noon. Boys all excited and in good health.

June 8

Ordered to report with the battery at the levee at 7 o'clock AM. Assigned to the Jacob Strader, a fine boat. 1st Missouri Battery go with us. Boat not yet ready to receive us and we encamp on the levee for the night.

June 9th

At 10 o'clock AM are embarked. At 12:30 PM start for Vicksburg. Col. Hillier and Lt. Col. Duff of Gen. Grant's staff are with us.

June 10th

Arrived at Helena, Ark. at 5:30 AM . First Missouri Battery left at Helena. Left Helena at 12 noon under convey of a gunboat.

June 11th

Arrived at Snyder's Bluff east bank of the Yazoo River, Mississippi at 5 o'clock PM. Could get no chance to disembark till dark. Rain, mud, darkness etc. At 12 at night we were off the boat encamped in the mud. Heavy firing at Vicksburg.

June 12th, 1863

Started at 3:30 AM. Took position on a high bluff about one mile from the river. Heavy cannonading at Vicksburg.

*** *** *** *** *** *** *** ***

Snyder's Bluff, Miss.
June 12, 1863

My dear Wife,

We arrived here last night at about 5 o'clock and worked till 12 o'clock. Were up again this morning at 5:30 o'clock and have just got into camp. Haynes' Bluff is two miles further up the river (the Yazoo).

Cannonading and musketry were heard all night last night till about 10 AM today, since which time we have heard nothing. It is now 2 o'clock PM. We are about 8 miles from Vicksburg and can see it through our glasses.

It does not look as though it was intended for our division to take part in the siege of Vicksburg, but to remain here to prevent the enemy's being reinforced. This is a very strong place and Gen. Grant is entitled to much credit for the taking of it.[i] The bluffs are very high and the country very rough and heavy timbered. The 13th and 46th are only a few miles from us and I hope to see them. You are perhaps aware that 6 companies of the 46th were taken prisoners the other day. My health is good. The weather is very hot indeed. I do not know when I can send this and will wait and write more before it goes.

Saturday Morning 15th

No news from Vicksburg yet. Some heavy firing this morning at 2 o'clock. Last night at about 6 o'clock there was some pretty sharp picket fighting in our rear. The enemy were repulsed. We now have an army whose front is toward Vicksburg and another fronting north. We are in the last, and on the left, on the east bank of the Yazoo River. The Yazoo is inhabited principally by crocodiles which may be seen at any time. They are beautiful animals.

Everybody is confident that Vicksburg will fall within a week. I could give you any quantity of camp rumors, but it is useless, as we place no confidence in anything unofficial. A mail goes out this morning and I must close. I am feeling well and hope to be able to stand the campaign. Give my love to the friends. Tell me how little Gracie acted after I left. I expect Royce will become quite a farmer. Add to the superscription on your letters "Near Vicksburg". The weather is hot. Good morning Mary. Courage.

Affy. your husband,
John

*** *** *** *** *** *** *** ***

June 13th

Commenced building a fort. Received a letter from home.
June 14, 1863

---

[i] Snyder's Bluff was the site of a battle April 29 to May 1, 1863. Naval forces and the 15th Army Corps, Dept of the Tennessee, Maj. Gen. Frank Blair's Division, under Maj. Gen. William Sherman under Grant, took Snyder's Bluff.

Worked on the fort. Are in good shape and hope *Johnston* will come on. We can give him a warm reception.

June 15th 1863

Johnston reported within 4 miles of us in force. We are notified to be ready at any moment. Gen. Sherman visited us. He complimented us on the excellence of our fort, and the condition of the battery generally.

Visited Col. Blake's (Secesh) plantation. Ripe pears.

June 16th 1863

Out at 3 o'clock AM to be ready for *Gen. Johnston* who is expected to give us a morning call. The siege of Vicksburg still continues and fall it must as *Johnston* cannot cut his way through us to relieve *Gen. Pemberton*.

The 9th Army Corps have arrived and I have found Brother James[i] who is a quartermaster. He spends the night with me.

*** *** *** *** *** *** *** ***

Snyder's Bluff, Miss.
Tuesday, June 16th 1863

My dear Wife,

Your kind letter of 4th inst. came to hand on the 14th and I was rejoiced to hear from you. Tell Gracie that Pa will come some day at 5 o'clock to sleep with her. I expect Royce will soon have green peas to sell. I am now waiting anxiously to hear from you again.

We are now fortifying here. If *Joe Johnston* comes, we will give him Hell. We can do it. Grant will take Vicksburg so sure as God lives. He is shelling them every night. *Pemberton* has tried 3 times in as many days to cut his way out of Vicksburg and as often has he been terribly repulsed. Vicksburg can be seen though a field glass from our camp. The terrible roaring of the dogs of war is terribly grand. I wish you could be here to see the smoke from the guns curling up above the doomed City of the Bluffs. Hear the roar of our siege guns and guns of our naval fleet.

---

[i] Lieut. James F. Briggs of Hillsborough, NH, Company S, 11th New Hampshire Infantry, the brother of Mary Briggs Cheney. At Vicksburg the 11th NH was part of the 2nd Brigade, 2nd Division, 9th Army Corps.

Troops are arriving almost hourly and all is bustle and animation. Health of men excellent and all in good spirits. Last night *Johnston's* advance guard had a skirmish with Gen. Kimball's division. All the officers of artillery were sent for to report to Gen. Smith. We went down to his (Smith's) quarters. Were given some instructions concerning what was necessary for us to do in action. Were told that in all probability would be called upon by *Johnston's* army. This morning we were up and stood to the guns at 3 AM, but no attack yet. We are strongly fortified. God knows I want him to come, for we are in good condition to fight and it is now time that we were at it.

Don't fear for me for I am all right. My health is quite good. I feel glad that you have got a home[i] in which you feel so deeply interested and one that suits you so well. I hope and pray that many years may be spent by us together in our home with our children. Mary, I expect it, and it is hope that makes war endurable. Give my love to all the friends. Tell Mrs. Adams that as often as I partake (which is often) of horseradish, I do it in remembrance of her. I must close to get my letter in the mail. Write often. How is my colt? We expect to get paid in a day or two.

Affectionately your husband,
John T. Cheney

*** *** *** *** *** *** *** ***

June 17th 1863

Spend most of the day with the 9th Corps among whom I found many acquaintances from New Hampshire.

June 18th 1863

Visited by Jos. Morrill,[ii] Charlie Benjamin[iii] and Remington[iv] of the 13th Illinois and Lieut. Snyder of the 46th Illinois. Blackberries ripe. Magnolias in blossom. Weather hot. *Johnston* didn't come.

---

[i] John Cheney and family had rented house and in 1863 purchased a one
[ii] Pvt. Joseph R. Morrill of Dixon, IL, Co. A, 13th Illinois Infantry
[iii] Pvt. Charles A. Benjamin of Dixon, IL, Co. A, 13th Illinois Infantry
[iv] Pvt. Edward V. E. Remington of Dixon, IL, Co. A, 13th Illinois Infantry

June 19th

With Lieut. Snyder visited the 9th Regiment New Hampshire Infantry. Troops look well; well disciplined. Flag of truce came in from *Johnston* with a notice that no more flags of truce will be received from us by way of the Yazoo River. Have permission to visit Vicksburg tomorrow.

June 20th 1863

In company with Brother James, Lt. Burton and Capt. Galvin went to Vicksburg. No man can conceive under what difficulties Gen. Grant has labored, without visiting the works of the enemy. Visited the 13th Illinois and find enough to interest us. Only regret that I cannot remain a week.

June 21, 1863
Vicksburg, Miss.

Spent the night with the 13th Illinois Infantry. Lieuts. Dement and Pinkham[i] made us feel quite at home. This morning Maj. Bushnell of the 13th went with us to visit Gen. Sherman's 15th Army Corps and Gen. Logan's division particularly, which for daring and endurance during this siege, is not surpassed if equaled. Started for home at 4 o'clock PM where we arrived at 7.

June 22, 1863
Snyder's Bluff, Miss.

Went to Chickasaw Bayou[ii] on the steamer Armenia after quartermaster stores. On my return found orders to move tomorrow at 3 AM with 3 days cooked rations.

*** *** *** *** *** *** *** ***

---

[i] Lieut. (later Capt.) A. Judson Pinkham of Dixon, IL, Co. A, 13th Illinois Infantry
[ii] Chickasaw Bayou, MS is also know as Walnut Hills; located north of Vicksburg, MS

My dear Wife,

Your kind letter of the 9th inst. was received on the 17th inst. and if ever a man was glad to hear from home it was me. I am very glad to hear that you are getting along so finely and know you will make yourself as happy as is possible (under such circumstances) for you to be. I am glad to be able to tell you Mary that I am quite well and in as good condition as I have been in at any time since I enlisted.

On the 16th inst. I learned that a portion of the 9th Army Corps (Burnside's) had arrived. Just at dark in the rain I started for the levee and almost the first man I met was Brother James. He went to our camp and slept with me. The next morning we went to the boats and found Billy Franklin.[i] James and Billy are well and are in camp about 2 miles from us. On the 20th in company with Jim, Lieut. Burton and others went to Vicksburg. Met the 13th, saw Lieuts. Dement, Pinkham, Col. Gorgas, Joe Morrill, Charlie Benjamin, Alex Pitts,[ii] Ed Remington and many other Dixon boys. All well except Pinkham who has been unwell some days.

It would be almost impossible for me to give you any idea of the condition of things at Vicksburg. I can only say that the daring, energy, endurance, confidence of our troops has no equal in history. Think of two lines of fortifications being within 20 yards of each other. Rifle pits lined with sharp shooters ready to pop the first head that shows itself. Of saps[iii] being cut by our men across the ravine between the two lines of works (by night). Of our soldiers undermining the enemy's forts with spades while they could drop any substance on their heads, did they dare reach over to do it, and you can begin to form some idea of what warfare is. This is the condition of things in Gen. Logan's division. Vicksburg must fall, but the intention undoubtedly is to drive them to a surrender without making a charge, as many lives must necessarily be lost by charging their works.

I spent most of two days in examining the works and many bullets whistled through the air close to me. With proper caution no man need be shot unless by a shell bursting in our works. Many horses and mules are being turned loose by the Rebels and come into our lines looking as though forage was getting very scarce. I saw Mrs. Burk's son yester-

---

[i] James Briggs' mother was Nancy (Franklin) Briggs; possibly Billy Franklin is a cousin of James

[ii] Corp. Alexander Pitts of Dixon, IL, Co. A, 13th Illinois Infantry

[iii] Saps are trenches

day. He is quite well and is getting very fat. I never saw him look so well. I also saw Mat Adams who is well. I had not time to visit the 46th but heard from them, all well.

It is reported that *Johnston* is passing our right toward Black River. If this be true, we will soon be on the move again to attack his rear. Gen. Grant is very anxious to have him come down and visit him, feeling confident that we can finish up a large job by whipping him and *Pemberton* at the same time. We have not a sick man, boys feeling first rate and anxious for a fight. If there is anyone North who thinks Gen. Grant is moving slow, wish they would come down and see what a Gibraltar he has to contend with. If Gen. Grant and his assistants never take Vicksburg, they have already accomplished enough to entitle them to the respect and esteem of the American people.

I am very busy. My work is never done, but I will take time to write you as often as possible. Write often and remember me to all the friends. I miss my dear family more than ever. God bless you each and all. We will be the happy family when the war is over and peace once more restored.

I have tripe for dinner today. We expect to be paid in a day or two when I will send you $100. Have you had green peas yet? Will the strawberries live? Are the apple trees all alive? How high have the willows grown?

Affectionately your husband,
John T. Cheney

*** *** *** *** *** *** *** ***

June 23rd 1863
Snyder's Bluff, Miss.

Moved at 3 o'clock AM in an easterly direction expecting to meet *Gen. Johnston* who is reported to have crossed Black River.[i] 14 miles to Oak Ridge. Terrible rain. Beef plenty and good. Earthworks being thrown up. Heavy cannonading at Vicksburg.

Oak Ridge, Miss.
June 24th 1863

An official dispatch from Maj. Gen. Grant saying that Port Hudson[ii] is ours. Fortifying and ready for *Johnston*.

---

[i] Black River is east of Vicksburg, MS, between Vicksburg and Jackson

[ii] Port Hudson, Lousiana battle was May 21, 1863 to July 9, 1863, i.e., it did not fall until July 9

Oak Ridge, Miss.
June 25th 1863

Went to Snyder's Bluff after stores. Met Brother James of the 9th Army Corps. Terrible hot day.

*** *** *** *** *** *** *** ***

Snyder's Bluff, Miss.
June 25, 1863

My dear Wife,

On the evening of the 22nd inst. we received orders to be ready to march without tents at 3 o'clock AM of the 24th. At 3 we started in an easterly direction toward Black River. It was fully expected that by 8 o'clock AM we would meet and engage *Johnston*. But *Johnston* learned of our coming and immediately re-crossed the Black. We had but 3 days rations and today I am back after rations and forage.

I have just seen Jim. He is well. Our camp is now at Oak Ridge some 8 miles east of here. We have just received official information of the fall of Port Hudson. All hands jubilant. Vicksburg must fall within 3 days.

Your kind letter of the 14th I have just received. Mary you cannot imagine how much good your letters do me. I feel so proud of you in your noble expression of self denial for the benefit of our country that I cannot, nor will I attempt to, give expression to my feelings. I have but very little time to spare and cannot write you at length. My health is good. Can stand the weather much better than the cold. Blackberries plenty and good beef in abundance. Boys all well. Rebels are planting batteries on the Mississippi above us. No boat can pass without a gunboat as an escort. Don't worry about me, I am all right. Remember me to all friends. To our children give a thousand and one kisses.

Affectionately yours,
John

*** *** *** *** *** *** *** ***

Oak Ridge, Miss.
June 26, 1863

Went out after beef. Got a fine yoke of oxen. An attack expected tomorrow. We are ready.

Break in diary starts here – diary lost.

On July 4, 1863 Vicksburg surrendered. At the time of Cheney's next letter, Battery F was east of Vicksburg and moving east toward *Gen. Johnston* at Jackson, Mississippi

Edward's Ferry Black River, Miss.
July 6th 1863

My dear Wife,

The enemy dispute our passage across the river. 50,000 men want to cross and we are going. Last night we shelled them. This morning our brigade, while attempting to cross, were repulsed temporarily. Six were wounded. I am well. Jim is well. The boys are well. We are getting into a warm place, but will push them back. At Jackson, where they are strongly fortified, we will play Vicksburg with them. All is hurry. My trains go to the Bluffs after rations. I cannot write but a few lines. I will write you often. Although my letters must be short, I keep a diary from which I can gather all of interest and you shall know it all.

I received your letter of the 22nd. Was very sorry that you are suffering with your head and eyes,[i] and hope you are better. Be careful of your health. I will come out all right. Love to all friends and the children. Jim F[ii] is along and well.

Yours truly as ever,
John T. Cheney

~ ~ ~ ~ ~

In Camp near Jackson, Miss.
Sunday, July 19 /63

My dear Wife,

After an apparent neglect of a good many days, I will write you. The truth is Mary, it has been next to impossible for me to write earlier for the reason that you will see when you get my diary, if I ever get time to copy it.[iii] I will not attempt to give you an account of our march since we left Snyder's Bluff, more than to say that we built bridges,

---

[i] 'head and eyes' might be an indication of migraine headaches
[ii] James F. Briggs
[iii] Other parts of his diary exist as both originals and copies, or originals only; that volume of his diary is lost

raised sunken ferry boats, shelled the skirmishers of the enemy, and finally arrived within two miles of Jackson on Friday the 10th inst. You will recollect we started on Saturday the 4th. On our arms we slept, short naps till 2 o'clock, and at 8 o'clock next morning our line of battle was formed. We were ordered to follow Col. Hicks' brigade.[i] Our skirmishers were thrown out and soon the ball opened. The enemy being driven back. We made about one half mile that day to the front, but made marches by flanks right and left a full 3 miles through timber, cutting our road with axes. When we gained the hill opposite the enemy's works, the battery was not 5 minutes behind the brigade, though the day's work was hard. You ought to see my boys fell trees, tear up railroads, smash down fences and overcome any obstacle that comes in our way.

Harpers Weekly "Before Jackson"

Saturday night was up most all night superintending the building of bastions for the batteries. Sunday Morning the 12th we were ordered to open the ball with artillery at 8 o'clock. At that hour 16 guns[ii] of our division went into battery in one continuous line about 20 yards apart. All commenced to fire at will. Such a racket I never before heard. Soon the Rebs began to reply. We being on the top of the hill were only covered by a strip of woodland from their full view. Capt. Cogswell's Battery was on the right, Capt. Mueller (6th Indiana) right center, Cheney's left center and Capt. Bouton's on the left. Soon after we

---

[i] Col. Stephen G. Hicks commanded the 2nd Brigade, 1st Division, 16th Army Corps, Army of the Tennessee

[ii] 4 batteries with 4 guns each

commenced the enemy got our range, only shooting high, most of his shots went directly over my battery. The devils gradually depressed till they found where we lived. One 12 lb solid shot went directly through between Jim and Gates detachments on a line with the muzzles of the pieces. Strange to say no one was injured. Henry Horn and I were standing at the right of the battery when I saw a solid coming and concluded to let it come as I could not stop it. It passed about 3 feet from my number 1 piece and under Horn's horse, between his (horse) legs. I sensed my battery to be singled out as a target at which to shoot, but the only damage done was a spoke knocked out of a wheel, caisson slightly damaged, and one horse instantly killed. We were ordered to limber to the rear and drop under cover of the hill which we done and all firing ceased.

We urged the chief of artillery[i] to let us open again but he would not. We fired directly into the thickest part of the town. It has since proved that had we continued 15 minutes longer with our iron hail, *Johnston* would have run up the white flag. One of the enemy's batteries was driven from their works. Our infantry line of battle was in front of us and we had to shoot over them. Had it not been for this we would have driven them in a few minutes, but we did not dare to shoot lower. Our shell fired many houses. Spent the time till Thursday in cutting saps through hills, throwing up cotton bales in front to protect workmen etc. etc.

I went into a brick house to get a view of a fort that we were to operate against. I just opened the blind about 3 inches when a shell came through the observatory. We went out to compare notes under the hill when pop went a shell not more than 20 feet directly over our heads. Six horses were hitched just beyond us, but strange to say neither horse nor man was injured. The fort looked wicked with its black guns staring us in the face, through embrasures.

This afternoon Gen. Sherman ordered a charge to our right by Col. Hicks' and Col. Sanford's[ii] brigades. The artillery could not move with them, but one battery could have taken position to assist. This was not done. Our brave boys marched boldly forward. Out came a Rebel brigade to meet them, when a masked battery opened on our men with

---

[i] Capt. William Cogswell was the chief of artillery, 1st Division, 16th Army Corps; Cogswell's Battery was at that time commanded by Lieut. Henry G. Eddy

[ii] Col. William W. Sanford commanded the 4th Brigade, 1st Division, 16th Army Corps, Army of the Tennessee

shell and canister,[i] killing and wounding one hundred men. The enemy attempted to outflank us, when the little handful of men led in to make a charge, were forced to retreat or be annihilated. Gen. Sherman believed the enemy had evacuated but in this he was mistaken. 93rd Indiana and 46th Illinois suffered most severely in this charge.

Friday morning 17th, *Gen. Johnston* with his 50,000 men have evacuated Jackson and are on the other side of the Pearl River. The batteries go into town kiting. The boys are just raking things. Safes being broken open. Stores relieved of dry goods, sugar. A complete army of men going to and fro loaded with all kinds of plunder. Buildings enveloped in flames. My God Mary you can't conceive what a destruction of Rebel property. It is beautiful, sublime, glorious, just. The nest in which treason has been nursed for years is about broken up. In two days more the once beautiful capital of Mississippi will be among the cities that were but are not.

You will know that I would not injure the property of my worst personal enemy. But believing as I do that the Rebellion will be sooner crushed by laying waste their property, I rejoice in it, believing many valuable lives will be spared.

Since writing the above I have taken a ride about town. Find the cotton is being scattered and is already on fire by order of the commanding general. I expect by tomorrow we will get orders to go north or rather perhaps west to Vicksburg, and from thence wherever we may be needed, possibly Kentucky. I have learned not to trouble myself about when we go, but be always ready, and go good naturedly wherever ordered.

The boys behaved splendidly. I would designate some names, but would hardly know where to stop. You can tell the friends in Dixon that their sons, brothers, husbands will never disgrace them on the field. My health is good. Have had a little ague, one light shake in consequence of being out in the dew, but am all right and feel well and strong. I am all right and am taking as good care of myself as possible.

I am not a major nor do I wish to be at present. I prefer active service. Have had it, and am very likely to have it this summer.

I send you a paper in which you will find some seeds to plant next spring; a dish similar to string beans, boiled in the pods. I also send you a few pits to plant this fall without cracking. They are a tree similar to a peach. The fruit is much like a peach, called plumb peach. I have a nice pony that I am taking along, ride him on a march. I have also a mag-

---

[i] Canister is a cannon round consisting of a number of pin-pong ball sized balls, and functions like a huge shotgun; used at close range

nificent silver teapot given to you by one of the boys. Also a splendid cologne stand of china given to you by Henry Goshen. I will try and get them home.

The last letter I received from you was written July 2nd and I was rejoiced to learn that you are better. Take good care of yourself. Be assured I am coming out all right. Jim is hearty as a buck and so are all the boys from Dixon. We have captured a CSA hospital mess chest, and have a good supply of nice china crockery. We will use it here as I think it looks quite as well as to send it home. I saw J.F.[i] and Billy[ii] day before yesterday. They are near us and well. I have not had time to visit them. The 13th and 46th are near us but I have not had time to visit them. They are well.

Remember me to all the friends. To the children give a thousand kisses. Royce I suppose is busy farming. I am glad to hear so good a report from him though it is just what I expected. Tell Pers and Marg I would like to have them write. Reported that Richmond is taken,[iii] hope it is true. Not less than 1,000 of *Johnston's* men have deserted and come into our lines. Two regiments of Mississippi troops were forced to leave Jackson at the point of the bayonet swearing if they could not hold the capital of their own state they would fight in no other, but go they had to. The Rebellion is getting weak. In less than a year I will be at home, say in season to make a garden next year.

I am just called upon to make a report of our march: distance, engagement, etc. etc. and must conclude my letter to you promising to write as often as possible. But you must not be surprised if I do not write for some time as everything looks like moving in the morning. Good night my dear. That our love will (if possible) be strengthened by separation is certain.

Affectionately yours,
John

Summary

Cheney's health held. His spirit was noticeably better when actively participating in an engagement as at Snyder's Bluff during the Siege of Vicksburg. It was excellent after he and

---

[i] J. F. is James F. Briggs, John Cheney's brother-in-law
[ii] Billy Franklin
[iii] Richmond was not taken

166

Battery F were for the first time actively engaged in the thick of battle at Jackson, Mississippi. Cheney "saw the elephant." Militarily, the Union was achieving significant results. Personally, Cheney had successfully withstood the test of combat. He had behaved well. His personal and public honor, and that of his men, was demonstrated.

John Cheney criticized the decision of his superior, Capt. William Cogswell, to move the battery out of the line of fire in front of Jackson. Cogswell was division chief of artillery, a position typically held by a major. Cheney expressed that he preferred the active service of captain (head of a battery) over the more headquarters focused role of major (chief of artillery). Still rank and advancement were generally important to soldiers. The notion of promotion to major may have been on his mind.

Cheney's lack of respect for the personal property of Southern civilians was again seen. He described the burning and looting of Jackson as "beautiful, sublime, glorious, just." He was pleased to accept items looted by his men to be given to his wife, i.e., a silver tea pot and a cologne stand.

Chapter 12 - Inactivity in Mississippi

July 25, 1863 to September 23, 1863

Background

After engaging in combat for the first time in the war, Battery F next began a period of inactivity in the area between Vicksburg and Jackson, Mississippi. Over a period of 2 months John Cheney wrote 14 letters to his wife. As little transpired, only 6 are included in this chapter.

Battery F was part of Brig. Gen. Ewing's 4th Division, Maj. Gen. Sherman's 15th Army Corps.

Black River Missungus Ford, Miss.
Monday Morning, July 27th 1863

My dear Wife,

I have received your letter of July 2nd and was more than ever (if possible) glad to hear from you. Sorry to learn that you are suffering with your head and eyes. I hope that you have been governed by the doctor's directions and are well by this time. Do be careful of your health Mary. I know what a feverish state of excitement you have been in since we left Memphis. Also know the effect that it must have had upon your head. But Mary all will yet be well. And I hope you may be well.

I had not seen a paper since the 4th of July, till last night. You can imagine what a treat to me, after having had a morning and evening paper for years and then not seeing one for nearly a month, to get hold of a Chicago paper. I wrote to you on the 19th and my only apology for not writing again sooner is we have been on the move. I will give you a little history of what has transpired since the 19th.

On the 20th, the 9th Army Corps left for Hayne's Bluff at 4 PM. I expected we would follow them and did not even see Jim to bid him good-bye. But all is uncertainty in war. We will not probably meet again during the war, as I learn that they go up the river to Columbus, Ky. in a day or two. In the evening Col. Jones, Maj. McCracken, Capt. Marble, Lieut. Bullock, Lieut. Woodbury of the 46th and Capt. Rodgers of Rodger's Battery visited us. We had a pleasant time. Jackson has suffered from fires today and scarcely a business house is left standing.

July 21st a terrible hot day. Men on half rations ordered to be ready to move at any moment. Good supply of roasting ears of corn, green apples and peaches. Also fleas, mosquitoes, flies and what the Negroes call jiggers,^{i} a sort of gnat of less size than a pin head and operate some like a wood tick. Great country this.

July 22nd full rations of bread. Gen. Smith goes home sick. We are under command of Brig. Gen. Ewing attached to the 15th Army Corps and designated as the 4th Division. Ordered to move at one o'clock AM in the morning.

July 23rd no sleep last night. Started at one o'clock. My battery leading the column. Marched 10 miles to Clinton,^{ii} arrived at 8 o'clock AM. I laid down and slept soundly during which time I had a pleasant dream of being at home with my dear family. Would to God it was real, but I am content with my lot, hard as it is. Had dinner of an ear of corn and a cracker, with a cup of tea. Looks like a slim meal, but just as good as anything else if a man only thinks so. Ordered to move at 2:30 AM tomorrow.

July 24th got up at 1 o'clock but owing to some mismanagement did not get started till 5 o'clock. I suffered with the colic^{iii} last night. Am not yet relieved and ride in the ambulance. A terrible hot day. We marched during the hottest part of the day, 12 miles to a point north of Bolton, 5 ½ miles east of Black River. *Joe Davis'* house has been burned since we went out.

July 25th marched at 3 AM, crossed the Black at Missungus Ford at 8:30 AM. I am better today though compelled to ride in the ambulance, part of the way. Visited the 13th and found the boys all well, only tired and willing to rest. It has been a sad sight to see our ambulance train pass with sick and wounded. The train was nearly a mile in length. One regiment was detailed to carry on stretchers many of our men who had had limbs amputated and could not ride in an ambulance. Such a train in a Northern city would not be as beneficial to a recruiting officer as a drum and fife. Two of our trains sent to Snyder's Bluff tonight to get our baggage.

Sunday July 26th I am (after a good nights rest) entirely free from colic and all right again. Have drawn full rations of bread, 2/3 of salt meat, ¾ of sugar and coffee. The boys have been out and drove in 12

---

^{i} Jiggers are chiggers, also known as redbugs

^{ii} Clinton, MS is 13 miles west of Jackson, MS

^{iii} Colic is abdominal pain

head of good beef. I have milked a quart of milk from the cows. With green peaches, milk, beef, sweet potatoes, coffee, and bread and milk, my God Mary only think of it. And a full set of china with plated forks, an Old Dominion coffee pot, all a fellow lacks of being in heaven is the want of my wife and Royce and Gracie. Our knapsacks and tents have got here, horses have got oats to eat, and all merry as a marriage bell.

I have given you a brief history of our march, which has been rather severe, particularly so on account of our rests being broken by being up nights so much. It is truly a great wonder that our men should keep so healthy. We have not a single case of sickness that amounts to anything. I have often wondered at our good fortune and feel thankful that it is as well with us as it is.

It is highly probable that we will remain on or near to Black River during the hot weather. We are about 20 miles from Vicksburg and some 9 miles from the railroad bridge across the river. My health is now first rate. The only cause of my colic was I could not get food such as I ought to eat. Neither could I eat at proper hours. We hear with pleasure that Gen. Meade is doing a good thing for *Lee*, but our Army must have been severely punished at Gettysburg. We are expecting to hear soon that Charleston has been taken. Could we only hear that Richmond was taken, then we would go and finish up Mobile and the thing played out.

Morgan[i] does not seem to like the climate in Indiana. I hope he may be compelled to remain there for a while. I wish a good strong raid could be made into southern Illinois. It would teach some of the Illinois Copperheads what war is. The riot in New York has evidently been terrible, but will result in good as the more Northern traitors get punished, the better. After the Rebellion is once crushed, traitors will have learned that the government of the United States can withstand all the powers of Earth and Hell combined in their efforts to crush her, and come out without the loss of a single star. I am glad to see so perfect a union of all the imps of the Devil, in an effort to crush this government. I doubt not that the spirits of the damned in Hell are today raising their utmost endeavors to assist the Confederacy in breaking the government down. A large number of Northern politicians, who ought to be hung, will be politically dead. Whatever is, is right.

It is reported and undoubtedly true, that furloughs of 20 days will be given to 10 per cent of the enlisted men. I do not know whether Jim will go home or not. 20 days is a ridiculous length of time to give a man as it will take from 5 to 7 days to go, and the same to come. It is

---

[i] Confederate raider *John Morgan* of *Morgan's Raiders*

probable that Lieuts. Burton and Smyth will go home on furlough. We expect a mail today and I am so anxious to hear that it has come, that I can hardly wait.

I have two letters at last. Such a feast as I will have only a soldier can enjoy. I had got the skirt of my coat torn so badly that I had it cut off and now have a jacket. If Gen. Ewing gets up a review and wishes me to come out in a uniform or regulation coat, all he has got to do is furnish me with one and I will wear it with pleasure. I was very sorry to hear of the accident that occurred to Jed and hope it may not be so serious as you feared when you wrote. Give my love to him and also to Marg, Lib, Mother, Pers and Hat, and all the friends.

[There was no closing or signature on this letter]

~ ~ ~ ~ ~

Camp Sherman, Miss.[i]
August 1, 1863

My dear Wife,

Since I wrote you last, I have received four letters from you. I have had a very rich feast over them, I assure you. I selected the oldest and read them in the order in which they were written, from the 8th to the 19th of July. When I wrote you last, we were on Black River. We are now about 2 ½ miles west of the river on a hill in the timber. Have a pleasant camp, the only objections being we have to go two miles for drinking water and to the river to water our horses. There is but very little air in circulation but good shade. My health was never better since I came into the service than now. I think I wrote you that I had an attack of colic. Well I got over it and am feeling first rate.

I have applied for furloughs for Lieuts Whaley and Smyth. I think Lt. Smyth will get leave, but am doubtful about Lieut. Whaley's success, as it would leave but one officer in the battery. As Capt. Cogswell, chief of artillery, expects leave of absence, I would have to act as chief of artillery and Lieut. Whaley would have to take command of the battery. Lieut. Burton I have nothing to do with, but have no doubt he will be able to get leave from headquarters. Sergt. Vesper will undoubtedly go home about the middle of next week, as I have applied for a leave for him and have the promise of it. It would be a great pleasure for me to go home, but Mary I never again want to break away

---

[i] Camp Sherman was in the area of the Black River (between Vicksburg and Jackson, MS)

from home to go into the field, nor to go anywhere else, to be gone more than one day at longest. With my present feelings, I will not probably return till my labor is finished, unless sick or wounded.

We have thousands of rumors in camp, one of which is that Gen. Sherman and his corps are going East to assist the Army of the Potomac. We are (as I believe I wrote you) in Gen. Sherman's corps. My opinion is that we will remain here till the last of September or first of October, unless the movements of the Rebels (who appear very busy now) make it necessary for us to move to the assistance of the Army of the Cumberland, Potomac or Southwest. I do not think the Army of the Mississippi will be troubled any by Rebels this summer. The Rebels think undoubtedly as I once said to a blue racer,[i] "Let me alone and I will you." They do not love Gen. Grant's army.

Our boys are all well and I don't see why hardly that it is so. Battery I (Bouton's) just by the side of us, with the same rations, surgeon, the same water and only 85 men present, have today 23 sick men. We are certainly the luckiest set of fellows in the whole army. It is evening. We have had a fine shower, and the air is cool and comfortable. The boys are talking, laughing, singing, boxing, wrestling, playing euchre[ii] (not for money), dancing and occasionally one writing. All seem cheerful and happy. Be assured when this is the case, and my own health as good as it is now, it is a pleasure to be with them. I do not desire to leave so long as I can remain in justice to Lieut. Burton, who is entitled to the command of the battery as soon as a vacancy occurs in the line officers of the regiment.

Mansel Burr has come from near Vicksburg today to visit his father. Both of them are well. Dr. Hollister amounts to about no man at all, as anyone I ever met. He has I understand reported that I was using sanitary stores referring to my eating the horseradish that Mrs. Adams was kind enough to give me. I gave some of it to some of the boys who have been unwell, but did not give any to him. That's what's the matter.

You may hear that I gave James E. Taylor[iii] a whipping; well I did. The corporal of the guard reported to me at 1 o'clock in the morning that he was asleep on the gun trail[iv] while on duty as guard over the guns. I have had considerable difficulty in inducing him to do his duty

---

[i] Blue racer is a variety of American Blacksnake

[ii] Euchre is a card game

[iii] Pvt. James E. Taylor of Dixon, IL, Battery F, 1st Illinois Light Artillery

[iv] Trail is the end of the gun carriage – the part that sits on the ground when the gun is in use

and I concluded to wake him up with a mule whip. I whipped him severely and after jerking him to the ground 3 times, asked him if he was awake. He said yes and since then he has been a good boy. I could have court-martialed him, and either imprisoned him during the time of enlistment taking his pay, or he might have been sentenced to be shot. But I took the shorter and better method in my opinion. I only write you this because he may write home about it and if he does I will court-martial him yet. I have just received notice that tomorrow we will be inspected by Maj. Gen. Grant. I will lay my paper aside and finish my letter after the inspection.

Aug 2nd 4 PM, we have been ready and waiting for Gen. Grant all day, but on account of rain he has not come. I suppose we will be inspected tomorrow. Tell Gracie to help you write to papa. Ask Royce how many potatoes he will have to sell. I think it is too bad after he has worked so hard to raise them that it should be so dry, but we will have better luck another year. You did not mention the peach trees.

I have been very anxious about Daniel and am very glad to hear that he was not killed or wounded at Gettysburg. But don't see why in the world he does not write if he is all right. I wish you to get for me a nice piece of fine flannel similar to that Jim had, and make me a pair of shirts to send by Lieut. Smyth or Jim. I would send home after a new uniform if I could get one to fit me. If I thought Jed's size was near enough to mine for his measure to answer for me I would send at once, as I am nearly naked. At least I have nothing suitable to appear on review in.

About the money I sent. I don't much care what is done with it only that it is invested safely where it will earn something, and the more the better. I have got one dollar (the silver one) and that is all I have got, but I can borrow. We expect the paymaster in a few days when I will send you some money, but cannot tell how much. Charlie Kennedy is very healthy indeed. Don't look like the Charlie Kennedy that you used to know, has thickened up so. I would mention the names of all the boys, but it is unnecessary as they are all well. Remember me to all the friends and our own family in particular. Lieut. Smyth has not received a letter from home since last April. I do not see why it is, as we all get more or less letters. I am so glad that you are so prompt in writing as I am every day now watching the mails, and with an anxiety that you fully appreciate. Continue in well doing. You will now be able to hear from me oftener than you have for the last two months. I hope

Roxie[i] will come home. Good night my dear wife. Kiss our children for me and imagine yourself kissed by me.

John

~ ~ ~ ~ ~

Camp Sherman, Miss.
August 26, 1863

My dear Wife,

It is now two o'clock PM. I have just returned from headquarters. Thought I would spend a few moments in writing to you. Last night I received your letter of the 12th inst. and had a good treat. Mary, I feel so much better contented when I am hearing from you often, that I am a different man. Write on larger sheets. My health is fine and when the letters come regularly and contain news that you are well, I am happy.

This morning I wrote to Adj. Gen. Fuller to use his influence with the Hon. Secy. of War to induce him to issue an order to let me fill up the battery with volunteers instead of taking drafted men. I took it to Maj. Taylor and he endorsed it and gave our battery a standing second to none from Illinois. He gave me a very high recommend. I hope we will be allowed to recruit. Should we be, I doubt not I will come home and try my hand at it again. Do you think I could succeed in getting men? I have not time to write much tonight as I have to get up early in the morning, but thought I would write a few lines as I know you are always expecting a letter and often disappointed.

I am glad to get something to wear again, but rather have your letter of last night than all the uniforms in Christendom. I am glad Royce's potatoes are doing better. Suppose Jim is about starting for the battery again. Well I don't envy him his happiness in leaving. Mary if I had one sweet kiss from you tonight, I would give you a dozen in return. I am anxiously waiting for the pictures. Good night my darling. Health and happiness be yours till we meet, and then Heaven will be ours. Remember me to all friends and the young Cheneys in particular.

Affectionately your husband,
Jno. T. Cheney

---

[i] Roxana (Briggs) Fitch, the sister of Mary Briggs Cheney, had lived in John Cheney's household when they relocated from New Hampshire. Roxanna married Pvt. James Fitch of Chicago, Co. C, 127th Illinois Infantry. Roxanna retuned to live with Mary Cheney while their husbands were off at war.

~ ~ ~ ~ ~

Camp Sherman, Miss.
Sunday night, 11 o'clock PM
August 30, 1863

My dear Wife,

Lieuts. Smyth and Whaley arrived on Friday. I was pleased to see them back again I assure you. I think those photographs are beauties. I never seen better. I would not take any money for them. I regretted that you did not have yours taken. Wish you would do so and have it sent in a letter. My uniform is a perfect fit and a very nice one. I am very busy as my monthly and tri-monthly are due. Also muster and payrolls; consolidating the same for all the batteries etc, all come in a heap. I have 4 batteries to muster tomorrow and one of them 10 miles off, so you see I have plenty to do.

It is rumored that the general will keep me as chief of artillery. I do not know that it is true, and do not care to serve in that capacity, however will obey orders. Should I be ordered to take that position I would consider it as a testimonial of confidence on the part of the general. If I was Capt. Cogswell, I would resign if I was superseded by one inferior to me in rank. It would be very humiliating for him to be under my command after commanding me so long. You need not mention this just at present, but the general told me today that if Capt. Cogswell should return during the day, he desired me to muster the batteries tomorrow, and this looks like a change.

We are allowed to inscribe "Siege of Vicksburg" and "Jackson" on our flag. My health continues fine. All in all we are all in good condition except a little ague. There is considerable sickness, but it has not reached us to any extent. I wish you and the children had come down. Had I known we would have remained here so long would have sent for you. Even now I wish I had sent to have you come down with Lieut. Smyth, but dare not send for you now. My God Mary I almost get blue when I think of you, and of the distance between us. But that is of no use so I will grin and bear patiently as possible our separation, knowing that when the war's over, we will neither of us regret that I came from a home made so happy by you. We may hope that a little has been done toward giving to our children the same blessings that our government has given to us. For what our government has done for us even, we owe her our best effort in suppressing this rebellion.

Gracie has grown and it seems as though Royce had run up a little. Wish he was here. Sam thinks Gracie is a brick. The nights are quite cool, so much so that we need two blankets to keep warm. The days are very hot. The evenings are beautiful. I think every night, if you was only here to walk out with me, I would be the happiest man living. I always think of home on a moonlight evening, more than any other. I hardly know why. But Mary I must not get sentimental for such letters do not induce hilarity or mirth, but on the contrary gloom and discontent. Be assured I was glad of my bitters and am taking them selfishly. I suppose Jim will be back in a week. Will be glad to see him. He will be awful homesick for a few days. I am glad to learn that Roxie is coming back. Give my love to her, and request her for me not to go to the Waverly House or any other house to work at present. I was also very glad to hear from Sam and Daniel. Think Sam would be better off in his regiment than in his sheep's pen. Daniel seems cheerful and happy. I am very glad to hear it. I will write him soon and wish you would.

Grace Cheney taken on July 8, 1863 – her 2nd birthday

Mary I have written a long letter and said nothing. Give my love to all the friends and kiss the children for me. We will meet before many months, no more to be separated. I feel just as though something was going to occur, by which our separation would be of short duration. I don't know why, but it is so. Have you got your dress? Good night my angel wife.

Affectionately your husband,
Jno. T. Cheney

~ ~ ~ ~ ~

Camp Sherman, Miss.
Sept 5th 1863

My dear Wife,

It is Saturday evening between 9 and 10 o'clock. All is quiet in camp. I thought a few moments of my time might be spent in communication with you, as it seems like it to me, when I am writing to you. I often feel lonely, particularly in the evening. I get relief by writing to you. I have been homesick for the last week. Only for the reason that the battery needs my attention in being got in readiness for a winter campaign, I would certainly come home.

I am relieved as chief of artillery by Maj. Barrett[i] of our regiment. Lieut. Whaley has today been ordered to take command of Company I (Bouton's old Battery) leaving Lieut. Smyth and myself with my battery. We were yesterday reviewed by Gen. Sherman. He said to my battery that we have as good a battery as was in the corps, and our horses the best. We are drilling every day and are getting to A No. 1. Jim has not arrived yet, but we are expecting him every day. I have not yet heard from the Secretary of War, but should I get orders to recruit, will come home as soon as the order arrives. Our camp is but a few rods from Gen. Sherman's. While I write, he is being serenaded by the band belonging to the 13th Regulars. They are now playing "Do they miss me at home, do they miss me,"[ii] and I can answer they do. It is one of the finest bands that I ever heard play.

Had I known that we would have remained here as long as we have, I would have had you come down by all means, but it is so near cool weather that I dare not send for you. I have got one of the finest horses in the department, at a very low price. He is gray and up and coming. I could hardly take Gracie with me on him as I used to on Dan. Tell John Adams I call him Dandy.

There is an owl that comes into the tree but a few feet from my tent every night and keeps up a noise about half of the night. He is hollering now. The health of the men is generally good. Mr. Burr is some sick, but is getting better and will be about again in a few days. My health is pretty good, but for the past 4 days I have not been quite as well as usual, though I think I will be hearty again soon. I feel better than when I commenced this letter. If I could only see you and the children, I would make one desperate effort to embrace you all at once.

---

[i] Maj. Samuel B. Barrett of Chicago, IL, HQ, 1st Illinois Light Artillery
[ii] First line of the song *Do They Miss Me at Home* by Caroline A. Mason and S. M. Grannis

We were paid yesterday up to June 30th, 2 months pay. I sent you two hundred dollars. I have but a few dollars left, but if I get short I can borrow. The government now owes me $270, so we are getting ahead a little in money matters. If I get home all right (and I will), we will have a pleasant home and a little money to do with. Won't that be a happy day for us Mary, when this war is over and peace restored. When we, with our boy and girl, are at home and I hope to be no more separated. I hope for and expect all this. It is this hope that buoys me up and makes our separation endurable, though hard.

I hope Roxie is with you by this time. Do as well by her as you would by one of our children for she seems like one to me. If Marg or Mother need anything, be sure to get it for them, for they have been very kind to me, particularly during my sickness last summer. I wish also to make Lib and Ruth[i] a present, but what I hardly know. The band are now playing a medley and I am glad of it, for "Lieut. Howe" and "Do They Miss Me" make me sad. When I sat down, I hardly knew what to write. Although I have said but little of importance, still my sheet is almost full and I almost feel loath to quit. I will bid you good night asking you to give my love to all the friends. Give Gracie a kiss and Royce a kiss with my thanks for his letter. I often see you in my dreams. Hope I may tonight. God bless you.

Affectionately yours,
John

~ ~ ~ ~ ~

Camp Sherman, Miss.
Sept. 16, 1863

My dear Wife,

Your kind letter of 5th inst. came to hand yesterday. I was very glad to know that you were well and in good spirits. Since I wrote you last, I have not been very well, but am better and only want a little strength to make me all right again. You must not worry about me for if I am sick I can come home any day that I wish to. If I get sick, I will certainly come. I am anxious to get the battery in the best possible trim preparatory to leaving it, as I am sure to do so before three months. It is also necessary for me to settle my accounts with the government for every article I have ever received or else it will be deducted from my pay.

---

[i] Ruth Briggs Shepard, the sister of Mary Briggs Cheney. Ruth lived in Dixon, IL. It is unknown when she relocated to from New Hampshire to Illinois.

Therefore I will not come at present. When I get my commission, I will come home before I enter upon my duties as a major.[i] I would rather you would not say any thing about my promotion to anyone out of the family till it comes. Jim is well and sits by my side, sends his love to you all. I regret very much that I cannot consistently come home now for I feel very anxious to see you all. But I know that it is better for me and for you that I should stay at present. One thing is certain, when I get my promotion it will have been earned. No influences either personal or political have been brought to bear to get it for me.

I wrote you to get me a pair of boots. If you have not got them, you need not get them as I bought a pair of Snyder's. We are drilling every day. The boys are kept quite busy most all the time. The health of the boys is generally pretty good. Mr. Burr is now sick with diarrhea, but I think he will come out all right. I wish he could be at home and have tried to get him home, but could not. Will Loveland has been sick, but is all right again. The weather is very hot and we are having no rain though it looks like rain tonight. I hope we may have some, as it will be so much more healthy. Tell Mrs. Kennedy that Charlie is well and fat. He is as good a non-commissioned officer as I have got. Oh Mary if I could slip in and see you all tonight, but I can't and I won't allow my self to dwell upon it. On the contrary will make the best of our separation for a while longer. When we are all together again, we will just begin to live won't we?

When I remember how many came from Dixon to this war and left wives and children and friends, who are now widows and orphans, I feel that we are well situated comparatively. We hope and expect to meet again and be happy for many years in each others society. God grant that it may be so. I cannot think of more that will interest you and therefore will bid you a happy good night. Give my love to all the friends and particularly to our own family connections. Royce and Gracie come in for a large share of my love. Be careful and happy as you can. Good night again my dear.

Affectionately yours,
John T. Cheney

---

[i] Cheney is anticipating a promotion and leaving Battery F. A major would not command a battery; a major would be a chief of artillery for a division or an army corps.

Summary

Cheney's health troubled him some even though it was not as poor as it had been. In anticipation of being promoted to major and leaving the battery, Cheney wanted to ensure that Battery F was in good shape. To that end he had not taken a furlough. That in turn made him more lonesome. Cheney missed his wife and children very much.

Chapter 13 - March from Memphis to Chattanooga

October 11, 1863 to November 19, 1863

Background

On September 19-20, 1863 Maj. Gen. William S. Rosecrans' Army of the Cumberland was defeated at Chickamauga by *General Braxton Bragg's* Army of Tennessee. Rosecrans retreated to Chattanooga, Tennessee to regroup. Maj. Gen. Grant replaced Rosecrans with Maj. Gen. George Thomas.

Battery F left Black River, Mississippi and returned to Memphis, arriving by riverboat in early October 1863. They then marched across country as part of Sherman's movement to support Thomas at Chattanooga.

Memphis, Tenn.
Sunday morning 4 o'clock
Oct. 11th 1863

My dear Wife,

We arrived at Memphis Friday. Since then I have been very busy night and day in preparing for a winter campaign. At midnight I was awakened by an orderly and found that at 5 o'clock we are to march toward Corinth, probably to Rosecrans. We are now about to start and I thought I must drop a few lines to you. Yesterday I received your kind letter of the 2nd. Be assured I was never in my life so glad to hear from home as I expected to leave without hearing from you. My health is good again and I will stand the march first rate. I will write to you just as often as I can send a letter, but I fear that you will not hear very often for a week or two.

Don't believe any rumors about the battery, for if we get into an engagement you will get the particulars sooner by me than by the papers; if any serious papers are sustained. I was sorry to hear that Royce was sick, but hope he is well again. Get him his overcoat. I would tell Pers take him into Chicago and get him a good outfit. He is a good boy. I have not time to write you much.

Mary I am unfortunate in loosing my overcoat and had to buy a new one for $35.00. My expenses have been terrible. When we get paid, I don't know how much I can send home. I have already borrowed $75. Now my darling I must bid you good-bye, but in a few weeks I will be at home recruiting. You must expect me for I am coming sure. The boys are all well and in fine spirits. You are doing me lots of good by writing so often. I will do my best to get letters to you as often as possible. Give my love to all and our little ones particularly. Oh Mary if I could only have you with me, I could endure anything without murmuring. It is hard for me to be away from the best family that any man ever had. God bless you my dearest wife.

Affectionately your husband,
John

~ ~ ~ ~ ~

Chewalla, Tenn.
Oct 16th 1863

My dear Wife,

On Sunday the 11th inst. we left Memphis for Corinth. On our arrival at White Station we heard heavy cannonading. Soon the artillery received orders to pass the column and go to Germantown soon as possible. We went kiting. On our arrival we learned that a fight was going on at Germantown. My battery and the 90th Illinois were ordered to go by railroad to Collierville.[i] In a few moments we were on the way. When within one mile of town found the railroad bridge on fire. Disembarked, formed in line of battle. Advanced on the enemy as we supposed, having been informed that they had surrounded the town and Gen. Sherman had surrendered. But were surprised to learn that Gen. Sherman with 450 men and not a piece of artillery had repulsed 25,000 at least of mounted infantry. I saw many dead and wounded. Had I time could fill a volume with incidents connected with the fight. Our usual luck! The Rebs knew we were coming and skedaddled.

We went on our way the next morning. We are now 10 miles from Corinth. Nothing of unusual interest has occurred. We have the most terrible roads that I ever saw. I wish you could see some of the bridges and creeks that we have passed through this week. We broke through two bridges yesterday. Had 3 horses taken out from below. Did not delay the column one hour in the whole. I have been formally complimented by the general for the good condition of my trains, the willing-

---

[i] Collierville, TN

ness of my men to work and the promptness with which every order is executed.

We will go to Corinth tomorrow. Where we will go from there is more than I can tell, probably toward Rosecrans. But the fighting will be done before we get there. I am well except that I have a terrible boil on my posterior, which troubles me about riding. It is late and we move at 4 o'clock in the morning. Have just got our tent up. I thought I must write you a few lines tonight, as I know just how you are worrying about me. I do not know when I will get a chance to send this, but suppose from Corinth when I get there.

Don't believe any rumors for if anything befalls me or any member of the battery from Dixon, you will hear it from me as soon as from any paper. We are all in good health, not a man sick. Mary I sometimes think I cannot stay away from you any longer. Still I can't leave the service and feel as though I was doing right. I would willingly endure all the hardships of war if I could only have the approving smile and society of my wife and our children. I often see you in my dreams. Oh Mary when I am awakened by the sound of the bugle and find that 'tis but a dream, I am glad to rush into work and bury in the cares of the day all thoughts of home. Sometimes again I love to go out alone (and I think sometimes not alone in spirit) and think of you all at home and hold communication with you. You have been my wife, my angel of mercy, Mary. God grant that I may get back to repay you by kindness and protection for the fine woman's love you have bestowed upon me.

It is getting near 11 o'clock and we must load the wagon. The desk was taken out for me to write on. Our little ones you must remember for me. Oh how I wish I could see them. Love to the friends. I expect we will be paid at Corinth. I will have some to send to you, but not much as it has cost me most awfully to live on Black River this summer. Good night my darling.

John

~ ~ ~ ~ ~

Iuka, Miss.[i]
Oct 21st 1863

My dear Wife,

I have just received your kind letter of the 13th inst. and was rejoiced to learn that you are still well. Hope you may be as well contented with your lot, as you possibly can be, both for your own sake

---

[i] Iuka, MS is 22 miles southeast of Corinth, MS

and for mine also. Mary I do tell you how I am. You know the worst at all times, so when you receive a letter from me you may rely upon knowing just how I was when I wrote. I wrote you last from Chewalla. At the time I had a boil on my posterior that troubled me some. It became worse till I could scarcely ride my horse.

On Saturday we arrived at Corinth and went into camp two miles east of town. Sergeant Raub and I went back to town to make arrangements for forage for the horses. My saddle blanket got loose and I dismounted to arrange it. I had on a heavy overcoat. In attempting to mount, just as I threw my leg over my horse, Sergt. Raub's horse took fright and jumped against my foot pushing my spur into my horse's hip. Being already lame and bundled up in my overcoat I failed to get my leg over, and was thrown to the ground. My horse stepped on my leg with both his fore feet. I held him and soon mounted him not thinking I was much if any injured, but next morning I could scarcely step. How in the world I escaped having my leg broken is more than I can tell. But the only injury received was of the cords and muscles.

I was not able to ride my horse and was allowed to go to Iuka by railroad, which I considered a very great favor. At 4:30 PM Sunday evening I was on the tender of an engine filled up with the wood. I was better provided for than any other man on the train. We started, went one half mile, found we had too heavy a load for our engine. We cut off three cars and went on our way rejoicing for a full half mile when we got set. Stopped till a little more steam could be got up and started again.

The story of our trip to Iuka can be told in a few words. We made details to pick up wood. Finally tore down a building to get up steam with. After all got stuck on a steep grade. The front half of the train went on to Iuka arriving at 12 o'clock at night. 20 miles in 7 ½ hours. It may be very fast time but I couldn't see it. I soon found Lieut. Risley[i] who had been sent through by railroad from Memphis in charge of camp and garrison equipage. Found a good fire. Also Mr. Carey[ii] with the box of grapes that you sent me. I soon opened the box and we soon devoured the grapes.

I could neither walk or sit for two days, but laid on my side or my back. Last night the battery came up. Having got a hole in my boil, I am today able to get round. Feel pretty well considering all the circumstances. The roads have been terrible from Memphis. I have suffered

---

[i] Lieut. John W. Risley of Jacksonville, IL, Battery F, 1st Illinois Light Artillery
[ii] Pvt. Benjamin Carey of Dixon, IL, Battery F, 1st Illinois Light Artillery

everything, but in a day or two will be as well as ever. I had the misfortune to lose my overcoat and was obliged to buy a new one for which I paid $30.[i] I have never since I have been in the army had to pay such exorbitant prices for everything as in the last 3 months. I tell you it has cost me most terribly although I have tried to be as economical as possible.

I have just been paid and can only send home $125, which I will send by express tomorrow. I will have due to me two months pay on the 30th of this month. We have the promise of getting it on the 20th of next when I hope to be able to send $200 more. You ask if Capt. Waterhouse's commission prevents my getting one. No it does not. Nor have I expected one till Col. Adams is mustered out as lieutenant colonel of our regiment and in as colonel of the 2nd Tennessee. I understand his (Adams) regiment is nearly full. As soon as it is filled, he will be mustered. I am in no hurry about the matter. Let it come when the time comes right.

I am very sorry that you were feeling so badly when you wrote and hope you are now looking on the bright side of the picture. I am all right with as good general health as I could wish. They say a boil is worth $5 every time[ii]. (I would sell mine for half the money.) I have no cause of complaint. I am coming out all right. We will spend many a long evening as we used to, only we will talk on difficult subjects – say boils, crying wives, war, cripples. We will have that old crutch hung up to look at if Jed has taken care of it. I will stick my feet up on a chair (I couldn't do it tonight) and load up my meerschaum[iii]. While the smoke goes up, we will laugh and grow fat over the little (not very little either) annoyances that we are subjected to now.

I was very much pleased with your photograph, but regretted that it was not full length. I only wish you would have one taken full length and send it in a letter. Mary I love home and you and our children more as time passes. Nothing but a sense of duty and a determination not to put my hand to the plow and look back, could induce me to remain away from you for a day or an hour. Your encouraging words to me are doing much toward making life endurable while absent from you. You have my prayers, thoughts and love. I hope ere long you will have my presence in person.

---

[i] Cheney may be repeating what he wrote in his Oct. 11, 1863 letter of losing his overcoat and needing to buy a new one for $35

[ii] A common expression

[iii] Meerschaum is a pipe for smoking, carved out of the mineral meerschaum

Remember me to the friends and particularly to the children. We do not know how long we may remain here but probably nearly a week. I will write as often as possible. Good night and may I be allowed to see you in my dreams.

Yours,
John

Mary (Briggs) Cheney about 1863

In Mary's photo, she is wearing a pin at her throat that contains a picture of John

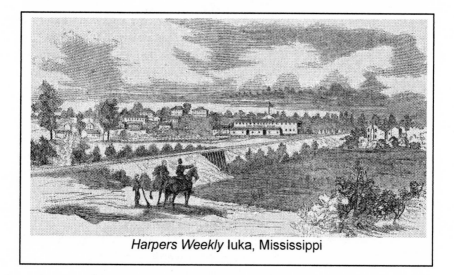

Harpers Weekly Iuka, Mississippi

~ ~ ~ ~ ~

Iuka, Miss.
Sunday evening, Oct 25th 1863

My dear Wife,

I have been at work today on ordnance returns. Lieut. Smyth and myself have been out to ride for exercise after sitting at the table since morning. I thought I would sit down and talk with you for a little while.

I can see you, the work out of the way, sitting and reading. Or talking with some friend who has happened in, or perhaps telling a story to Gracie about going to Memphis. Occasionally a halt in your reading or talking. Asking yourself where John is, and how is he?

Well I will answer your questions. I am all right, well and at work getting ready to visit you at the earliest possible moment consistent with my duty. I have been unfortunate in one sense, and in another how fortunate. I was allowed to quit my command and go to Iuka by railroad. Then (as good luck would have it) we remain long enough for me to recover. Had I been forced to move with the battery it would have been the roughest soldiering I ever did. I do not know that I ever was better since in the service than now.

Last night we had a rich treat of fresh oysters. I fried one can and Adam stewed another and we had a fine feast. One section of the battery (Lieut. Whaley's) have gone to Eastport[i] about 10 miles northeast of us on the Tennessee River. They have a very pleasant

---

[i] Eastport, MS is on the border with Alabama, 8 miles northeast of Iuka, MS

place, and are enjoying themselves finely. How long they will stay or how long we will stay here we do not know, but probably not more that a week. I do not think our division will go to Chattanooga, but will go to the right to prevent *Bragg* from turning Gen. Rosecrans' flank. I have learned not to care but very little where we go. The most of my care being ready to go wherever and whenever ordered.

I have just been out and had my supper of stewed apple, hard bread, cold boiled beef, butter and coffee. I tell you Mary it is good enough for anybody, only the hard bread is animate[i] a little, which quickens digestion. I have got my pipe lighted. All I lack of being happy as a clam in high water is your presence and our children's. I would sacrifice anything but honor to be with you the rest of my days. But I will neither disgrace myself or you and our children by crying baby and resigning while I have my health. If I could see you all tonight, I would give my best horse. You would get such a smack and embrace, as you never got yet. The children would be allowed to pull all the hair out of my head, if they could get hold of it. It is cut close.

But Mary I can't see you and the next best thing is to write. Though I have but little to write, I often keep at it even after I have said all I have to say, for the reason that I feel better for having written. Indeed I almost feel that I have really had a chat with you. If it be at night, I often dream of you.

You have forgotten to tell me about our onions that we planted last spring. Do they amount to anything? Have the willows made a line of it? My God Mary I wish I could give you my arm and walk round with you. Look over our pleasant little home and lot. That spot has become a perfect Eden to me. Only I have no one who will tempt me to wrong, but instead an angel to assist my counsel. Well Mary, one good result this war has produced is we know how to appreciate each other and also how to appreciate our children. I do not think we needed this lesson as much as many, but still we even needed it. As severe as it is, when I get back we will thank God for it. Whatever is, is right.

I did not send you any money this time as I bought a fine horse. Was offered $25 more than I gave for him the same day I bought him. I now have two fine horses. One of them only cost me $10, and I would not take less than $200 for him. I expect to send about $300 the next time I get paid. About my promotion; I expect it within two months. Before I enter upon my new duties I will try hard to get a leave of absence, and doubt not will be able to get it.

---

[i] Animate is live, i.e., infested

Henry Horn is quite sick with pneumonia, but I hope will recover and think he will. All the other boys are well. Good night my dear. If you can, be of good cheer. My love to all and the children in particular.

Affectionately your husband,
John

~ ~ ~ ~ ~

Iuka, Miss.
Sunday evening, Oct 25th 1863[i]

My dear Wife,

Since I wrote you, I have learned that we go to Eastport and cross the Tennessee River. From thence east about 120 miles to Athens.[ii] Your map will give you our route. Where we go to from there I do not know. The news I give you is contraband even in camp. But there is no order against writing to one's wife so I have told you.

I feel fine and would much rather march than be idle in camp. I will write you as often as there is any possibility of sending a letter to you. But you must not be surprised if you do not hear from me for the next twenty days, as there will probably be no possibility of getting a letter to you in that time. The time will undoubtedly seem long to you, but it will seem doubly long to me, as when I cannot get a letter to you, I cannot receive one from you.

All hands are now busy making preparations for a move in the morning. I have much to do and must bid you good night. Don't worry about me Mary for I feel that I will come out all right. But should the worst happen that can, even in war, our separation could be but temporary. Remember me to the friends and to the children particularly, all in good health and spirits. We are well supplied with clothing, rations, and everything else except tents. The boys are much better off than 9/10 of the army having good paulins[iii] for shelter.

Affectionately your husband,
John T. Cheney

~ ~ ~ ~ ~

---

[i] Note, this is one of two letters with this same date
[ii] Athens, AL is about 90 miles east of Eastport, MS; Cheney's march while not in Tennessee is parallel to the Tennessee boarder
[iii] Paulin is tarpaulin; a sheet of waterproof canvas

On the March
Nov. 11th 1863

My dear Wife,

Yesterday morning at daylight I heard that a mail had come up. I lost no time in finding it and was made glad by the reception of your letter of the 27th ultimo. You say war widows only know how to appreciate a letter, but Mary I can tell you of another class who appreciate letters, war widowers. Never in my life was a letter more acceptable than yours of the 27th ult. At the moment I got it, our brigade was ordered to take the road if we could get it on account of the 1st Brigade being late. We get the road and as soon as we get it I might have been seen anxiously perusing the letter from you. I was so glad to know that Gracie was smart again, and to hear that you were all in good health, that I had to tell all the boys of it.

We are now between Winchester and Decherd[i] and expect to be ordered forward at any moment. I thought I must stop and write you a line, as I know how very anxious you must be to hear from us. Jim cannot get time to write but he is well and in fine spirits. I do not know anything of our destination but am ready and willing to go wherever duty or orders call and thank God for the words of cheer that I received from you. We have had a terrible rough march so far as roads are concerned, but have had plenty to eat. We are now only dinning ½ rations but with our usual good luck have a surplus of hard bread and have plenty of beef and pork. We have no fear of starvation. I have the credit of having the best horses in the department, but it begins to look as though we will get short for forage. Still the boys will have it, if it is to be had. Gen. Sherman has repeatedly complimented us as being equal if not superior to any battery in the corps. My health is good and spirits also. You know long ere this that it will not do to place reliance upon any reports concerning our being whipped, forced to retreat etc. We have been annoyed some but not enough to cause any serious hindrance to our march. I am keeping a diary… .

[The letter ends here – probably there were additional pages that are lost]

~ ~ ~ ~ ~

---

[i] Winchester and Decherd, TN are about 65 miles west of Chattanooga, TN

Rye Creek, Tenn. 4 miles west of Stephenson
Nov. 14th 1863

My dear Wife,

It is a cold rainy night. We have just got into camp. We have crossed a spur of the Cumberland Mountains through what is called Montgomery Pass. I can never tell you so that you can possibly conceive what roads we have passed through. Horses have actually had to jump down descents of 4 feet and carriages come crashing after them. We got on the wrong road and too late to return so we put her through. Neither the battery nor transportation met with any loss or damage while others went to the Devil kiting. One battery broke 5 wheels, another broke one. Horses played out etc. The reputation of Cheney's Battery today is better than any other in this corps.

Mary I do so want to get a letter from you and hope in a day or two to get out of the wilderness when we will get our mail. I do not know when I will get a chance to send this but hope to reach Stephenson tomorrow where I expect I can mail it. My health is good. We have had plenty to eat. Not a man sick. I have kept my diary up and you will know it all some time. We do not know where we go to, but expect to go to the southeast somewhere in the neighborhood of the right wing. Gen. Sherman is with us and in high glee.

I expect it must be very cold up there in Dixon now as it is quite cold here. I am glad you have such a nice little home and plenty to do with. When I get back, I think we will enjoy it some. Remember me to all. Tell Royce I am very glad to hear that he is making so good progress in studies. Tell Gracie papa will say 'oh how nice', when he sees those furs. I will write to you often and hope my fingers will be warmer next time. Good night my darling Mary.

Affectionately your husband,
John T. Cheney

~ ~ ~ ~ ~

Trenton, Georgia[i]
Nov. 19th 1863

My dear Wife,

At Bridgeport on the 15th inst. I received 4 letters from you. I was never more pleased in my life than then and there. We came across the Tennessee at Bridgeport on pontoon bridges, and found a terrible road to Trenton where we arrived yesterday. Our battery was in front. When

---

[i] Trenton, GA is about 20 miles southwest of Chattanooga, TN

we came near town the enemy's pickets were in sight and a signal gun was fired by the enemy. We were ordered to open fire which we did. As they skedaddled through the timber we threw 19 shells at them, killing three. The infantry did no firing as they did not get within range of them.

We are now in quiet possession of the town. On our right is Lookout Mountain and on our left Shell Mound. We are in the valley. Lookout is about two miles from us and the camp fires of the Rebs can be distinctly seen. It is going to be a terrible job to dislodge the Rebs, but time and labor will do it. My health is good. We have had a hard march, but our usual good luck; men all well. Plenty to eat, and plenty of grain for horses most all of the time. Where we go from here depends upon circumstances of course. I am sure we will make no more long marches toward the enemy, as we are now looking each other full in the face. We will have to fight like demons or rather heroes, for we could not get out on the top of the mountain in our rear in 12 hours with our artillery. I have seen rough roads in New Hampshire but nothing to compare with these. Multiply Stuls Hill by the White Mountains the 6th product by the Allegany's and you will begin to approach somewhere near an idea of the roughness of northern Georgia. The idea of a man's going from the South to visit the White Mountains and expecting surprise at them is simply ridiculous. The White Mountains are as much smoother than Cumberland as Illinois prairie is smoother that White Mountains.

Capt. Cudney[i] of Battery I has been relieved, and Lt. Burton put in command. He will undoubtedly be commissioned as captain. As soon as the fight is over, I will apply for a leave of absence and come home if possible. I would not be surprised if there was no general engagement for two months. One thing is certain; Gen. Grant will never attack till he gets ready. I do not think we are likely to be attacked. Still we may be awakened at day break by the boom of cannon. All is uncertain as the fortunes of war always are. I am ready for the trial although not so anxious as I used to be. I have the same feeling of safety that I have ever had. We will try and make a reputation for us that we will not be ashamed of.

We are now very busy in putting in good order everything appertaining to the thousands of little and big traps[ii] that go to make up a battery. I was obliged to leave two wagons, and my trunk and uniforms and everything except what I had on, but expect they will reach us at

---

[i] Capt. Albert Cudney of Chicago, IL, Battery I, 1st Illinois Light Artillery
[ii] Traps are belongings, goods, luggage

some time. The weather is not so cold as it was a week since. Trenton is a small town, the county seat of Dade County. I am very comfortably situated in a good house with good bed to lie on. The town is almost deserted. Oh Mary I wish I could be with you. God only knows how I long for home. But Mary we will just have the happiest home when I do come that this world ever knew. Give my love to our children and friends. Good night Mary. I will write as often as I can send a letter.

Affectionately yours,
John T. Cheney

Summary

Cheney continued to miss his wife very much, but on the move again, his good sprits returned. He anticipated further combat soon. Having had battle experience he was ready for the coming trial but not as eager for it as he had been in the past.

Chapter 14 - Missionary Ridge

November 21, 1863 to November 28, 1863

Background

At Chattanooga, Capt. John Cheney and Battery F were under Capt. Henry Richardson, chief of artillery, Brig. Gen. Hugh Ewing's 4th Division, Maj. Gen. Frank Blair's (later Logan's) 15th Army Corps, Maj. Gen. Sherman's Army of the Tennessee, Maj. Gen. Ulysses S. Grant commanding the Western Armies.

Confederate forces were positioned on the high ground outside of Chattanooga – on Lookout Mountain and Missionary Ridge. They were commanded by *Gen. Braxton Bragg.* *Bragg* was feuding with his subordinate generals after several of them tried unsuccessfully to get *Jefferson Davis* to remove him. The resulting lack of cooperation between *Bragg* and his generals was of significant advantage to Grant and his generals.

Cheney's diary resumes.

Saturday, Nov 21, 1863
Trenton, Georgia

At 6 o'clock AM were ordered to march (we know not where) at 7. Rain falling in torrents and roads very muddy. Anything but a pleasant prospect. Our train has come up and we must dig out as this valley will not always support us. After marching a mile, learn that we go to Chattanooga.

Drag along 11 miles when we meet the 2nd Division (Gen. Morgan L. Smith's). Go into camp. Met Maj. Barrett and Lieut. Blaisdell.[i] The rain has ceased to fall and moon shines beautifully. Seems that we have to run the gauntlet under Rebel bats to get to Chattanooga. We have

---

[i] Lieut. Timothy M. Blaisdell of Chicago, IL, Battery B, 1st Illinois Light Artillery

been in sight of Rebel pickets and campfires all day on the mountains. We are told that we are just in season for an engagement that may commence at any moment.

At Trenton resides *George Hains* the brother of Lieut.[Leregoats?] [Sterns?]. He has a son *George Jr.* Col. Cockerel asked him if he was a Confederate. Answered yes. Colonel told him he ought not to be. When he said if you had a mother who was a Rebel, a brother in the Confederate army and a father who sympathized with them, wouldn't you be a Rebel? Colonel answered no. When the little rascal said, "what if you was a little fellow wouldn't you." Colonel was nonplused.

Trenton is the county seat of Dade County. Gen. John A. Logan is to take command of the 15th Army Corps and relieve Gen. Blair.

Sunday, Nov. 22, 1863

At 1 o'clock PM immediate orders to march. Started in a northwesterly direction. Crossed the Tennessee River near Chattanooga. Marched over terrible roads a distance of 12 miles. Received orders to prepare for an important movement in the morning. Three days cooked rations in haversacks.

Mr. Henderson of the "N.Y. Tribune" stopped with us. We have had a severe march today.

Monday, Nov. 23, 1863

Went to the Tennessee River with Col. Taylor.[i] Have taken shelter under a hill to wait till evening and then take positions to protect Gen. Sherman's army while crossing the river. Also to protect Gen. Hooker while coming down the valley on the other side of the river from Chattanooga. Can distinctly see the Rebels in line of battle on the mountain opposite. Shells thrown from Chattanooga can be seen to burst in the camps of the enemy.

We are getting ready for an engagement the result of which must be a glorious victory or a terrible defeat. God grant that we may be successful in achieving a victory that shall result in disheartening the Rebels and be the beginning of the end. On our right the ball has opened and heavy cannonading is now (3 PM) going on and off.

---

[i] Col. Ezra Taylor, 1st Illinois Light Artillery

Musketry is being discharged volley after volley. J. E. Remington[i] and son[ii] are here and it seems good to see familiar faces.

The result of this evening's work has the taking of the 1st line of works and capture of a Georgia regiment. All by a brigade. In the evening ordered to report at Chattanooga with battery horses and drivers to handle a battery for Gen. Hooker. Most of the horses in his department have starved to death. My battery put in position on east side to protect Gen. Sherman in crossing. This was accomplished at midnight. The order to send my horses and men away to handle another battery is terrible. I have determined to go to Chattanooga and try and save my men or take the rest of them and handle the battery ourselves.

Chattanooga, Tenn.
Thursday, Nov. 24, 1863

At 2 o'clock AM started for Chattanooga with 56 horses and 28 drivers. Crossed the river on a steamer. Succeeded in getting 32 horses and all the drivers back. Gen. Sherman has crossed the river and met with little resistance as yet, but they are getting ready to give him a lift.

Today an attack has been made on the right. A terrible conflict has raged the result of which is we occupy Lookout Mountain. Have captured 2,500 prisoners, 7 pieces of heavy artillery. We have driven with our battery, one Rebel battery from a position they had taken on Missionary Ridge. 21 shells thrown.

Battleground, Chattanooga, Tenn.
Wednesday, 25 Nov. 1863

At 7 o'clock the engagement became general on the left. Gen. Sherman made the attack and drove the enemy before him. No tongues can express or pen record the awful grandeur of the conflict. We have done well our part, having driven away one battery that took the same position that it took yesterday. We can reach them and cannot be reached by them. Hooker's men keep the valley, ascend the mountain, took the forts. Stars and Stripes on Missionary Ridge.

1st Brigade 2nd Division of the 4th Corps scaled the ridge under a galling fire, led by a hero with the Stars and Stripes floating in the breeze. Captured 7 pieces of artillery with horses. 1,500 Prisoners. Now we occupy Missionary Ridge.

---

[i] Quartermaster John E. Remington of Dixon, IL, 75th Illinois Infantry
[ii] Thaddeus Boardman

Chattanooga, Tenn.
Thursday, Nov. 26, 1863

Learn that the enemy have left bag and baggage. At 7:30 AM ordered to report to Col. Cocherill[i] our brigade commander. Our horses have just been returned to us. We are ordered to go light in pursuit of skedaddling *Bragg*. Crossed the Tennessee on a pontoon. Find that our division have left, and the 3rd between us and it. Now is the time to try what our horses can do. At 12 noon we were with our brigade having passed 3rd Division and two brigades of our division. Marched 12 miles to encamp 3 miles southeast of Chickamauga Station.

At Chickamauga the Rebels have set fire to corn, meal, etc. but have left plenty to feed with and we load up our pieces and caissons. Boys have found plenty of meal, beef etc. Our result of the rout is we will begin to live again.

Col. O'Meara is dead. Gen. Corse wounded. Col. Heath of the 100th Indiana mortally wounded. Lt Col. Stewart[ii] of the 90th Illinois dangerously wounded. Some 400 in our division[iii] killed and wounded. Visited the hospital.

The Rebels left their dead unburied and robbed our dead of their clothing. Cut open the jackets of those whom they had not time to strip of their clothing.

The roads are strewn with ammunition, broken wagons, caissons, pieces etc. etc. etc. showing that the rout is complete. We hear heavy firing in front.

Jeff C. Davis leads and he is having work to do. Wish we were up to help him.

Met Dr. Abbott.[iv]

In pursuit of *Bragg*
Friday, Nov. 27, 1863

Col. Taylor came around and expressed much surprise that we are here. Learn that Gen. Osterhaus engaged the enemy last night at Graysville and captured one battery. Beauregard and we move to the front. Had scarcely got started when we heard heavy cannonading in front. Got ready to take a hand. Arrived at Graysville, Ga. at 12 noon.

---

[i] Col. Joseph R. Cocherill, at Chattanooga commanded the 3rd Brigade of the 4th Division, 15th Army Corps, Army of the Tennessee
[ii] Lieut. Col. Owen Stewart of Chicago, HQ, 90th Illinois Infantry
[iii] Cheney was in the 4th Division, Brig. Gen. Hugh Ewing
[iv] Surgeon Nathan Abbott of Alma, IL, 80th Illinois Infantry

Distance 6 miles road terrible. Gen. Osterhaus has had a serious fight at Taylors Ridge. Charged the Rebels 3 times before he succeeded in holding the hill. 7th and 4th Iowa have lost terribly. 13th Illinois was around here but they were not in the engagement. Learn tonight that our advance is at Ringgold.[i] Have captured 900 prisoners, 26 pieces of artillery. Are crowding the Rebels terribly. Gens. Grant and Sherman are in front. We remain here till further orders. Roads terrible. We fear that we cannot get our rations up and will be obliged to retrace our course to follow the enemy.

Found one of the Rebs who had his leg most terribly shattered. My boys took a stretcher and went after him. Brought him to the [___] [___] and our surgeon amputated his leg. Doctor dissected his leg and gave us a lecture in physiology. I have much sympathy for this poor fellow as he is young and knows not what he does.

Prisoners are coming in. I have been out and talked with them. They have got enough of war. One of our trains have come up.

Ordered to report the operations of the battery on the 24th and 25th inst. Have made the report. We are now ready to go at any hour we may be called upon which may be at any time tonight. Some possibility of our being obliged to take the back.

Graysville, Georgia
Saturday, Nov. 28, 1863

A cold rainy day. Short rations; men with one blanket; no overcoat. Railroad torn up; bridges burned. Reported that we go back to Chattanooga. Artillery gone except one battery from each division.

Received orders at 10 PM to move at daylight.

*** *** *** *** *** *** *** ***

Graysville, Georgia
Nov. 28, 1863

My dear Wife,

I have nice comfortable quarters in an old home with broken windows, a good large fireplace in which we have a good fire. We left our tents behind more than a week since and have been sleeping in the open air. As we have a cold northeast storm tonight, it seems good to get under shelter by a good fire. You will think we have suffered, but Mary

---

[i] Ringgold Gap where the Western & Atlantic Railroad passed through Taylor's Ridge

we have not. We have been continuously on the march now for two months, only stopping to fight two days and all well. Are in fine spirits ready for another march, which commences tomorrow morning.

I suppose you have had dreams of broken legs, amputated arms, surgical instruments, bandages, crutches, wooden legs, disfigured countenances, distorted features, etc. etc. And awakened and found it only a dream, and thank God so far as my boys and myself are concerned it is but a dream. Mary many a family circle has been broken, many a wife tonight mourns the loss of a hero husband, many a child mourns the loss of a noble father or affectionate and favorite brother. Many fathers and mothers have given a son to their country and now mourn the loss. Thousands of hearts are broken and bleeding. Many a poor wounded soldier is now suffering from the wound of the leaden bullet or the bursting shell. Some from the thrust of the glittering steel – the saber or bayonet stroke. We all get an unbroken family only by distance. Oh my God Mary, how thankful we ought to be and are. I received your letter of the 14th on the 25th while the battle was raging. I wished you could have been there (at a proper distance) to have witnessed the awful grandeur of the scene.

I will try and give you some idea of the tack we took in the battle and also of the whole thing. First then, the plan of attack was for Gen. Sherman to cross the Tennessee on pontoon boats with the 15th Army Corps (that is the infantry) under cover of night. While this crossing was being effected and some earth works thrown up, Hooker was to attack the right to attract their attention from the left. As soon as Gen. Sherman was ready, he was to make an attack on the left, not intended to be general unless absolutely necessary. Gen. Thomas was to come down through the valley and while Sherman was calling a feint[i] one way and Hooker calling a feint to the right. Thomas was to scale the mountain. You can see the plan.[ii] Your map will show just the situation of things and the difficulties attending the attacks, if the plan worked well. All agree if a mistake was made, the whole scheme failed. From our position I could see it all and watch every movement. Such anxiety as men felt, God only knows. Now Mary I will try and tell you how the plan worked.

On the night of the 23rd we with other batteries were stationed on an eminence on the east side of the river. Ordered to cut out the brush

---

[i] Feint is feigned action, a deception

[ii] The battle occurred as Cheney described it, although Grant had not planned for troops in the center to scale the steep slope of Missionary Ridge; they did so on their own

and take position during the night. At 12 o'clock we went up and got in position without being discovered, all our fires being back under the hill. The next morning we can see Gen. Sherman on the other side with a line of rifle pits a full mile long. A good pontoon bridge on which artillery was crossing. A heavy fight going on on the right, so that we could attend to the gentlemen on the left quite comfortably. Hooker has done a terrible but glorious day's work and Lookout is ours. So far all is well. We have captured many prisoners, much artillery. The entering wedge is in. Every man elated, determined and will fight with distinction.

Now Gen. Thomas must pass through the valley or into it to be ready to scale the hill at the proper time. The valley is heavily timbered, only an open field between it and the river. It might well be called the dark valley of the shadow of death.[i] On the morning of the 25th (a morning that will never be forgotten by the thousands who were participants in one of the most strongly contested battles on record) at 7 o'clock the earth was fairly shaken by the roar of hundreds of pieces of artillery and incessant volleys of musketry right and left. Gen. Thomas came down carefully but quickly under our guns (we firing over him) filed to the right into the timber. Soon four columns of infantry could be seen marching up the hill, led by a hero (who should be rewarded and will be) with the Stars and Stripes floating in the breeze. Never did that flag look so supremely beautiful as it steadily moved up the sides of Missionary Ridge. That may well be called Missionary Ridge for such a mission as that flag went on is only equaled by the missions of Christ to the world.

They are discovered. A galling fire is opened upon them. Shells are lighted and thrown down the precipice by hand; rocks are thrown down. The enemy are harder pressed on the right and left. Some going to the right, some to the left, they are confounded. The time for the exertion of every muscle in every man has come and most nobly has the call been responded to. Every man feels that the responsibility rests on him. The columns of infantry turn neither to the right or left but move steadily on. The color bearer nears the top. Will he live to plant that flag on that fort or must he fall and another do it? It must, will be done, are our thoughts. God grant he may. He[ii] leaps upon the parapet.

---

[i] Though I walk through the valley of the shadow of death – Psalm 23:4.

[ii] Arthur MacArthur of the 24th Wisconsin is generally credited with being the first flag bearer to reach the top. He remained in the army after the war and rose to the rank of lieutenant general. Arthur was the father of World War II Gen. Douglas MacArthur.

The battered and torn, but honored flag waves in triumph over their fort. A moment and another flag floats from another fort near at hand. We have captured artillery, infantry and Missionary Ridge is ours. Column after column are forming a line of battle on the crest. Where we last night saw a few fires of the enemy are now a line of fires from right to left. Thanks be to God and the brave hearts and strong arms of the people of the North.

On the morning of the 26th we are ordered to march in pursuit of the enemy. Leaving transportation, tents and off we go. We overtake him and are forcing him to destroy ammunition, wagons, artillery etc. Yesterday they made a stand at Taylors Ridge near Ringgold. They made a desperate resistance but were forced to yield.

The loss on our part has been severe. I do not know what the loss of the 34th was. The 13th I learn lost 62 wounded and 4 killed. During the engagement we knocked a battery out of position in about 4 minutes. It was plying upon the 5th and 7th Iowa and an Illinois regiment. We just got their range and threw 40 shells as fast as they were ever thrown since God made the world. We were songed by two of those regiments and received their thanks for the splendid manner in which we did our work.

I have orders to move at daylight in the morning. Expect it is on a raid. Not in the direction of retreating Rebels but northeast. Only one battery of our division go, and we are separated. The other batteries have gone back to Chattanooga. The railroad is being destroyed. One gunstock factory has been burned. I think the property in this section will suffer singularly. If not more, I saw 14 generals together today, Gen. Grant among the rest. I have hastily given you some idea of the Battle of Chattanooga. I have said but little of our own work. Let the official report tell, not me. Good night. It is late and I must retire. Dixon will never be ashamed of the men of Cheney's Battery, sure.

John

Summary

John Cheney's health and spirits were good. The hard work and danger he and his battery experienced were welcome because they produced results. They were moving against the Confederate forces and were achieving success.

Chapter 15 - Relief of Burnside at Knoxville

November 29, 1863 to January 1, 1864

Background

Gen. Longstreet had Maj. Gen. Burnside bottled up at Knoxville, Tennessee. Maj. Gen. Grant, following the success at Chattanooga, focused his army on the relief of Burnside at Knoxville. Battery F marched in a northeast direction from the Chattanooga area toward Knoxville.

Sunday, Nov. 29th 1863

Cold as Greenland. We are bound for we know not where. We are marching northeast at 8 PM. We are within one mile of Cleveland. Tenn. having marched 24 miles over terrible roads. We are out of rations, that is government rations, but we have confiscated corn, meal, flour, beef, pork, honey, chickens, sheep etc. It is a terrible cold night and many must suffer.

It is reported that *Longstreet* is on the retreat from Knoxville to reinforce *Bragg*. Reported the impossibility of his crossing the Tennessee on account of his pontoons having been destroyed by our cavalry. The 11th and 14th as well as ours is near us. We may have work to do.

Near Cleveland
Monday, Nov. 30, 1863

A bitter cold morning. The infantry are tearing up the railroad between Cleveland and Dalton.[i] No rations yet. At 10 AM started again and marched 12 miles to Charlestown.

Cold, no tents, sleep in the open air.

Short rations. Foraging. Awful.

---

[i] Dalton, GA is south of Cleveland, TN and southeast of Chattanooga, TN

Tuesday, Dec. 1, 1863

Our division train has come up after a march of 42 hours without halting. At 12 noon we start and march over terrible roads to Athens.[i] Mule lost with rations, mess kit, etc. Distance 16 miles. Ordered to move at daybreak in the morning. Supposed that we would buy *Longstreet* if quick enough.

The roads have been bad, particularity after dark when we have some terrible places to go through. 300 beefs.

Wednesday, Dec. 2, 1863

At daylight we start and start in a hurry. Reported that *Longstreet* has been repulsed by Burnside and we are just in time to do him good. Learn that some 500 Rebel cavalry encamped about 4 miles from us last night. They have undoubtedly reported our coming to *Gen. Longstreet* encamped at Philadelphia, Tenn. Distance 20 miles.

Thursday, Dec. 3, 1863

Started at daylight. Marched to Tennessee River near Morgan-town, Tenn. Bridging commenced. Distance 11 miles.

Friday, Dec. 4th 1863

Gen. Sherman has allowed us to attempt to ford the river. We have sent our ammunition chests on a float across a stream 200 yds. wide, and 4 ½ feet deep. We have passed without any damage to any property except destroying 4 prolonges, the men actually pulling them to pieces.

The bridge is completed. We are waiting anxious for the division to get across that we may catch the bird *Longstreet*. Plenty of forage, but our horses need shoes not forage. Distance 1 ½ miles.

Saturday, Dec. 5th 1863

Started on the ridge road for Maryville. Marched six miles when we learn that one column is on our right and one on our left. We have to stop and communicate with the other columns.

Find many places, homes from which Union or Federal flags are floating. We begin to see that Parson Thomaston told the truth when he said "let the Federal army pass through eastern Tennessee and the Old

---

[i] Athens, TN

Rags will come out." Referring to American flags that had been concealed for the reason that they dare not bring them out.

At one place found a lady with two children whose husband was in the army of the Union. She had lost 4 horses by the Rebels. I gave her two good horses and supplied the difference by taking two horses from the Rebs. *Bob Thompson* a noted Rebel had his home skinned but no Union family was disturbed or molested.

4 prolonges condemned by Capt. Clune.

Arrived at Maryville at dark and went into camp. The bird *Longstreet* has flown, but not till Burnside had given him a good whipping, capturing his train and is now pursuing him. Where we go to, is now the question. We were not in season to help whip *Longstreet*, but were in season to relieve Gen. Burnside who was really in a bad fix.

Maryville, Tenn.
Sunday, Dec. 6, 1863

Learn that at a distillery some three miles distant there is some whiskey. I am ordered to go with one wagon and a party of Gen. Ewing's[i] scouts to get it. Whiskey gone. Found many real Union families with one of which took dinner. God only knows the persecutions that the Union men of east Tennessee have suffered. Many incidents are so strongly impressed upon my mind that I need not write them now, as they will not be forgotten while life shall last.

Wagon load of oats.

Cold night. Have a kettle of coals in our tent and are comparatively comfortable. Awfully dread to go back over such terrible roads. Don't know as it is of use to fret but how can a man help feeling that soldiering is rough.

Burnside is giving *Longstreet* the devil, capturing his wagons, artillery etc.

Maryville, Tennessee, about 15 miles south of Knoxville was as far as Battery F needed to go in support of Burnside. They then started back toward Chattanooga.

---

[i] Brig. Gen. Hugh Ewing commanded the 4th Division, 15th Army Corps – the division Cheney was in

Monday, Dec. 7th 1863

Marched on the backward track to near Morgantown. Distance 15 miles.

Foraged off the country. No rations. Sergt. Raub captured a mounted and armed Rebel today with an empty pistol. Not a particle of powder or ball on Raub's person, while his captive was well armed.

Tuesday, Dec. 8th 1863

Crossed the Little Tennessee in advance of the division. Followed the Tilico Creek up some 6 miles. Distance marched 12 miles. Instead as we had supposed of going into winter quarters, we are after *Brecken-ridge and Wheeler*. Go to Tilico Plains to hold the gap while Davis and Morgan L. Smith go to the right. We hope to bag them, but bagging is about played out.

Wednesday, Dec. 9, 1863

Marched by a circuitous route to Madisonville. Distance 12 miles. Turned over No. 1 piece. Met with but little delay. Roads terrible. Detail was foraging and came up late. 260 pounds flour etc.

It is supposed that the march is for something but we can't see it. We supposed we were on the road to Tilico Plains. But when a man thinks he is, he ain't also. More'n spite of Hell by a damned sight.

A terrible day for horses and men. Getting diarrhea. Dough gods[i], corn, coffee and no sugar. Forage plenty.

Thursday, Dec. 10th /63

Sun rose beautifully. A range of mountains in full view east of us. Query – "Has not our bay a hole in both ends and one end always left open? Echo answers often."[ii] Well we are living off the country having drawn no rations since Dec 2nd.

Marched over good roads to Athens. Distance 16 miles. Sent for to report in person to Gen. Ewing.

---

[i] Dough gods are bread dough fried in a skillet
[ii] This seems to be a reference to diarrhea – the bay being the body, the digestive system

Friday, Dec. 11th 1863

Informed that we remain here for a few days. Sent out for forage and got a good supply of flour, meat, corn, hay, etc. Went to brigade headquarters and having an invitation to spend the evening and night there, accepted. Took dinner with Dr. May a sound Union man. Spent the evening very pleasantly playing whist, poker etc. Undressed and slept in a bed. Such a luxury is duly appreciated.

We are all impatient to get a mail. The 11th Army Corps are here and we learn they leave tomorrow.

Athens, Tenn.
Saturday, Dec. 12, 1863

Have had a good nights rest. Slept with Lieut. Nelson. Moved our camp one mile west of town. Rain. 11th Army Corps have left.

Athens, Tenn.
Sunday, Dec. 13, 1863

Rainy day. Wrote to my wife. Went to headquarters and slept. Sick. Orders to march at 8 o'clock tomorrow.

Still foraging off the country.

*** *** *** *** *** *** *** ***

Athens, Tenn.
Sunday morning, Dec. 13th 1863

My dear Wife,

I know how anxiously you have waited and with what hope and fear you have sent to the post office for many days past. But Mary all is well. There has been no possible opportunity to send a letter to you. Had there been I would have written if it had only been to say well. Two weeks last night I wrote you from Graysville. At that time I only knew that we were under marching orders. Well since then we have been to Maryville, some 10 miles from Knoxville. We have had no fighting, but the fact of our coming in the rear of *Longstreet* forced him to leave or do worse, leaving behind much of his artillery and most of his train. Gen. Burnside did a brilliant thing at Knoxville, but could hardly have held his position. Only that *Longstreet* knew it to be madness to remain for us to bottle him up.

We left Maryville last Monday, the work we came to do having been accomplished. Arrived here on Thursday Dec. 10th. We took a

206

circuitous route for the reason that we have drawn no rations since Dec. 2nd and are living off the country. Living pretty well except we need some coffee and sugar. Our battery wagon and forge and two mule teams were left at Chattanooga. I do not know when we will see them again. It is also impossible to tell when we will leave here or where we may go to. We will of course have to be governed somewhat by the movements of the enemy. I rather suppose we will go into winter quarters near Chattanooga. If so I will try and come home for a few days, but while I am needed here I will not apply for a leave.

The health of the men is excellent. My own is quite good, though I cannot stand winter as well as summer. Lieut. Smyth has gone out with a party foraging. Lieut. Whaley has gone to church. Lieut. Risley is lying down in the tent. The rain is falling in torrents and comes through our tent as it would through a sieve. I am engaged in writing to my angel. Mary it has been more than two weeks since I have heard from you. I think it has been the longest two weeks I have ever experienced. I hope and pray that we will soon be where we can again receive letters from each other at least. I also hope I may be allowed to come home and spend a few days.

If I could have my family with me, soldiering would be more endurable than it is. But when as much of a home body as I am is compelled to be not even within hearing distance of home, it is hard. I am not repining, only as I said, it is hard. Still Mary if you could visit east Tennessee and see the terrible condition of families here. Husbands forced to flee to save their lives. Even women whipped on account of their devotion to their country.

Thank God it is as well with us as it is. I now feel that when my three years shall have expired, my duty will be done. Then my dearest Mary we will spend (I hope) many years together in our own home growing onions. And scorning the cowardly pups who have remained at home during the terrible struggle in which we have been engaged.

Gen. Sherman told me day before yesterday in the presence of his staff, Gen. Ewing and several others, that my battery had often exceeded his admiration. Said particularly during this campaign, I have the best battery in the department, acknowledged to be so. For this reason it was the one selected to accompany the division. The batteries (except one) were all sent back to Chattanooga from Graysville.

I do not know when I will get an opportunity to send this letter, but thought I would write you a few lines and watch for a chance to send.

Dec. 22, Bridgeport, Ala.[i]

We got here night before last after a terrible march. Day after to-morrow we start again to go toward Huntsville, Ala. I have got every-thing to do and am tired but well. Short rations, but enough to sustain life. I have lived two days on hard bread, without meat and no coffee. We are off of the mountains and can get something to eat. I will be at home the last of January. Oh Mary, God only knows what a feast I have had on your letters and photograph. But your photograph don't do you justice. I think I know truly what soldiering is, but must close. Boys all well. Love to all. God bless you my darling wife. I can hardly wait to see you. Be patient and hopeful.

Affy. your homesick,
John

*** *** *** *** *** *** *** ***

Monday, Dec. 14, 1863

A cold wet unpleasant day. I have rode in the ambulance under the influence of morphine. Marched over bad roads to Calhoun, on the Hiwassee[ii] bank. Distance 15 miles.

Went into camp in a grave yard. Good taste.

Slept in a house. A very pleasant family named Katz. Gen. Howard's 11th Army Corps are on the other side of the river at Charleston. Leave tomorrow.

Tuesday, Dec. 15, 1863

Had a good breakfast with the family. Gave the old man some to-bacco. At eight o'clock took up the line of march, crossed the Hiwassee through Charleston. Feel some better today.

Passed through Cleveland and went into camp some 3 miles east of town. Distance marched 16 miles.

Wednesday, Dec. 16, 1863

Started at sunrise. Were ordered to turn out of the road to let the 11th Army Corps pass. Dr. Abbott of the 80th Illinois came up to visit

---

[i] Cheney starts this letter on Dec. 13, 1863 but does not send it right away. He adds to it on Dec. 22, 1863.

[ii] Hiwassee River separates Calhoun, TN and Charleston, TN

us. Saw Gen. Carl Schurz, a nobler patriot than whom does not live. Also Gen. Hooker who is a fine looking officer. Also saw Gen. Howard commanding 11th Corps with only one arm. This corps do not compare favorably with western corps.

I am now seated in the ambulance looking over the 11th Corps and cannot help feeling that Gen. Sigel has not been fairly dealt with. He should have been allowed at least to command men who enlisted with the expectation of fighting with Sigel.

Passed through Ooltewah.[i] Went into camp having marched 14 miles. Rains most terribly. Fodder scarce.

Thursday, Dec. 17, 1863

Started at daylight and marched over most dreadful roads to Missionary Ridge. Looked over the battle ground. Can say truly we are terrible fellows and can whip the Rebels under any and all circumstances. *Bragg* ought to be superseded.

Marched 14 miles. No feed for horses.

Friday, Dec. 18, 1863

Moved at 8 AM. Went to Chattanooga. Got a small feed of corn for horses. Turned over all my ammunition. Dismounted my pieces and sent them on 4 pontoon boats to Bridgeport with a detail of 20 men commanded by Sergt. Raub. We go across country. Just as we get ready to start, out goes the pontoon. We must remain here till it is repaired.

Cold. No wood. A very gloomy prospect generally. We have drawn two days rations and the boys can have coffee and sugar again. We do not admire the situation of things, but suppose it to be part of a good soldier to thank God that it is as well with us as it is. If old theology is true we might have been dead and in Hell years ago whereas now we are alive and on praying ground. Thus we cogitate. Nary a letter from home.

Battery wagon and forage teams etc. have gone to Bridgeport. Chattanooga is anything but a pleasant town. We sign for the Department of Tennessee. Oh for some lost wilderness in which to rest, anywhere but here. There is more than [pastry?] in soldiering today. Don't know where our feed is coming from. Met Remington and think I will stay with him tonight.

---

[i] Ooltewah, TN is next to Chattanooga, TN

Lieut. Risley introduced us to the medical purveyor. We slept on a good mattress.

Saturday, Dec. 19, 1863

Got across the Tennessee at 4 PM and went 4 miles. Encamped near Gen. Hooker's headquarters. I am the ranking officer, the others having gone to Bridgeport on a steamer. Tomorrow morning I will lead the column if I can get the road.

Rations paid out.

Sunday, Dec. 20, 1863

Started at daylight and got the road. Such a road; oh awful. I tell the boys we will be in Bridgeport[i] tonight. We reach Whiteside at 12 noon. Find 16 sacks of grain. Go over the mountain arriving at Nicka-jack Cave at dusk. Stopped and fed our horses. Pull through murderous rocks. Got safely to Bridgeport at 9:30 PM to the surprise of all who supposed we would be at least 3 days.

Distance 26 miles. My horses are terribly used up but will be all right again in a few days.

Monday, Dec. 21, 1863

Spent the day in making arrangements for clothing. Men getting quartermaster stores etc. etc. Kept none for me.

Cheney left the battery to go home to Dixon on recruiting service. Battery F moved to and wintered at Scottsboro, Alabama.

Tuesday, Dec. 22, 1863

Drew clothing and got ordered home on recruiting service. Slept in a freight car at 10:30 PM. Arrived at Stephenson[ii] at 2 AM of the 23rd. Took the train at 6:30 AM and arrived at Nashville at 6 PM. Have to wait till 7:30 24th for a train. Go to bed and the clerk neglects to awaken

---

[i] Bridgeport is just over the border from Tennessee in Alabama

[ii] Stephenson, TN is between Manchester and Monteagle, TN – on the way to Nashville

us and we have to wait 24 hours longer. Remain at the St Cloud till the morning of the 25th when I give the clerk a drumming and refuse to pay him. How do you do St Cloud!

25th took the train at 7:30 and arrive at Louisville at 6 PM. Left for Indianapolis at 8:30 PM arriving at 3:30 AM of the 26th. Left Indianapolis at 10:40 AM arriving at Lafayette at 3 PM where we remained till 10:30 PM taking the train for Springfield where we arrived at 7 o'clock AM of the 27th. Reported to Lt. Col. Oaks. Must wait till tomorrow for orders.

A wet gloomy day and terrible lonesome one. So near home and must stop over on account of the carelessness of a drunken clerk in Nashville.

Summary

Cheney was by this time a veteran soldier. He had been in the army almost 2 years and experienced both combat and inactivity. Battery F was a good unit. Cheney was proud of the complementary remarks about the battery from Gen. Sherman.

Cheney served out of a strong sense of duty, but he was being worn down. His definition of duty was changing. He now felt that when he completed his 3-year enlistment, that would be sufficient to fulfill his patriotic obligation to his country.

John Cheney spent the winter of 1864 in Dixon, Illinois. On January 4, 1864 Sergt. James Vesper, husband of Lib (Briggs) Vesper, was discharged and returned home to Dixon. February 13, 1864 John Cheney was promoted to major, but not mustered in as such at that time. That same day Lieut. Josiah Burton was promoted to captain and given command of Battery F. Sergt. Theodore Raub was promoted to lieutenant.

After spending the winter in Dixon, John Cheney had orders to return to the front on April 7, 1864 to be mustered in as major and assigned duties as a division chief of artillery.

Chapter 16 - Atlanta Campaign – Dallas; Kennesaw Mountain

April 7, 1864 to July 2, 1864

Background

John Cheney did not leave Dixon as planned on April 7, 1864. About a week prior to that date, his wife Mary composed the following poem. The poem speaks of 'we' (Mary) missing 'thee' (John). One interpretation is of a wife who will miss her husband when he is away at war. A closer reading of the poem points to Mary anticipating her own death.

We miss thee when the spirit sighs
And gathering teardrops dim the eyes
When naught around our grief can calm
We miss thy words of healing balm.

We miss thee ever – joy's not true
Unless dear one, thou'rt happy too
And hours of grief more quickly fly
If thou art near to chase each sigh.

We miss thee ever, yet again
We hope to meet where tears nor pain
And partings no more chill the soul
But floods of bliss forever roll.

The day Cheney was to return to the front he sent the following letter to his recruiting service superior.

~ ~ ~ ~ ~

April 7, 1864
Dixon, Lee Co., Ill.

Lieut. Col. James Oaks
Supt. Recruiting Service Ill.
Springfield, Ill.

Colonel

My wife died this evening. If possible I wish you to order me to report on the 20th inst. that I may have an opportunity to provide for two children. I have the honor to be Colonel

Yours truly,
Jno. T. Cheney
Capt. and recruiting officer

~ ~ ~ ~ ~

Mary Cheney's obituary does not indicate her cause of death. She was buried in Oakwood Cemetery (lot 291) in Dixon, Illinois.

John delayed his return to the front by a month. Two-year-old daughter Grace was left in Dixon. She may have been cared for by John's brother Person Cheney and his wife Harriet. Alternatively in one place or another in and around Dixon resided Mary Cheney's mother Nancy Briggs and sisters Lib, Marg, Roxana and Ruth.

Eleven-year-old Royce Cheney went with his father off to war. It was the beginning of Sherman's Atlanta campaign. Sherman moved his army out of Chattanooga, south toward Atlanta. Battery F, which Cheney no longer commanded, was part of Brig. Gen. Harrow's 4th Division, Maj. Gen. Logan's 15th Army Corps, Maj. Gen. McPherson's Army of the Tennessee, Maj. Gen. Sherman's Military Division of the Mississippi.

Grace and Royce Cheney about 1864
Dog is Nero

Have been home on recruiting service from Dec. 25, 1863 to May 5, 1864, which explains the vacuum in my diary.

Thursday, May 5[th]1864
    Left home at 12 noon. Arrived at Decatur at 6 PM. Royce accompanies me.

Friday, May 6th
    Left Decatur, Ill. Arrived at Springfield, Ill. at 7 AM.

Saturday, May 7th

Spent most of the day in settling recruiting acts. With Royce went to Chathamⁱ to visit Dr. Wright. One month ago tonight Mary left me. Shall I say alone? It seems so but I have much to live for.

Chatham, Ill.
Sunday, May 8th /64

Spent the day with Dr. Wright and family very pleasantly.

Monday, May 9th

Left Chatham at 11:30 AM; arrived at Springfield, Ill. Wrote home. Will probably get orders to go to the front tomorrow. Good news from the Army of the Potomac. Gen. Butler occupies Petersburg.ⁱⁱ

Springfield, Ill.
Tuesday, May 10th 1864

Have concluded my business. Start for the front at 11:20 AM via Western Railroad.

Wednesday, May 11th 1864

Arrived at Louisville AM and at 7 PM leave for Nashville.

Thursday, May 12th 1864

Arrived at Nashville 6 AM. Reported to Gen. Sherman's headquarters. Saw Capt. Cogswell, Lieuts. Eddyⁱⁱⁱ and Elting, Capt. Price. Went to the Old Nashville Theater in the evening: Macbeth by Adams.

Friday, May 13th 1864

Left Nashville at 6:20 AM via Nashville and Alabama Railroad. Arrived at Huntsville 7 PM. Met the 13th Illinois Infantry. Left for Stevenson at 9:30.

ⁱ Chatham, IL is just south of Springfield, IL
ⁱⁱ Not so
ⁱⁱⁱ Lieut. Henry G. Eddy of Lockport, IL, Cogswell's Battery, Independent Illinois Light Artillery

Saturday, May 14th / 64

Arrived at Stevenson at 2:30 AM. Bridge across the Tennessee at Bridgeport so badly injured that trains dare not cross. Here we are, no hotel and we must go to the Soldiers Home for something to eat.

Arrived at Chattanooga at 1 PM. Left my trunk at the transportation office. Procured blankets, grub etc. Went to hotel and had a good night's rest.

Sunday, May 15th

Went to depot to take a train for the front. Accommodations not all that could be desired, but as good as can be expected.

Passed through Missionary Ridge, Tunnel Hill, Buzzard Roost, Ringgold, and arrived at Dalton at two o'clock. Met Maj. Watson[i] of the 75th Illinois. Accepted his invitation to stop at his quarters. We have to take the chances in finding our corps, which is in the advance.

Monday, May 16th 1864

Found the ordnance train of the 4th Division, 15th Army Corps. Got our traps on the wagon and start on foot back for our division. A very hot day. Learn that the Rebels have evacuated Resaca[ii] and our corps are giving chase on the right toward Rome, Georgia. All is action. Brigades, divisions and corps moving hurriedly. Such trains I have never witnessed before. God grant success to our armies this time is my prayer.

Maj. Watson treated us very kindly last night and this morning. The question is how we fare tonight. Our food consists of crackers, cheese and codfish, no tea or coffee, but we relish the food.

At Resaca learn that our command have moved. Our boys having heard that we are on the way sent back an ambulance and met us. Good luck has attended us and we reached the battery at 10:30 PM. Found the boys all well. Crossed the east fork of the Coosa River.

Tuesday, May 17th 1864

Started in a southwest direction chasing the enemy. Skirmishing heavy. Moved across creek 10 miles toward Rome.[iii]

---

[i] Maj. James A. Watson of Dixon, IL, HQ, 75th Illinois Infantry
[ii] Battle of Resaca, Georgia, May 14-15, 1864
[iii] Rome, GA

Have many old friends and am improved in health. I will be assigned to duty as soon as mustered. General Thomas has done some fighting in the center. Have not heard from the right.

Wednesday, May 18th 1864

Am kindly received by Col. Taylor and Maj. Stalbrand. As soon as mustered I can be assigned to 2nd or 4th Division as I may select. Took a detour to the right and at night find ourselves 2 miles beyond Adairsville[i] together with the 4th Army Corps. There is a Rebel line of battle 2 miles south of us, but it being dark we cannot attack. Gen. Wilder with his brigade of cavalry have cut the railroad between us and Rome. The enemy have evacuated Rome.

Majs. Stolhand and Waterhouse and Capt. Wilkinson have had supper with us. It has been a very hot day, health improving. Royce is very well pleased with soldiering though he is not very well, being troubled (as all new recruits are) with diarrhea. Not having any command I have been all over the lot and met so many kind friends and acquaintances that time has passed quite pleasantly. How strong are the attachments formed in the field, none but a soldier knows.

Thursday, May 19th

Made a march of about 6 miles to Kingston. A portion of the 16th Corps have cut the railroad between here and Rome and captured a train if not two, laden with stores.

Rumored that we have taken 2000 prisoners at Rome, also that Richmond[ii] is evacuated.

Maj. Stalbrand has been captured today while alone just in front of our column. No enemy very near our front. Went to see Capt. York, mustering officer and have got my papers started for mustering.

Kingston, Georgia
Friday, May 20th 1864

Mustered in as major by Capt. York. Assigned to duty as chief of artillery in the 4th Division, 15th Army Corps.[iii] Have reported to Gen. Harrow and commenced my duties.

---

[i] Adairsville, GA

[ii] Not so

[iii] 4th Division (Harrow), 15th Army Corps (Logan)

We are to remain here for a short time to get in shape for a long march. I have got two good six-gun batteries[i] and will have a pleasant command. Charlie Lowe detailed as clerk.

John Cheney in major's uniform

Saturday, May 21, 1864

We are getting in shape for a march, inspecting etc. Went to the Etowah River the east branch of Coosa River and had a good swim. The battery that I recruited and commanded is one of my command.

---

[i] The two batteries were 1st Battery, Iowa Light Artillery, Capt. Henry H. Griffiths and Battery F, 1st Illinois Light Artillery, Capt. Josiah H. Burton. Note Battery F, which Cheney formerly commanded, started the war as a 4-gun battery. It became a 6-gun battery as a result of Cheney's recruiting.

Just now I am quite at home with officers and men with whom I have long associated.

Sunday, May 22nd 1864

Inspected two batteries. Capt. Burton turned over two James Rifles and drew 2 Twelve Pound Light Guns.[i] Received a letter each from Mother Cheney, Mrs. Vesper, Margaret, and Brother James. The arrival of the mail tells me again in trumpet tones that my Mary's letters will no more come by the mails. Thanks to the kind friends who have not forgotten me in my solitude.

Orders to march at 6 tomorrow morning.

Monday, May 23rd 1864

Started at 8 AM; traveled southwest 19 miles. Encamped in a field near a beautiful creek – Euharlee. Have passed through a good country. It has not been divulged where we go.

Georgia
Tuesday, May 24th /64

Started at 8 o'clock AM southeast through Van Wert.[ii] Distance 9 miles. Encamped on a creek.

2nd Division have come up and we are concentrating. No enemy here.

Went to Gen. Harrows headquarters to mess. Am in a mess with Lt. Col. Wright,[iii] assistant inspector general; Dr. Cake, medical director; Capt. Percy, engineer corps.

Wednesday May 25th /64

Started at 8 o'clock AM. Made a slow tedious march of 7 miles over rough roads. Water scarce; forage scarce. Went into camp a little before dark. Have heard heavy cannonading in the center by Thomas'

---

[i] 12 pound light guns were smoothbore Napoleons; a compromise between a gun (long barrel and flat trajectory) and a howitzer (shorter barrel and arched trajectory)

[ii] Van Wert, GA

[iii] Lieut. Col. George W. Wright, 103rd Illinois Infantry, in 2nd Brigade of 4th Division, 15th Army Corps

army, which continued till 10 o'clock PM. At 9:30 PM we were ordered out and moved about 1 ½ miles through a drenching rain. Went into line of battle and slept on our arms. My first night in the open air.

Enemy reported to be in force at Dallas.

Thursday, May 26th 1864

Morgan L. Smith, 2nd Division took the advance, Gen. Osterhaus, 1st Division next, and Gen. Harrow (ours) follow. Moved at a snail pace getting into Dallas at 4 o'clock PM. Distance 3 ½ miles.

We have been held now at least 24 hours by what now looks like a small force. Later, 9 PM, have found that a short distance east of south are Rebels, whether in force or not is to be yet determined.

10 PM, the length of the Rebel lines proves to be not less than 3 miles, but the depth is yet to be determined. A line of battle has been formed and our skirmishers ordered to advance. We find the Rebels are here and probably in force.

Lieut. Gen. Joseph Johnston replaced *Gen. Braxton Bragg* as commander of the Confederate Army of Tennessee. *Johnston* blocked Sherman's path to Atlanta and Sherman was attempting to flank or go around him. *Johnston* fell back to the Dallas, Georgia area and entrenched. Maj. Gen. Logan's 15th Army Corps entrenched opposite the Confederate lines. Brig. Gen. Harrow's 4th Division (including the two batteries under Cheney's command) was in the weakest part of Logan's line – a place where the Villa Rica road runs up the backbone of a ridge.

Lieut. Gen. Johnston ordered *Lieut. Gen. William Hardee* to test the strength of the Union line. On May 28, 1863 *Armstrong's* Brigade of *Brig. Gen. William Jackson's* cavalry division, part of *Maj. Gen. William Bate's* division of *Hardee's Corps*, attacked. *Armstrong's* Brigade was dismounted and attacked like infantry, at the weak point in the line occupied by Harrow's division.

Friday, May 27th 1864

We find that a formidable work has been erected by the Rebels and here they try us on. Laboring hard, entrenching, getting batteries in position etc. Heavy skirmishing all day. An artillery duel between DeGress'[i] Battery and a Rebel fort.

Saturday, May 28th 1864

Have been busy in getting batteries in position. Skirmishing till about 4 o'clock PM when a cannonading commenced. Shortly the Rebel infantry came out of their works and charged our whole line. A terrible conflict opened lasting some 45 minutes, during which time we were severely punished.

The enemy most terribly punished and driven back to his works. In Cheney's Battery,[ii] one man Thomas J. Mitts[iii] hurt badly. Had my bay horse Pacer shot through the head.

Three guns of the 1st Iowa Battery had been positioned on the skirmish line, i.e., in front of the main entrenchment. Those three guns were overrun by *Armstrong's* Brigade.

Maj. Gen. Logan's official report describes the fighting as "close and deadly." *Armstrong's* Brigade was driven back and the three 1st Iowa guns recovered.

Hardee tested other points in Logan's line, and was also unsuccessful. The Battle of Dallas was over. Sherman then continued his efforts to flank or go around *Johnston's* army.

---

[i] Capt. Francis DeGress of Cape Girardeau, MO, Battery H, 1st Illinois Light Artillery

[ii] Battery F is still called Cheney's Battery

[iii] Pvt. Thomas Mitts of Springfield, IL, Battery F, 1st Illinois Light Artillery, recovered from his wounds and returned to the battery

Harpers Weekly depiction of the defense of Logan's position

Sunday, May 29th

All parties on both sides at work. Sharp shooters and skirmishers at work.

At night I am notified that we are to withdraw our corps and move to the left. Batteries withdrawn and sent to the left of the corps when at about 10 PM an assault was made on Gen. Dodge commanding 16th Corps just on our left. From that time till 12 a most terrible cannonading was kept up. All were certain the enemy had learned that we were evacuating and had massed columns to break our lines. Heaps of Rebel dead were expected to be found, instead of which not a dead Rebel so far as I can learn was found. The 4th Division did not participate in the fight. That an assault was made on Gen. Dodge is doubtless true. It being dark our men did not wait to learn whether their fire was being returned or not and we therefore expended much ammunition to little purpose.

Monday, May 30th 1864

Heavy skirmishing and sharp shooting with a vengeance. We are evidently going to the left, as a heavy detail is made to throw up rifle pits to use in case of necessity.

11 PM ordered to get the artillery out at daylight tomorrow morning.

Tuesday, May 31st 1864

For some reason we do not move today and instead a heavy cannonading and severe skirmishing.

Later ordered to leave tomorrow morning at daylight. We have had many sleepless nights and much hard labor but are hoping that it will pay.

Wednesday, June 1, 1864

Started at daylight toward the left. Take the position occupied by Gen. Joe Hooker. He going still further to the left to turn the Reb's right.

We go into a sharp place in which a man has to go low.

Thursday, June 2nd 1864

Find that our lines are from 75 to 250 yds. distant from each other. Worked in getting guns in position. Work all night in strengthening our works.

Gen. Hooker has gone to the left with the 20th Corps to turn if possible the enemy right. A heavy cannonading at 4 o'clock PM. Later 10 PM reported that Hooker has been partially successful, having surprised the enemy and taken 5 pieces of artillery. A heavy rain this PM. A small mail has arrived today, but none for me.

Friday, June 3rd 1864

Much work has been done. Two more guns are in position and the works strengthened. Also rifle pits advanced. A beautiful morning. The 40th Illinois have just arrived and among them I find many old and valued friends.

Our boys are throwing messages attached to darts over to the enemy's works inviting them to come over and take a cup of coffee etc. etc. Heavy rain. Reported that Grant occupies [   ].[i]

---

[i] In the East, Grant had fought at the Wilderness May 5-7, 1864, at Spotsylvania Court House May 8-21, 1864 and was starting the engagement at Cold Harbor

Near Dallas, Georgia

Sunday, June 4th 1864

Has been a very rainy night and but little accomplished toward finishing our new line of work.

Spent the AM in selecting positions for batteries. Went to headquarters for dinner. Had a smoke and was very quietly wending my way to the front when a volley came from the Rebels and all was action. Shot flew like hail. Lasted but a few minutes when comparative quiet was restored.

Sharpshooters troublesome. We opened 3 guns on the Rebels works, which had a tendency to quiet matters very materially. Soon after Gen. Harrow ordered a charge to be blown by the bugler when every man was ordered to shout at the top of his voice. At a signal "all hands and the cook" gave a shout.

Considerable consternation was caused in the Rebel lines. Skirmishers withdrawn, all in readiness to resist an expected charge.

Any amount of ammunition expended and nobody hurt or very few. Another rain has set in retarding our movement. The night will be spent in getting guns in position.

Near Dallas, Georgia

Sunday, June 5th 1864

During the night the enemy have evacuated. Their pickets in our front (some 30) have been captured with one lieutenant. We have done a large amount of labor, but would rather they would be flanked and then assault their works. I go to look over their works.

Have found that the enemy had strong works and embrasures for 21 pieces in front of two brigades of our division. In case we had assaulted their works a most terrible havoc would have been made. We have captured some 300 Enfield[i] rifles; many entrenching tools.

The retreat of the Rebels was hasty and well done. We are expecting orders to move at any moment.

Moved at 11 o'clock AM in a northeast direction toward our left. On account of the heavy rain we find hard[ii] roads. Make about eight miles. Learn that Capt. Remington is near us. After getting the batteries in park, I went to his train but could not find him. Have left word for him to come to our headquarters and hope to have a visit from him this

---

[i] Enfield is a British made musket used by both the Union and Confederate armies

[ii] Hard in the sense of difficult, not hard in the sense of firm

evening. Met Mr. Thaddeus Boardman, Capt. Remington's son, but hear no news from Dixon, as they are like us, cut off from mail communication.

Capt. Remington and Mr. Boardman have visited me. It seems good to see old friends down in this wilderness.

Monday, June 6th 1864

Started at 6 o'clock. We expect to reach Acworth today. Gen. Osterhaus 1st Division leads and we follow. Roads rather hard but better than yesterday. Moved through Acworth to a crest of hill about one mile south of town. Acworth is a small town on the railroad and is about like most Southern towns, far inferior to Northern. Enemy reported to be but 3 miles from us in force and entrenched. The enemy's cavalry in sight when we come into town.

Oh how we wish for a mail and hope to get one tomorrow. Learn that the railroad will be open to this place tomorrow. The train (wagon) has come up but no letter for me. Oh can it be that I will no more receive my accustomed letters from Mary? Will my sisters understand me? Mary has gone to her home beyond the grave. I can no more hope to receive her cheering letters, but the sisters will not neglect me. I will yet look with anxiety for letters from them.

Tuesday, June 7th 1864

Reported that Gen. A. J. Smith has come to Vicksburg from the Red River expedition with 20,000 men. Will move east to divert the enemy then come northeast to join us. We remain here for a day or two. A train has come up from Kingston with supplies and has gone immediately back again.

Received a letter from Sister Roxie dated May 18th. Am pleased to learn all were well at home. I was quite sick last night but feel much better this morning. We expect the railroad to be open in two or three days. How cheering it will be to again listen to the whistle from an engine.

Two months ago tonight Mary's spirit took its flight to that world to which we are all hastening. Today I have received two white flowers, the first that bloomed over the grave that contains the casket[i] in which the jewel dwelt for thirty four years. Sister Roxie I thank you for the beautiful white flowers. I doubt not that the wreath that encircles

---

[i] Casket refers to Mary's body not her coffin

her spirit brow is composed of similar flowers. Oh that I could see her as she is.

Wednesday, June 8th 1864

Maj. Gen. Sherman has issued an order in which he expresses the opinion that the enemy have retreated across the Chattahoochee. Still we are warned to be ready to move at any moment and to fight if called upon.

We move tomorrow morning. I have written a letter home to the friends there today. The 17th Army Corps have joined us today. Maj. Gen. Frank Blair commanding.

Acworth, Ga.

Thursday, June 9th 1864

Went to corps headquarters. Also to the 17th Corps. Met Capt. Cooper[i] of Company D, 1st Illinois Artillery. Wrote to Brother James. Gen. Garrard in command of cavalry has gone to the front with a large force. Also Col. Walcutt with 2nd Brigade of our division and one section of guns from Battery F, 1st Illinois. In the afternoon went to the front. Find that our advance have skirmished 3 ½ miles and driven the enemy into their works some 5 miles distant. Threw a few case shot[ii] and then came back to our old camp.

Friday, June 10th 1864

Received orders to march at 6 o'clock AM. Brig. Gen. Morgan L. Smith in advance. Moved about 3 ½ miles when we came in contact with the enemy's skirmishers. Spent most of the day in forming line of battle. After forming a line of battle we were ordered to advance some 200 yards to take position on the crest of a hill in front. In our front is Kennesaw Mountain, on the highest peak of which is a signal station.[iii] We can see the signal flag and its workings.

Considerable difference of opinion exists as to whether the enemy are in force or not in our front. We will probably know by tomorrow as

---

[i] Capt. Edgar H. Cooper of Plainville, Battery D, 1st Illinois Light Artillery

[ii] Case shot was a hollow cannon projectile, filled with small balls and a bursting charge ignited by a fuse, that dispersed the balls. Case shot was used at longer range.

[iii] Confederate signal station

our lines are being advanced. We will either find a clear way or find the enemy in force.

Maj. Gen. Sherman is very cautious and seems to be determined to sacrifice as few lives as possible. I have had a hard days work and feel fatigued. Still I have work to do tonight to advance the batteries as our line of infantry advances.

Brig. Gens. Wood and Osterhaus are at our headquarters. As Gen. Wood formerly commanded a brigade in which my battery was, I am very glad to meet him. Gen. Osterhaus is a very pleasant gentleman and a good soldier.

Maj. Gen. Thomas in the center has advanced his column some two miles to the right and front of us. We hear the report of his cannon. Our lines were advanced some 300 yds. Was out with Gen. Harrow till late in the night. A mail has come. Received a letter from Cousin Sarah[i] dated May 27th. How kind of her to write me. A heavy rain has fallen today that has retarded our movements considerable.

Big Shanty, Ga.
Saturday, June 11th 1864

The enemy are here in force with works some 5 miles in extent near the base of Kennesaw Mountain. Here no doubt will be the great struggle with *Johnston.*

The Army of the Ohio occupy our right. Army of the Cumberland the center. Army of the Tennessee the left. The Army of the Cumberland are a little in the advance and the flanks are governed in their movements by the center. It now seems to be impractical to flank the enemy and the fight must come.

A very hot day. A train of cars has arrived and cheer after cheer goes up from our boys. An engine is detached from the train and run down to within a few yards of the enemy works. The whistle and bell are vying with each other to see which would or could make the most noise.

---

[i] Cousin Sarah might be Sarah (Cheney) Abbott of New Hampshire, daughter of Moses and Abigail (Morrison) Cheney

Harpers Weekly drawing of Big Shanty station

Big Shanty, Ga.
Sunday, June 12th 1864

Rain has fallen in torrents during the night and is still falling. Think there will be but little fighting done today but all are preparing for the contest.

Wrote to Brother George and Sister Eliza Ann.[i] It has been a very cold day and rain has fallen incessantly. Have really suffered with the cold on the 12th day of June in the sunny South. Have got thoroughly wet while visiting the lines. Heavy cannonading on our left this evening.

Big Shanty, Ga.
Monday, June 13th 1864

Aroused at 3 AM with orders to be ready to move at a moment's notice.

Rain is still falling. Sharp shooting and skirmishing has commenced.

Daylight we are ready to move. I will take a cup of coffee and look out a road for the artillery through the forest. Royce is anxious to

---

[i] Eliza Ann (Cheney) Applebee (married to George Applebee) is John Cheney's sister in New Hampshire or Vermont

228

go with me but I dare not let him. Was it not for the rain I would expect to make a terrible record in my diary tomorrow.

Big Shanty, Ga.

Tuesday, June 14th 1864

Rain has fallen all day and a very cold rain at that. Seems more like November than like June. Some cannonading and sharp shooting, but the weather is such that little can be done. A mail has come and no letter from home for me. Oh how lonely, how hard to be deprived of Mary's cheering letters.

A Rebel captain, lieutenant and 31 men comprising a full company of the 54th Virginia Infantry came into our lines last night, who report the Rebels evacuating. It looks, when a full company desert and come over to us, as though the Rebellion was trembling. This company were out on picket and deliberately left preferring not to go further south with *Johnston*. They report that the brigade to which they belonged would come if they could. The weather is better today. We are feeling our way up to the Rebel lines.

We are in the reserve today but expect to be called in tomorrow. Received a letter from Sisters Lib and Roxie tonight. All are well at home. Wrote to Sister Lib. It is a beautiful evening and the most perfect silence is in our front, except the sharp crack of a musket or rifle occasionally. Brother Charlie and Sister Mary[i] are visiting at Dixon. How I would love to be there to see them.

Rev. Leonidas Polk, lieutenant general in the Rebel army has been killed this day in our front, as we are informed from corps headquarters by a circular. If reverend gentleman such as him go to Heaven, all I have to say is I pity the poor fellows in Heaven who have to associate with him.

At midnight we are informed that Gen. Thomas will work his artillery against the enemy during the night. Seventy-one deserters have come into our lines (15th Corps) this day.

---

[i] Mary (Cheney) Wright the sister of John Cheney; her husband Charles Wright of NH; they would be visiting her brother Person Cheney at Dixon, IL

Brig. Gen. Harrow's Division was moved to the extreme left of the Army of the Tennessee where it formed perpendicular to the main line of Maj. Gen. Blair's 17th Army Corps. Harrow's Division was directly across the right flank of the Confederate line. Part of Harrow's Division, supported by Cheney's artillery, charged the Confederate line and drove them from their position.

Big Shanty, Ga.
Wednesday, June 15th 1864

At 2 o'clock AM heavy musketry firing on our left. Some fear that the enemy are trying to turn our left. Firing seems very near but till 3:45 AM becomes more distant. We hear what appears to be 2 pieces of artillery probably belonging to Gen. Garrard's cavalry. Must be some 3 miles from us.

Rather a sleepless night last night, although Gen. Thomas did not open his artillery

At 9 AM ordered to be ready to move at 11 AM.

Move promptly at 11 o'clock on the road toward our left. Moved some 2 ½ miles. Had a hard fight to get a position on the left of the 17th Army Corps.

At this engagement we lost some 60 men killed and wounded, and killed as many Rebels. We captured some 400 prisoners, this by the 4th Division. The Rebels opened a battery with which they could enfilade[i] our line of infantry and did so for about 2 minutes. I crowded Capt. Burton's Battery[ii] into position, and the Rebel battery, considering discretion the better part of valor, limbered to the rear.

Lieut. Grimes of the 6th Iowa, an eternal friend, has been killed today, a ball going through his head. Gen. Osterhaus had done some good fighting. We have not heard from the center and right. Our division have done a fine day's work and have done all that we were ordered to do. At 8 PM we left the position we fought so hard for the 17th Corps to hold and withdrew to the rear of Osterhaus' rear. Tired, hungry and sleepy, but pleased with our day's work. One of Capt. Burton's guns disabled by having a trail broken.

---

[i] Enfilade is to rake your enemy's line with gunfire in a lengthwise direction
[ii] Battery F, 1st Illinois Light Artillery; John Cheney's old battery

A private in the 48th Illinois Infantry was wounded in the leg and sent to hospital, when to his surprise and joy, he met a brother, a Rebel who had been shot through his arm. Such is one of the incidents resulting from this unholy Rebellion.

20 commissioned officers have been made prisoners of war today, 31st and 40th Alabama. War seems to be much like a game of checkers, in which the best man wins. Artillery practice practically is reduced to a science and we do not suffer by comparison with the Rebels. Our artillery practice is far superior to the enemy's and acknowledged by them (even) to be so.

Never since I have been in the service (save at Missionary Ridge) has my admiration for our volunteer soldiering been so intense as today when our charge was made. I saw one man belonging to the 46th Ohio Infantry who had been wounded in the leg, run to the rear to have his wound dressed. He was moving to the front when Maj. Gen. Logan accosted him, learned the facts, and had to promptly order him to the rear before he would go.

Near Big Shanty, Ga.
Thursday, June 16th 1864

A fine morning. We have heard heavy cannonading in the center, but have not yet heard what the results of our yesterday's work was on the right and center.

No positive official information concerning Gens. Thomas and Schofield. We are in the reserve having done a brilliant thing yesterday and resting today. Visited the lines in company with Gen. Harrow. Had a fine view of the enemy's works and witnessed some pretty good artillery practice between Gen. Osterhaus and Rebel guns.

We are under marching orders not knowing at what moment we may be called upon to go in.

At about 9 o'clock PM a heavy fire of musketry was opened on Gen. Osterhaus. Rockets went up. In company with Gen. Harrow rode to the front. Osterhaus soon silenced the Rebel crew. Comparative quiet during the night save heavy firing on our center and right.

We are having beautiful evenings, therefore are expecting, or rather always ready for, night attacks. Got back at about 12 midnight and got a very good rest. This is a hard campaign and tells upon our troops, they having to spend so may sleepless nights continuously on the watch.

God bless our noble soldiering.

Near Big Shanty, Ga.

Friday, June 17th 1864

A beautiful morning. Some artillery practice is going on but no general engagement. A mail has come but no letter for me.

2 PM another mail has come up and no letters for me yet. Disgusted with mails generally and today's particularly.

I send for Capt. Griffith[i] and with him and Royce went to the extreme left of our line. Followed to the right of Gen. Osterhaus' line, and witnessed some fine artillery practice in which our artillery excelled. Reported that Gen. Thomas has broken the lines of the enemy and has formed a line of battle perpendicular to theirs. If this be so, and the information is semi-official, we have a decided advantage. Also reported that Gen. Osterhaus is to make a charge on the enemy's works at 5 PM. After having seen the works in front of Gen. Osterhaus, I think it will be a hard job to do. It seems to me to be almost impossible that the lines of the enemy can be carried in front of Gen. Osterhaus, as the enemy have as good works and as much artillery in his front as in any place on the entire line.

While I write, shells are being exploded very near us, but so far nobody hurt.

Gen. Osterhaus did not make an assault, but merely advanced his skirmishers. Heavy artillery work, but little musketry.

No further news from the center or left. A rain storm has commenced. We are fearful that our work is to be delayed as the roads are already bad and another storm will make them almost impassable.

Royce has today for the first time gone to the front during an action and has witnessed a sharp artillery fire, being in the fort with our guns.

Near Big Shanty, Ga.

Saturday, June 18th 1864

A heavy rain is falling and our men being without tents are suffering. Nothing is being or can be done. It is believed that a large part of the Confederate army have fallen back to Marietta. Was the weather good, we would soon ascertain. Soldiering in times like these is not pleasant, but as there is no help for it; every man is making the best of it.

---

[i] Capt. Henry H. Griffiths, 1st Battery, Iowa Light Artillery

Have rode round our lines and find the creeks very much swollen, so much so that my horse got mired and I well wet. Rain falling copiously and a gloomy appearance generally. All quiet in our front.

Met Lt. Allison W. Cheney[i] of the 30th Illinois Infantry who was born in Merrimack County, New Hampshire, removed to Sangamon County, Illinois. Knows Dr. Wright. Looks and talks like our family of Cheney's. He buried his wife last July and has two children whom he sent back to New Hampshire to his friends. His time is out in September next, when if living he will go back to New Hampshire. How curious he and I should meet, both similarly situated in family relations. I pity him and am glad to make his acquaintance. What would life be worth only for sympathy with each other? Friends whom one year since I thought once dear, now seem doubly dear.

The storm continues, as also does the artillery firing.

Near Big Shanty, Georgia
Sunday, June 19th 1864

Rain has fallen during the entire night, and such roads I have not seen in a long time. Our movements are checked. I only hope that the enemy have been delayed in their work as much as we have.

No official information from Gen. Thomas, or Gen. Schofield. Tomatoes and blackberries for breakfast. Telegraph wires down, and no railroad train yesterday. Supposed that either the storm or Rebels have made a break between us and Resaca. This is a lonely day and six months[ii] since I could have spent an hour or two in writing to Mary and relieved the loneliness that will come in spite of my best efforts to be cheerful.

8:30 AM, I am relieved; ordered to be ready to move at a moment's notice.

9 AM, we are on the move. Arrive at the base of Kennesaw Mt. at 10 AM. The Rebels open upon us with artillery from the mountains. Our skirmishers are advanced to feel the way. We occupy the works that the Rebels occupied yesterday. Is possible that their interior lines may be on the mountains. We soon will know.

---

[i] Lieut. Allison W. Cheney of Loami, IL, Company B, 30th Illinois Infantry, was the 5th cousin once removed of John Cheney

[ii] December 1863, six months ago, would have been the last time Cheney was in the field writing to his wife

The whistling of bullets and shells is not the most pleasant music in the world, but far preferable to sitting down in camp and reflecting, thinking and sometimes almost mourning.

Learn that the railroad train has come in and we will soon get a mail. Hope to get a letter from home. A most terrible shower has come up and all work is suspended for a time.

12 o'clock noon, the sky is clear again and work resumed. Royce accompanies me round the lines, and seems to be entirely fearless of the enemy's missiles. This day's work reminds me of Missionary Ridge.

5 PM, it rains again and our headquarters are established in the mud. A mail has come, no letter for me.

Big Shanty, Georgia
Monday, June 20th 1864

Firing has been kept up during the night without any particular result, further than that the enemy have not entirely evacuated. Reported they have marched by the right flank. Their left now rests at Marietta, and right extends far beyond our right. If this be so we will soon change position.

The sun shines and our wet clothing is being dried. A Yankee dinner of baked beans.

4 PM, a terrific cannonading on our right, indicating that we are in the advance.

9 PM, heavy firing. I mount and with an orderly go to learn what is the [___]. Learn that the 14th Corps have taken another line of the Rebel works with some artillery. The Rebs are striving to retake it, but do not succeed. Get back to camp at 12 o'clock just in time to prevent getting wet through again.

Rain has fallen every day since the 10th inst, and still it comes.

Loaned T. W. Raub $10.00.

Big Shanty, Ga.
Tuesday, June 21st 1864

Have had a very uncomfortable night having been out riding and also sick. This morning we are almost submerged in water and mud. Rain still falling.

Heavy work on our right. Cannonading all day. Rain falling in profusion. At 4:30 PM with Capt. Burton and Lieut. Smyth go to the front. I remain out till nearly dark and think proper to cut across lots to get back to camp.

Encounter a creek and as the water runs swift, think there is not danger of miring. Start in, water very deep. Horse goes in all over. I get well wet but cross the creek. Capt. Burton and Lieut. Smyth think best not to cross after seeing me well wet through. Get back to camp at a late hour. Change clothing, get my supper and write up my diary thanking good luck that it is as well with me as it is.

If *Johnston* cannot hold such works as he has evacuated, I cannot see where he can sustain himself. I think he displays more generalship in selecting, than in holding, positions.

Railroad cut again and no mail today. I begin to think it makes but little difference to me as I get but little mail matter nowadays. I am tired and sleepy. Although musketry is distinctly heard, I expect some rest.

Near Big Shanty, Ga.
Wednesday, June 22nd/64

Rain has fallen during most of the night, but sun rises clear. We have a prospect of a fine day.

Work has commenced in earnest this morning. 8 AM the Rebels have opened as many as 12 pieces of artillery from the top of Kennesaw Mountain. A terrific cannonading is going on. Our right is being moved forward. If we do not get another rain today, a terrible battle will be fought.

We are notified to be ready to move to the right.

6 PM severe fighting has been done on our right in which we have been comparatively successful. At 7 PM firing ceases. All quiet till 11:45 when a terrible artillery fire opened by the enemy from Kennesaw Mt. Their railroad trains are busy, whistles being distantly heard. I got up and witnessed the work. No one can describe the terrible grandeur of an artillery fight at night. This lasted till 12:30. I returned thinking that a good sleep would only be disturbed by more of a fight than I have witnessed yet.

Near Big Shanty, Ga.
Thursday, June 23, 1864

At one AM received an order that the enemy are massing on Gen. Thomas. We must be ready to take a hand. 7 AM all quiet save a skirmish fire. A lovely morning, birds sing, sun shining brightly.

Everything in nature beautiful, while two armies are almost within a stones throw of each other, eagerly watching for an opportunity to annihilate each other by strategy if possible or by deadly conflict if necessary.

4 PM with Royce visit the front. Quite a little scare but nobody hurt. Heavy artillery firing. Letter from Brother Pers.

Near Big Shanty, Ga.
Friday, June 24th 1864

Has been very quiet during the night. Royce has suffered with a toothache all night. This morning had the tooth extracted. A fine morning and roads getting quite good again.

Wrote to Brother Pers. A signal officer reports Kennesaw Mt. evacuated. Gen. Osterhaus' skirmishers ordered to go to the summit, which could not be reached till after dark, and they were ordered back.

Near Big Shanty, Ga.
Saturday, June 25th 1864

A fine morning. Heavy skirmishing in front indicating the Rebels have not entirely evacuated Kennesaw.

Heavy artillery firing during the entire day in which we hold our own though the enemy have a decided advantage in position. At 3 PM we are notified to be ready to move. Seems that our division go to the center to relieve Gen. Jeff C. Davis' division. We go into a pretty hot place, but feel ourselves equal to the task.

4 o'clock PM a mail has come in and I received a letter from Brother Pers saying that he has received a letter from Brother Daniel saying that Brother Sam of the 12th New Hampshire Infantry fell into the hands of the Rebels, wounded[i] at Cold Harbor, Va. on the 3rd inst. I have a strong hope that almost amounts to a belief that he will come out all right, and I will yet meet him. Daniel's blanket saved him, it being too much for the bullet to penetrate, that lodged in it.

It does me good to learn that Daniel and Samuel are doing their duty fearlessly, regardless of personal consequences. God grant that we may all again meet at the old house at home. Mary cannot be with us in the flesh but should the members of Father Cheney's family who have

---

[i] Samuel Cheney, 12th N.H. Infantry, died June 3, 1864 of wounds received at Cold Harbor

been engaged in this terrible conflict meet under the old roof, Mary will be there to cheer us.

I look upon Mary's death (and it seems to me always must) as one of the results of this slaveholding Rebellion. Feeling this terrible result in addition to my natural and acquired hatred of slavery in any of its forms, my arm is nerved and my spirit strengthened to do my utmost toward the extermination of the Slaveocracy. God grant victory.

I have today received my trunk from Chattanooga. In it I find many a little (in the common explanation of the word) treasure put into it by my angel wife. Can it be that I will no more meet her on the shores of time. Mary has gone but a little (at longest) before me and will be waiting to extend to me a waiting hand, and warm reception to that world to which we are all hastening, and only for Royce and Gracie, to which I would willingly and gladly go.

Royce has got a change of clothing from our trunk, as also have I, and we both feel better. While I write, a heavy cannonading is going on, and rather than think and reflect upon past joys, present afflictions, and future uncertainty, I prefer action, let the consequences be what they may.

At 7 PM started and at 1 AM on the 26th, got battery under cover. Not having headquarters established, took my saddle blanket and overcoat and went into camp on my own hook.[i] Not a very pleasant trip winding among the mountains, crossing ravines etc.

---

[i] On foot

Trunk used by John (and Royce) Cheney during the war.
The initials on the lid were changed at a later date
from JTC (John) to RLC (Royce)

Near Big Shanty, Ga.
Sunday, June 26th 1864

Got up at 4 o'clock, well wet with heavy dew. Soon find the general and his staff. Get breakfast and cogitate thus. Such trips as last night's are not pleasant while being made. The only pleasure that I can see that can result from them, will be the driving of the Rebels, and should we survive this conflict, reflecting upon the pleasures of warfare generally, and this campaign in particular.

An order comes for a readiness for assault tomorrow morning at 6 o'clock AM. Have to work all night to get guns in position.

Monday, June 27th 1864
Kennesaw Mountain, Ga.

I have command of twenty four guns[i] in position to play upon the Rebel artillery. 12 of these guns have been in position during the night.

---

[i] Cheney had 2 6-gun batteries in the 4th Division; it is not clear who the other batteries were

Some delay has occurred this morning. We are waiting for our assaulting columns to start.

At 9:30 AM the Rebels opened their embrasures, mount the parapet and unfurl a Rebel flag, as much as to say "we are all ready, do not wish to take advantage of you" so "look out there now we's a goin' to shoot." We profited by the notice and had every gun loaded. The Rebs opened and we replied. Result after a conflict of about 10 minutes, the Rebs had 3 guns dismounted, works torn to pieces, and left in disgust, not even waiting to show that flag to us. Not a gun have they fired at us since, during the whole day.

One assaulting column consisted of the 2nd Division of our corps (Gen. W. S. Smith's) with the 2nd Brigade of our division (Col. Walcutt), Col. Walcutt taking the advance.

We were repulsed, Col. Walcutt losing in killed and wounded 205 officers and men, among whom are many of my friends and acquaintances. Col. Barnhill,[i] 40th Illinois killed. He leaves a wife and two children. Col. Walcutt wounded. Lt. Col. Wright 103rd Illinois wounded.

Our left are the 16th and 17th Corps who have made but little progress and not much finished. The 4th and 14th Corps have done heavy fighting and gained in position, but lost heavily in men. 4th Corps 600 and the 14th not much less. In the batteries of this division[ii] no casualties. We have not done what we attempted, but have done well. Neither a success nor a repulse. Has been a very hot day.

Our loss in killed and wounded will reach near 3,000.

Tuesday, June 28th 1864

The Rebel artillery, having been driven from the crest of Kennesaw, are seeking places at different points to stick in guns. We are attending to them as fast as they get positions to be driven from. We have sought out caves in which they burrow, and drive them out, often punishing them severely. There has been but little fighting today.

Some of the killed of yesterday are now within 40 yards of the Rebel works, and we cannot get them away.

Received a letter from Sister Lib dated June 22, 1864. All well at home.

---

[i] Lieut. Col. Rigdon S. Barnhill of Fairfield, IL, HQ, 40th Illinois Infantry
[ii] 4th Division, 15th Army Corps

Near Kennesaw Mt.

Wednesday, June 29th 1864

A fine day. We hear no more from the artillery in our front. Have received various orders from corps headquarters. Made tri-monthlies etc.

Visited the front and shelled Kennesaw some. At about 4:30 started for headquarters. The Rebels had not opened a gun from the north side of Kennesaw since the morning of the 27th when we gave them a most terrible whipping. The "Atlanta Appeal" says we killed 18 men and one lieutenant in one battery.

When about 100 yards from the batteries, the Rebels opened upon our batteries. A perfect storm of shot and shell fell in all directions. Secured a place for Royce behind a large tree with shell exploding all around it, and went to the batteries. It was the work of but a very few moments to drive them from their positions and quiet again reigned.

Came to headquarters and got supper. Went out again. The Rebels had moved their guns to the southwest span of the mountain and opened on our right. Our guns opened upon them, throwing over the highest point of the mountain. In five minutes they were compelled to desist. This last engagement was after dark and a more beautiful sight I never witnessed in artillery practice. I predict that the Rebels have learned that a summer residence in 1864 on Kennesaw Mt. is too hot for them, and they will speedily evacuate. We shall see. I feel tired, exhausted, pleased with our day's work. Hope we may be allowed to sleep tonight, but that is very doubtful.

At 11:40 PM a most terrific fire of musketry and artillery on our right calls us up. With general and staff go to the right where we can see the flash from the guns. Lasts about 40 minutes. Our artillery get the last shot, indicated by the flash from the guns. It is probable that the enemy assaulted our works. If so were cuttingly repulsed.

Probably the 4th and 14th Corps were engaged. Saw an "Atlanta Appeal" of 24 inst. in which a correspondent says that they (the Rebs) thought it impossible for the Yanks to throw shells to the top of Kennesaw Mt. In this they were disappointed as our Parrotts reach them with apparent ease.

Near Kennesaw Mt.

Thursday, June 30th 1864

In company with Capt. Percy visited Gen. Osterhaus' headquarters to consult with Maj. Langraeber, chief of artillery 1st Division. Result is we now hold every piece of the Rebs batteries in check. Best to keep quiet at present. This is the day for muster and inspection, monthlies, etc. All quiet along the lines and a good day to write up.

Near Kennesaw Mt.
Friday, July 1st 1864

A very hot day. Met Maj. Maurice, corps chief of artillery. Visited the lines with him. He is satisfied with the position of my pieces.

At 5 PM ordered to open our artillery and did so. A most thundering roar. Some likely hurt, but how many we do not know.

Near Kennesaw Mt., Ga.
July 2nd /64

In accordance with orders, opened at daylight with artillery. Skirmishers advanced on the left to make a diversion in favor of Gen. Schofield on the right.

I hope for good results today. During the charge on the 27th we lost nearly 3,000 men. Today many valuable lives must be sacrificed, but results cannot fail to be good. A summer residence in this country is often desirable and pleasant, particularly on the mountains, but I would rather be excused from residing on Kennesaw this season.

After cessation of firing I went to Capt. Burton's quarters to enjoy a little rest, when an order came assigning me to duty as chief of artillery 17th Corps, Maj. Gen. Frank P. Blair commanding. This assignment is favorable,[i] but at the same time I would much prefer to be left in command of a division as here are many acquaintances and friends with whom I have long been associated.

Obedience of orders is the first duty of a soldier and I go as cheerfully as I can. A mail has arrived and no letter for me. Royce does not like to leave the 4th Division as he has become acquainted with all the officers and men. It may be possible that all is for the best. I may yet fully realize that whatever is, is right. A truth (perhaps) that many accept till something occurs in their own corner which makes it almost impossible to make it seem so to us.

I will get my dinner and at once report to Gen. Blair. I will strive to do my duty. If I succeed in pleasing Gen. Blair, I will be glad, if not I will do my duty as best I may understand it.

Reported to Gen. Blair. We move to the right.

---

[i] Cheney had been chief of artillery for a division; being chief of artillery for an army corps is a more important position

Started at 9 PM, very dark and bad roads. Made about 3 miles. At 2 AM spread my blanket and covering myself with my overcoat, went to sleep.

Summary

Royce experienced the danger of combat being in the fort with the guns during an action on June 17th. On June 29th Royce was present for a "perfect storm of shot and shell." John Cheney secured a place for his son behind a large tree.

The arrival of his trunk was a moving event to John because it contained items packed by his now deceased wife Mary. He missed her very much and couldn't envision a future without her. His health was bothering him. Action distracted him so that he need not "think and reflect on past joys, present afflictions and future uncertainty." In the past he had lectured others to remain stoic because "whatever is, is right." By July 1864 he was having trouble accepting that view.

Chapter 17 - Atlanta Campaign – Atlanta

July 3, 1864 to August 26, 1864

Background

In July 1864 Maj. John Cheney left the position of chief of artillery of the 4th Division, 15th Army Corps – including Battery F. He became chief of artillery of Maj. Gen. Frank Blair's 17th Army Corps. Both the 15th and the 17th Army Corps were in Maj. Gen. McPherson's Army of the Tennessee, Maj. Gen. Sherman's Military Division of the Mississippi.

Sherman's Atlanta Campaign continues.

On the Move
Sunday, July 3rd 1864

Woke up in the morning to learn that the Rebels had evacuated Kennesaw Mt. This morning the Stars and Stripes are on the summit where yesterday floated the Stars and Bars. We started at 6 o'clock. Find as we move along, the enemy have evacuated the lines nearly, if not entirely. I am much pleased with Gen. Blair and his staff. Doubt not that I will, after getting a start, like them perhaps as well as in the 15th Corps.

12 noon Marietta[i] is ours, the Rebs retreating. We have taken many prisoners and our forces pursuing. We are pressing toward the river on their left flank. Thanks be to God who giveth us the victory[ii] when we use the means within our power.

Saw Gen. Schofield for the first time. Like his appearance very much.

A fine country, for a Southern country. Met the enemy pickets at creek. Skirmished till near dark when we form line of battle and stop

---

[i] Marietta, GA, 19 miles northwest of Atlanta
[ii] But thanks be to God, which giveth us the victory through our Lord Jesus Christ. I Corinthians 15:57

for the night. Heavy firing northeast of us, probably between the enemy's rear guard and Gen. Thomas.

The body of Lt. Col. Barnhill of 40th Illinois was found where he fell, stripped of his clothing and unburied – Southern chivalry.

Monday, July 4th 1864

I am not well this morning, neither do I like to acknowledge myself sick at such a time as this. One year ago today we were driving *Johnston* back from Vicksburg and today finds *Johnston* in full retreat again. It is a very hot morning. Our corps are to make a demonstration.[i]

At 4 o'clock PM started for the front. Went out with 4 pieces artillery and Gen. Grisham's Division. Moved about one mile. Found the enemy's works about 600 yds. in our front. Opened with the artillery. Was soon replied to by artillery from the Rebels, apparently with two pieces. They served canister on us with little effect. Artillery ceased firing and our skirmishers deployed, with a line of battle in rear of our artillery.

Skirmishers advanced to within 200 yds. of Rebel works. Covered themselves as best they could while Gen. Dodge with the 16th Army Corps on our left, advanced and took a line of Rebel works with some 200 prisoners.

It being dark we rest for the night. I have come very near being struck by canister today and having been sick, have had a very uncomfortable day of it.

Near Sweet Water, Ga.
Tuesday, July 5th 1864

The 15th Corps are moving up. I have met many old acquaintances. Received a letter from Brother Thomas dated 23rd June in which he says that Brother Sam has not been heard from since June 3rd when the enemy's works were charged at Cold Harbor, Va. Sam at best is a prisoner and we fear wounded or killed. Should he be killed what a terrible stroke to his wife. I hope to learn that he still lives.

We start out for another move at 8 AM.

Our corps have advanced and taken the line of works that we worked at last night. Advance and find still another, strongly put up. Have a heavy artillery fire, which closed at sunset. The night is spent in fortifying. Guns in position ready for work in the morning.

---

[i] Demonstration is a show of strength without the intention to engage in battle

Go into a mess[i] with Maj. Pomitz, Lt. Col. Hibbe, and Capt. Miller.

Near Chattahoochee River, Ga.
Wednesday, July 6th 1864

This morning we opened upon the Rebel works. Fire at intervals during the day, without eliciting even a reply from artillery.

The enemy are crossing the river. Have got works that it would be wholesale murder to attempt to carry by assault. We cannot annoy them very much on the opposite side on high bluffs. We expect to be troubled in crossing, but cross we must.

The many incidents of this will often recur to my mind should I live to return to my home.

The right wing 15th Corps have moved to the left to relieve Gen. Hooker. What this means I do not know, but suppose Gen. Hooker will attempt a crossing at some point.

Near Chattahoochee River, Ga.
Thursday, July 7th 1864

Three months ago today just as the sun set, my wife's spirit took its departure for the world of spirits. Three lonely sad months have they been for me. How little had I dreamed 4 months since[ii] that it could be possible that Mary would be taken and leave me thus alone.

It is a very hot morning. Today it is probable that we will make an attempt to cross the river, after having driven the last remnant of the Rebel army, which I predict we will do.

We opened at 4:20 PM with artillery but with what effect cannot tell. Elicited no reply.

Near Chattahoochee River, Ga.
Friday, July 8th 1864

Gracie is 3 years old today.

A demonstration was made last evening, but it was impossible to drive the devils without a sacrifice of life that seemed unnecessary. So here we are, and a quiet day it has been. Maj. Gen. Sherman has been round the lines. A cannonading has been ordered at 4:00 PM today on

---

[i] Mess is a group of people who eat together, i.e., he is having a meal
[ii] Seems Mary was healthy 1 month before death

the right to create a diversion in favor of Gen. Gerrard who is to attempt a crossing on our left and up the river. I hope we may succeed in crossing this barrier to our progress without great loss of life.

If we can judge by smoke, much property is being destroyed in Atlanta. We learn that considerable damage was inflicted last night by artillery. This comes from deserters who are coming in every day.

A good deal of a mess has been created by our artillery. Fire and a perfect cloud of dust has been rising. We hope Gen. Schofield has affected a crossing.

Boil.

Chattahoochee River, Ga.
Saturday, July 9th 1864

Gens. Schofield and Gerrard are across the river on our left. We expect to move at any time. This is glorious news. We soon hope to be in Atlanta. I am sorely afflicted with boils. How I am to ride horseback I do not know.

It has been a very hot day. So far as we know nothing of importance has been done. Wish I could get a letter from home.

Had a very pleasant chat with Capt. Burr, AQM[i] who comes from western Massachusetts. Royce is taking sketches of the country as we stop along. I think he will make a good engineer.

Chattahoochee River, Ga.
Sunday, July 10th 1864

I have had a very uncomfortable night indeed on account of my boils. The Rebels have evacuated our front and crossed the river. This applies to the right. It is presumed that they are nearly all across. Some deserters are coming in as usual after the evacuation of position after position.

Now comes the struggle for Atlanta. The enemy have planted artillery opposite us on the other side of the river. We are getting in position to try them on. Wrote to Brother Tom, J. M. Publes and Sister Margaret. A mail has come. Royce has been to the 15th Corps. No letter for me, how lonely.

This PM we have had a fine shower. If I could get a letter from home or friends would feel better. We are 12 miles southwest of

---

[i] AQM is assistant quartermaster

Marietta. The railroad is in good condition 6 miles south of Marietta where Gen. Thomas' headquarters are.

400 factory operators (women) have been captured on our left. At their request sent north. The factories in which they were employed were burned. Thus another source of supplies for clothing the Rebel armies has been cut off.

Below is a letter John Cheney wrote to his sister-in-law Margaret Briggs

---

Headquarters Seventeenth Army Corps.
Department of the Tennessee
Office Chief of Artillery
Chattahoochee River, Ga.
July 7th 1864

Dear sister Margaret,

Some three days since, I received a letter from you 5 weeks old and thought it was a long time in reaching me. I was so glad to hear from you. You will see by this that I am at headquarters 17th A.C. and chief of artillery on Maj. Gen. F. P. Blair's staff. My duties are not as hard here as at division headquarters. I have two clerks and an orderly. The most writing that I have to do is to sign my name. During the campaign I have enough to do I assure you. For the last week have had to work exceptionally hard. Have not been very well though I am better now than I have been. I like my new position very well as it is honorable and was given me over a major nearly a year my senior. Charlie Lowe is with me.

I am very lonely much of the time, though Mary is with me ever – almost with me. It does seem to me that I must see her form again though I know that it is impossible. I often ask myself how can I go home and not find Mary there? Is it so? Can it be possible? And Mary seems to say I am with you John. I have not yet seen her, but am hoping to.

The Rebels are now crossing the river. So strongly have they fortified to cover their retreat that it seems almost impossible to punish them much. A demonstration is to be made at 4:30 this PM with what success God only knows. We can see the doomed city of Atlanta distinctly from the top of a hill a short distance from our headquarters.

A large fire has been raging there since yesterday morning, supposed to be their foundry and machine shops.

Royce is well. He has just got a new saddle and feels fine. Three months ago tonight Mary's spirit left the form and heaven gained an angel. Gracie will be 3 years old tomorrow. How I would love to see her, but these desires, hopes, longings, fears, regrets and lamentations are what I must endure and am trying to do the best I can.

I feel almost sure that Sam is not dead. I pity his wife as no one who has not lost a companion knows how to, but I hope all may yet be well with him. Write me as often as possible and I will answer. Remember me to all. Tell them all that Royce and I are all right. We intend to come home again soon after *Johnston's* army is drummed out.

Affy. your brother,
John T. Cheney

Sunday Morning, July 10th

Since writing the within, the Army of the Ohio, Maj. Gen. Schofield, have crossed the Chattahoochee. The Rebels have evacuated our front on the right and crossed the river. Atlanta is in sight. I predict that within two days we will be in possession of the city. I presume that we will move today, but do not know. I will be obliged to ride in the ambulance if we ride as I have a very large boil just where it might hurt my saddle, should I ride horseback. I am very anxious to hear from home, but do not know when that will be. One train was burned on the 5th inst. that had a large mail on it. It would be my luck to have letters on it. You and Roxie have not sent photographs yet.

Yours truly,
John

*** *** *** *** *** *** *** ***

Chattahoochee River, Ga.
Monday, July 11th 1864

Some rain has been falling during the night. We have a fine morning. Received a letter from Sister Eliza Ann and answered it. How glad I have been made by the reception of this letter.

Have been in my tent most of the day on account of my ugly boils, but tomorrow will be in my saddle, I hope. Had nice blackberries for supper. Charlie Lowe detailed by order from department headquarters to act as clerk for me.

Chattahoochee River, Ga.

Tuesday, July 12th 1864

A lovely morning. I fully expect to receive two letters (at least) to-day.

A mail and no letter. Have visited the front. We are sharp shooting across the river. We have a fine view of a Rebel fort only about 800 yds. from us. Opened on them without any reply. The 15th Army Corps have moved out at 3 PM to go up the river. We (the 17th) remain to attract the attention of the front till Gen. Stoneman (who has gone to the right) gets back.

Went to look for a letter now that the 15th Corps has gone. I don't know as my letters are still directed to the 15th Corps.

We are having a fine shower this evening.

Chattahoochee River, Georgia

Wednesday, July 13th 1864

A very warm morning. Royce and I have visited our lines from left to right. Had a very pleasant interview with Gen. Leggett. Was told of a little trading affair that his sharp shooters and the Rebs entered into yesterday. Yanks on one and Rebs on opposite side of the Chattahoochee River. Yanks shout for tobacco. Rebs shout for coffee. Matters arranged. Each party stack arms. Yanks wade the river, chat, trade etc. Yanks return, take arms and again they commence shooting at each other. This is true, as the general's picket officer caught the boys at the game.

We hear nothing definitive from Gen. Stoneman. Our right is annoyed by sharpshooters and skirmishers. Our 24 pounder is attending to them. Rather quiet in our immediate front. Gen. Thomas is yet on our left. As there has been considerable cannonading in that direction today, suppose he has had something to do.

Chattahoochee

Thursday, July 14th 1864

In company with Royce rode round the lines. Royce's pony broke through a bridge. Nothing heard from Gen. Stoneman yet. All quiet on our front or comparatively so. No word from home yet. Oh how terribly the flies do bother me.

During the evening a fine shower and considerable wind. Some artillery firing during the night. The 17th Corps has now a front of at least 7 miles, joining Gen. Thomas on our left. If the Rebs see this, they would not then dare to attack us.

Chattahoochee River
Friday, July 15th 1864

After a rainy night, the air seems cool and pure, but we will have a hot day of it. Rode during the AM with Royce. Spent the PM in reading, writing etc. Tomorrow we move at an early hour.

Chattahoochee River
Saturday, July 16th 1864

Moved at 6:30 AM in a northeast direction. Crossed the Nickajack. After a march of about 6 miles in the direction of Marietta, put up our flies and stopped to get dinner and pass the hottest part of the day. Roads hilly and uneven but otherwise good.

Started out at 4:30 PM. Went into camp about one mile from Marietta. Dark, raining. Pork, bread, and coffee for supper. Laid on some fence rails, rested but little. Distance marched 12 miles.

It is surprising what an amount of work the Rebs have done between Marietta and the river. Line after line of abatis[i] and every conceivable obstacle in our way, but we have served them as Jehovah did Adam and Eve. Snaked them out, or as the more common saying is, corkscrewed them out.

We hear of formidable works across the river. Query – "Will we ever see them?" I believe that flanking is not played out yet.

On the move, Ga.
Sunday, July 17th 1864

Column started out at 4 o'clock AM in a northeast direction. A fine morning. Spent an hour in Marietta, a very pretty town.

We hear of the Rebel raid in Maryland and Pennsylvania. Also of the defeat of Gen. Wallace on the Monocag River. Let those stay-at-home people take care of that, say me.

I hope to get within reach of the 15th Corps tonight. Oh how I want some letters.

Royce is enjoying the march first rate, and is in good health.

---

[i] Abatis are defensive obstacles made from felled trees with sharpened tops pointing toward the enemy

Passed through Roseville where were two cotton and one woolen factory burned by our cavalry. The Rebel's cavalry burned the bridge last Wednesday. Although the river is 800 feet wide, it is rebuilt and we are crossing.

We are 3 miles east of the river, in camp. Distance marched 16 miles. It has been a very hot day. Many men have suffered from the heat and fatigue. The 15th Army Corps are about 6 miles in advance of us. It is too late to go out to see if there is any mail for me, so I must wait another day. One year ago today we entered Jackson, Miss.

Monday, July 18th 1864

Moved at 6 o'clock AM in southeast direction, 15th Army Corps in advance.

Program: Dept. of Tenn. on the left. Ohio Center. Cumberland in right. Dept. of Tenn. to advance in the direction of a point between Stone Mt. and Decatur.[i] Gen. Gerrard's cavalry on our left, are ordered to destroy railroad. 15th and 17th Corps to render any assistance necessary.

5 PM Gen. Gerrard has destroyed 3 miles of railroad. One brigade of 15th Corps ordered to advance and assist in destroying all that can be done. Little resistance. Three trains have passed over the road this AM laden with machinery.

Today we have had a decided success. It is probable that we will crowd the gentleman very hard. The enemy have evidently been surprised by this movement as they expected to be attacked on the right.

This is gloomy country, less animal life than any in which I have been. No birds (even) to break the dull monotony. We have chiggers and wasps (Royce was stung by one today) in abundance. Blackberries in abundance.

Received a letter from Brother George and so much disappointed in not receiving other letters. When will I hear from home?

Tuesday, July 19th 1864

Started at 5 AM. Ran against the 15th Corps. Roads blocked up by train. Move toward Decatur. Skirmishing.

---

[i] Decatur is just west of Atlanta, Stone Mountain is further west of Atlanta

At 10 PM find ourselves in camp having marched 6 miles. 15th Corps in Decatur. Petersburg reported taken by Gen. Grant.[i] This has been one of the hardest days work we have had, very hot and dusty. Our camp is 1 ½ miles from Decatur.

No supper till 12 o'clock. Royce is very tired but does not complain.

Dr. Grimes went out foraging only a few rods from us and was taken prisoner.

Wednesday, July 20th 1864

Started at 6 AM. Passed through Decatur. Take position southeast of Atlanta. 17th Corps left, 15th Corps center, and 16th right. We move cautiously, little knowing what obstacle may be in our way. While I write, skirmishing has commenced.

It is hard to tell what may appear in my diary tonight, but God grant that I may be able to record a victory over the destroyers of our national peace.

We have secured a position, but have suffered some considerable. Up till midnight busy in getting works thrown up for batteries etc. General Gersham commanding 3rd Division badly wounded in his leg. Leg broken but amputation not necessary. He starts home in the morning.

Thursday, July 21st 1864

There is a hill about a mile from our batteries on which is a Rebel battery. To Gen. Legget is assigned the taking of it. An assault is made. We have full view and terrible is the contest. Our whole line advanced, but the right are forced to fall back. The left succeeded in carrying the hill occupied by the Rebels.

In a very few minutes we have a battery planted on the same ground. A glorious achievement, for which Gen. Legget is entitled to much credit. No time is lost in fortifying. At night we have 32 guns in position in full view of the Rebels next line of works.

Atlanta is a hard place to take, but fall it must. 15th Corps are not quite as far advanced as we are, but we can help them from our present position.

9 PM received an order from Gen. McPherson to withdraw 16 guns as he thinks we are risking too much.

---

[i] Petersburg, VA was not in fact taken until April 1865

Samuel B. Reed[i] of Cheney's Battery killed,[ii] both legs shot off.

On July 22, 1864 *Lieut. Gen. Hardee's* Corps came out from Atlanta and moved in heavy force into a gap in the Union lines between the 16th (Maj. Gen. Dodge) and 17th (Maj. Gen. Blair) Army Corps. The Confederates attacked the flank and rear of Blair's Corps.

Friday, July 22nd 1864

Went around the lines this AM feeling quite unwell. On my return to headquarters had to stop and rest in the shade. After starting again for camp, learn that the Rebels are moving by the right flank and will probably attempt to turn our left. The 16th Corps have taken position in our rear leaving an open space of about ¾ of a mile between the 16th and 17th Corps.

At 11:30 AM an attack was made on the center of the 16th Corps extending to our right. The line of the 17th Corps was completely enfiladed. A most terrible conflict followed, lasting till dark, and indeed after dark. We hold almost all the ground we did this morning. Have been severely punished, and have inflicted a terrible punishment upon the Rebels.

Maj. Gen. McPherson was shot through the heart, and instantly killed. His loss is terrible and has cast a gloom over his command, by whom he was immeasurably beloved. Gen. Logan assumes command. How well he brought victory out of almost a defeat, history will tell. We who are here, know.

Saturday, July 23rd 1864

We yesterday lost two guns[iii] from the 17th Corps, Battery F 2nd Illinois. One caisson of the 3rd Ohio exploded. 20th Illinois Infantry captured. 16th Iowa Infantry captured. Killed and wounded Rebels estimated 8,000.

---

[i] Pvt. Samuel B. Reed of Mendota, IL, Battery F, 1st Illinois Light Artillery
[ii] Charles Kennedy of Battery F was also killed July 21, 1864
[iii] The gun crews were killed or captured along with the 2 guns. The crew of two guns was approximately 1 lieutenant, 2 sergeants, 4 corporals and 26 men.

In front of the 3rd Division alone were 1,400 dead Rebels, 773 having been delivered to the Rebs under a flag of truce. 300 have been buried by our men.

Although we gained no ground yesterday, we succeeded in killing and wounding 7,000 Rebs.

Near Atlanta
Sunday, July 24th 1864

Nothing of particular importance. Quite unwell. Atlanta papers acknowledge a loss of 20,000 killed, wounded or missing on the 20th, 21st, and 22nd.

Monday, 25th July 1864

Some artillery practice. Lines strengthened. Sick. Wrote Sister Lib and Brother Jim.

Near Atlanta, Ga.
Tuesday, 26th July 1864

Making routine reports etc. Orders to move to the right tonight. Quite unwell, and don't feel like traveling.

Artillery moved out at dark, infantry at 12 o'clock. Went with artillery. Was awake joining the infantry at daylight. Dept. of Tenn. go to the right. Royce has rode in one of the wagons, and looks fresh and good this morning.

16th and 17th Corps got away all right, but the 15th got a severe shelling.

Near Atlanta, Ga.
Wednesday, July 27th 1864

Have had a fine rain this morning. We have stopped to get some breakfast. I have been sick during the night, but am better this morning. I now wish I had something good to eat. It seems as though Gen. Sherman is determined that the Department of the Tennessee shall do the marching as we are from right to left and back again often. There is a heavy artillery fire on our left.

Bread, pork and coffee are now ready and will partake.

Visited Gen. Sherman's headquarters. Saw the general who looks first rate. Maj. Gen. O. O. Howard assumes command of the Dept of the Tenn. by order of the President. Gen. Logan back to the 15th Corps.

At 11 o'clock AM start for a position on the right of our line. 16th Corps joins Gen. Howard's right. 17th Corps joins 16th, and 15th. The 17th go within range of enemy guns in full view of them. Amused some, but not much.

Near Atlanta, Ga.
Thursday, July 28th 1864[i]

Getting into position on the line where the Rebs are formed. At 1 o'clock PM they made a furious assault on our lines. Without works, on open ground, we handsomely repulsed the enemy. We have advanced our lines and are putting in works.

The assault has been repeated three times today. Never did men fight with more desperation than the Rebs, but not an inch could they gain.

Friday, July 29th 1864

We are today burying the Rebel dead in front of the 15th Corps where the heaviest fighting was done. Rather quiet on the right, but on the left heard heavy cannonading.

Saturday, July 30th 1864

This morning our lines have been advanced. We are putting in works that will never be taken.

Sunday, July 31, 1864

Siege continues. Nothing of special importance, only that we are working and extending our line to the right.

Singing during the evening. Pain and pleasure combined.

Can it be that I will no more hear Mary sing on this plane?

Monday, August 1, 1864

Line advanced. 23rd Corps moving to our right.

---

[i] Royce Cheney's birthday; he was 12-years-old.

Letter from Sister Margaret.

Artillery opened on Atlanta from whole line. Enemy reply with 32 pieces.

Tuesday August 2nd 1864

Rode to the front with Capt. Burton before breakfast.

Putting in batteries and advance line. A very quiet day.

Capt. Miller presented me with a razor strap, brush, box and clothes brush, also a nice pocket book. Wrote to Sister Margaret.

Wednesday, August 3rd 1864

A fine shower during the night and a fine cool morning. I have got washed and shaved and feel refreshed. I am anxious for this campaign to close, that I may go home and spend some time with our children and friends.

Near Atlanta, Ga.
Thursday, Aug. 4th 1864

23rd Corps ordered to our right. Quite a heavy firing. Gen. E. M. McCook just returned from a cavalry raid. They received 800 mules, burned headquarters train together with a lot of the enemy's transportation, took up railroad tracks, destroyed telegraph wire etc. etc. A success.

Near Atlanta, Ga.
Friday, Aug. 5th 1864

Three months ago today we left home expecting that ere this, the campaign would be closed, and Royce and I home. But here we are in the midst of a siege.

We are ordered to draw our lines a little closer round Atlanta. Have laid out a new line of works in full view of the Rebs interior works. That is we judge so. A fine point has been selected for batteries. I predict that we will have a heavy artillery fight when our works are completed. That is if the Rebs do not get out. I make this prediction. The siege will not last three days.

Why is it I cannot get a letter? Have my friends all forgotten me, or have my letters miscarried?

I do not like this skirmish line. They are too careless with their missiles.

Near Atlanta, Ga.
Saturday, August 6th 1864

Our work is ready to occupy but the 16th Corps are not ready, so we do not advance. A cannonading ordered on our line at 4 PM. Army of the Ohio has crossed the railroad and found the enemy's works.

I have received three letters, one each from sisters Eliza and Marg and one from Brother Pers. Folks well at home. A heavy rain falling tonight. A heaviness of spirit and almost despair at this time has come upon me.

His health poor and his spirit weakened, John Cheney submitted his resignation August 7, 1864.

Sunday, Aug. 7th 1864

Four months ago this evening Mary exchanged worlds, from the physical to the spiritual. How long will it be ere I follow? Be it long or short, how joyful the meeting.

Received a letter from Sister Eliza and Brother Tom. Wrote to Brother Daniel and Sister Mary Addie.[i] Rode round on our front. Advanced to new lines. Some severe sharp shooting. Heavy firing on our right. Enemy attacked.

My resignation forwarded today to Col. Taylor.

23rd Corps have advanced and taken one line of Rebel works. Heavy firing during the night.

Gen. Blair serenaded by band of 32nd Ohio Infantry.

Before Atlanta, Ga.
Monday, Aug. 8th 1864

A wet day. Some fighting on our right. Maj. Kennard[ii] of the 20th Illinois left us today for the North.

---

[i] Mary Adeline (Moulton) Cheney, of Lake Village, NH, widow of Samuel Cheney (John Cheney's brother)

[ii] Maj. George W. Keenard of Champaign, IL, HQ, 20th Illinois Infantry

I am still afflicted with boils and am unable to ride. Walked over to department headquarters. Made the acquaintance of Maj. W. T. Osborn of the 1st N.Y. Artillery, new chief of artillery of the department. Another advance of our lines ordered.

Before Atlanta, Ga.
Tuesday, Aug. 9th 1864

I have had a very uncomfortable night. Rain has fallen most of the night. A sharp skirmish fire all night. Rebels have been busy with railroad trains most all night.

Ordered to fire 50 rounds to the piece from every gun within reach of Atlanta, while Gen. Schofield feels of the enemy's left.

We have done that and evidently made it warm in Atlanta. What Gen. Schofield has done, don't know.

Before Atlanta, Ga.
Wednesday, Aug. 10th 1864

We have some siege guns coming up. The shelling of yesterday has evidentially had a tendency to provoke the Rebs as they have opened on the whole line with heavy guns. Although they have injured but few men, killed a few horses, still it is very annoying.

Rebs have kept up a shelling all night.

Siege of Atlanta
Thursday, Aug. 11th 1864

This Atlanta affair has assumed the shape of a regular siege and bids fair to be quite long duration. A heavy artillery fire from both sides and but little fighting with musketry. Some fighting between skirmishers who do the most at night. Being unwell have begun a course of medicine.

Friday, Aug. 12th 1864

Some siege guns have arrived and are being put in position. Heavy shelling last night. Wrote Henry Smyth and Mrs. Kennedy. Received a letter from Brother Pers containing $20.00. Folks all well at home. Artillery horses (210) have come and am trying to get our part of them.

Have succeeded in getting 90 horses for our corps.

Lieut. William Robinson from Dixon, now an aide on Gen. Jeff C. Davis' staff, has called on me this evening and took supper.

Before Atlanta, Ga.
Saturday, Aug. 13th 1864

Last night I was kept up most of the night to get the horses divided. This morning feel worse for wear.

The fight seems to be almost entirely confined to artillery. Some strategy is in the wind, all sorts of conjecture, but time will tell. Remained in camp all day.

Before Atlanta, Georgia
Sunday, Aug. 14th 1864

Wrote Sister Lib and afterward received a letter from her. Has been very quiet till about 5 o'clock PM when a heavy artillery fire was opened on the 15th Corps. For 30 minutes it was continued, our batteries giving as good as they sent. This has been rather a dull day. Have had a fine shower. A movement is on the tapis[i] but where is mostly a matter of conjecture.

Royce and I have been down to the creek and had a wash by moonlight. We feel refreshed.

R.I.P.[ii] Had a long walk apparently alone, but not alone. R.I.P.

Before Atlanta, Ga.
Monday, Aug. 15th 1864

A very warm morning. Not feeling well. Hospitals being sent to rear. Rather quiet on the lines.

Spent the morning playing muggins. Maj. T. W. Osborn, dept. chief of artillery, 1st N.Y. Artillery has visited me.

Before Atlanta, Ga.
Tuesday, Aug 16 /64

Had a sick night. Some rain has fallen during the night. Have a comfortable morning. All day have been in camp. 32nd Ohio band

---

[i] "On the tapis" means under consideration
[ii] R.I.P. is Rest in Peace, a reference to John Cheney's deceased wife Mary

serenaded us this evening. A party from department headquarters stayed till the small hours.

Before Atlanta, Ga.
Wednesday, August 17th 1864

I am decidedly out of fix, having another boil on my leg, or very near it. So very near that were I obliged to ride, it might hurt my saddle. Maj. T. W. Merrill of the 1st Missouri Regiment, chief of artillery of the 15th Corps has visited me. Capt. Edward Speer of the 15th Ohio Battery, chief of artillery 4th Division, 17th Corps has also been here.

Having drawn one hundred and twenty three (123) horses since we were in front of Atlanta, we are now in shape to do good field service. If I had health it would be a pleasure to lead my artillery into action.

Charlie Lowe (my clerk), is getting everything in order for circumstances that may arise. It is a very hot day. Occasionally I wish I was at home where I could rest and perhaps regain my health. All is (as yet) uncertain as far as our movements are concerned.

Thursday, Aug. 18th 1864

A fine day. Heavy artillery practice. I have been kept in camp all day. Am getting tired of confinement. Learn that Col. Ezra Taylor of our regiment has resigned and his resignation is accepted.

Before Atlanta, Ga.
Friday, August 19th 1864

Had an uncomfortable night and feel decidedly worse for wear. I am getting sick of being halfway between somebody and nobody. Capt. [Berk?] mustering officer of 15th Corps and Maj. Maurice spent the evening with me.

Sick all night.

Before Atlanta, Ga.
Saturday, Aug 20th 1864

A fine rain. Rheumatism has concluded to visit me again. I wonder what will come next unbidden.

The siege continues still.

Before Atlanta
Sunday, Aug 21st 1864

Henry Goshen[i] of my old battery was killed this morning by a Rebel bullet. Shot through the head and almost instantly killed. I have written to Sister Lib and requested her to notify his friends. I learned of the death of Capt. Percy of the 53rd Ohio Vol. and acting as chief of engineers 4th Division 15th Army Corps. Capt. Percy was a heroic officer equal to any task and ready for any duty. I believe him to have been, and yet to be, a warm personal friend of mine. We were on Gen. Lauman's staff together. Messed and slept together. I grieved to learn that he has been called from the exciting scenes that we are witnessing, to that country where wars, and rumors of wars do not come. I know however that our loss is his gain. Then why so selfish as to regret his departure? Thank God Capt. Percy has not left a family to mourn his loss.

I have this morning forwarded my resignation. Learn it has gone through 17th Corps headquarters all right. What the result may be at department headquarters, cannot tell.

Before Atlanta, Georgia
Monday, Aug. 22nd 1864

A fine morning. Save some artillery firing, all is quiet. I am waiting with some anxiety to learn what the result of my resignation is. I only wish that I felt able to go through with the campaign.

I learn that my resignation has passed the Artillery Office and I will soon receive my papers accepted.

Before Atlanta, Ga.
Tuesday, Aug. 23rd 1864

A warm day. Some movement coming off soon. My papers have gone to Chattanooga for record.

Wednesday, Aug. 24th 1864

Am advised to go to Chattanooga after my papers. Have been to see the boys at the old battery.

Supplement. Paid by Maj. Glenn 5 months to include the 31st day of July 1864, $801.

---

[i] Pvt. Henry Goshen of Sterling, IL, Battery F, 1st Illinois Light Artillery

Thursday, Aug. 25th 1864

Left headquarters for the rear at 11 o'clock AM. In company with Capt. Barlow, Lieut. Whaley, Royce and Max. Took a seat in dirty cattle car. After a tedious trip of 4 hours, arrived at Marietta.

After remaining till dark, spread our blankets on the floor of the car. Some time during the night got started. Had some rest but was quite unwell.

*** *** *** *** *** *** *** ***

Headquarters
Department and Army of the Tennessee

Chattanooga, Tenn.
August 25, 1864

Special Orders No. 191

The following named officers having tendered their resignations, are hereby honorably discharged the service of the United States, with condition – that they shall receive no final payments, until they have satisfied the Pay Department that they are not indebted to the Government:

John T. Cheney, Major, 1st Regiment Illinois Light Artillery Volunteers.

By order of Major General O. O. Howard.

Wm. T. Clark
Assistant Adjutant General

*** *** *** *** *** *** *** ***

Friday, Aug. 26th 1864

Had a wash, some lunch, but feel worse for wear. I will be glad when this trip is over, then I can get some rest.

Arrived at Chattanooga, Tenn. at 10:30. Went to department headquarters and got a certified copy of my discharge papers. At 1:30 PM got off for the North. Spread my blanket on the floor of the car. Am off of the bounds, off of duty of soldiering, off from a country that I do not desire to see again, unless there should be another rebellion, and off the hooks generally.

Summary

The war was over for John Cheney.

By August 1864 the will of the civilian population in the North to continue the war was wearing down. The North, with a larger population and greater manufacturing capacity, was in a position to eventually defeat the South. However if the price paid to win was too high, the North might choose to end the war rather than press on to victory. Ending it would essentially recognize the Confederacy.

In May 1864, Sherman had begun the Atlanta campaign in the West and Grant had begun the Wilderness/Overland campaign in the East. By August 1864 Sherman had not yet taken Atlanta and Grant was bogged down in the Siege of Petersburg. Union casualties over the summer had been very heavy. Lincoln was under great criticism in the press and from his own party. Unless something changed, it looked like Lincoln would be defeated in the November 1864 presidential election.

The influence of the Peace Democrats was increasingly strong. The Democrats incorporated a plank into their Presidential platform that viewed the war as a failure and called for a negotiated peace. Thus in August 1864 a negotiated end to the war was a distinct possibility.

It didn't happen. The Democrats nominated George B. McClellan who repudiated the peace plank. On August 23, 1864 Farragut's Union fleet prevailed in the Battle of Mobile Bay. On September 2, 1864 Sherman took Atlanta. Those victories reinvigorated Northern resolve and Lincoln was re-elected in November 1864.

While the North's will to fight had not worn out, John Cheney's had. He was going home.

Chapter 18 - After the War

John Cheney and son Royce arrived at Dixon, Illinois by train on August 31, 1864. John recovered from the internal ailment he suffered from. His sciatica (rheumatism) bothered him off-and-on for the rest of his life, being very severe at times.

On July 21, 1866 36-year-old John Cheney married 23-year-old Sylvania Severance. The family of John, Sylvania, Royce and Grace lived in the Dement Town section of Dixon. John and Sylvania had two children. Charles L. Cheney was born and died in 1870. Mary Maud Cheney was born in 1872 and died in 1874.

Grace, John, Royce and Sylvania (Severance) Cheney about 1874

After the war John Cheney was involved in a number of entrepreneurial activities including the manufacture of platform scales, carriages and a livery business. By 1875 his principal occupation was proprietor of the Nachusa House hotel in Dixon.

At some time after the war, John's brother Dan Cheney and family moved from Holderness, NH to Dixon, IL.

About 1877 Royce Cheney married a woman named Katherine who was from Illinois. By about 1878 the families of John Cheney, Royce Cheney, and Dan Cheney left Dixon and moved to

Sioux City, Iowa. For almost 2 decades after that, the Cheneys were in the hotel[i] business in Iowa.

In 1882 John Cheney purchased 200 acres of land in the Morningside section of Sioux City; southeast of the center of town. By the late 1880s he was dividing and selling that land as house lots. John Cheney's developments created streets in Morningside that he named after his family members. Over time all but Royce Street have been renamed.

John Cheney 1880s Sioux City, Iowa

John prospered from his various business ventures. By about 1888 he had built and lived in a very grand house in Morningside. In 1889

---

[i] One or all three of John, Royce and Dan Cheney were proprietors of the Depot Hotel, Merchants Hotel, Hubbard Hotel, and Booge Hotel in Sioux City, Iowa. At the same time they were affiliated with 2 hotels in Missouri Valley, Iowa – the Cheney Hotel and the Union Hotel. Person Cheney of Dixon, IL was also affiliated with the Union Hotel in Missouri Valley, Iowa while living in Dixon, Illinois.

Cheney was one of several investors that created the Sioux City Transit Co. They built an elevated railway from downtown Sioux City to Morningside. John was vice-president and then in 1891 president of that company.

"Cheney's Villa" – home of John Cheney
in the Morningside section of Sioux City, Iowa

John Cheney's economic prosperity proved to be fragile. In the Panic of 1893 he lost his wealth. In trying to regain his fortune, he is reported to have lost his health. By 1894 the Sioux City Directory had no listed occupation for him and he was no longer living in the grand house.

In 1895 John and his wife Sylvania left Sioux City and moved in with Sylvania's mother – Martha Severance – in Painesville, Ohio. In 1899 the 69 year old John Cheney was manager of the Black and Tan Polisher Co.; a Painesville manufacturer of novelty items.

In a September 1901 medical examination, his doctor reported that John Cheney was in very severe pain from his sciatica. Despite his pain, Cheney attended the September 1901 GAR[i] reunion in nearby Cleveland, Ohio.

John Cheney in uniform, probably taken at the time of the Sept. 1901 GAR reunion

On October 16, 1901 Person Cheney in Dixon, Illinois received a telegram from Martha Severance -- "J T Cheney dangerously ill and failing unconscious."

John Cheney died that day. He was buried in Evergreen Cemetery, Painesville, OH.

---

[i] GAR is Grand Army of the Republic; a Civil War veterans organization

Chapter 19 - Postscript

Royce Cheney:

As mentioned above, in about 1878 Royce moved to Sioux City, Iowa and engaged in the hotel business with his father and uncle. At some time between 1888 and 1891 Royce was no longer married to his first wife Katherine. He was married to another woman, also named Katherine, who was from New Jersey. Royce's second wife was 20 years his junior. They had one child, a daughter Marion Cheney born November 8, 1893 in Sioux City.

Royce left the hotel business and Sioux City in the 1890s. By 1900 Royce, Katherine and Marion lived in San Francisco were Royce worked for a mining company. Royce died in Santa Monica, CA in 1914.

Grace Cheney:

Grace Cheney married Charles Lozier in Missouri Valley, Iowa, on Christmas Eve 1881. On November 24, 1882 their first daughter, Cleve Lozier was born in Sioux City. A second daughter, Mary Lois Lozier was born August 5, 1892.

Charles Lozier operated a real estate and loan business with his father-in-law John Cheney, called "Cheney and Lozier." Charles and Grace Lozier and their daughters lived with John and Sylvania Cheney in the large Morningside house up to about 1894.

Charles Lozier and family left Sioux City, IA in the 1890s for Toledo, OH. They also lived in Cleveland, OH, Chicago, IL and in 1903 Waltham, MA. In 1905 they moved to Elyria, OH. Cleve Lozier married Lawrence Underwood in 1906. They had no children. Mary Lois Lozier married Elbert Hay in 1913. They had one child Nancy Hay born 1915 in Elyria, OH.

Grace (Cheney) Lozier, Charles Lozier,
Mary Lois (Lozier) Hay, Nancy Hay 1915

Nancy Hay 1990s

John Cheney's daughter Grace (Cheney) Lozier died in 1958. Grace's granddaughter Nancy Hay continued the practice of her grandmother to carefully identify, package and preserve their family possessions including the letters, diaries and photographs presented in this book. Nancy Hay, who had no children, died in 2001 in Newport, Rhode Island.

Jim Vesper and Liz (Briggs) Vesper:

Sergt. Jim Vesper was discharged January 4, 1864 and returned to Dixon, IL. His wife Liz (Briggs) Vesper died in 1868. By about 1876

270

the 49-year-old Jim Vesper was in Walnut, Kansas and married to his second wife, Mary aged 23.

Richard Petty:

In February 1865 Richard Petty was assigned to Battery E, 1st Illinois Light Artillery. He was discharged July 15, 1865. Petty remained a white person and lived in the North for the rest of his life. After his discharge Petty went to Ogle, Illinois where he worked on a farm. "Having never had any educational advantages, during the winter of 1865-66 he attended school and studied hard." In the spring of 1866 he moved to Dixon, IL and learned to be a blacksmith. Petty went to Philadelphia in 1869 and on April 25 of that year he married Martha Locke.

By June of 1869, Richard Petty and wife Martha lived in Morris, IL. They had three children, Harry, Minnie and Cora. In addition to working as a blacksmith, Richard Petty also bought and sold poultry. He eventually entered the grocery business full-time. In 1902 he shifted from grocery to dry goods. He retired in 1904. Richard Petty died in Morris, IL November 11, 1928 at the age of 87.

Battery F:

On August 25-30, 1864 Battery F engaged in a flank movement on Jonesboro, Georgia and participated in the Battle of Jonesboro August 31-September 1. The battery remained there until September 8 when it went into camp at East Point, just out of Atlanta. Battery F had lost so many horses that it was almost unserviceable. It proceeded to Nashville, TN to refit, and remained in Nashville on garrison duty until February 1865. On February 22, 1865 the 3-year enlistments of its original members were up. Those who re-enlisted or whose enlistments were not up, were transferred to other batteries. Battery F ceased to exist. In its 3 years of operation it had 8 members die of wounds and 24 die of disease.

Officers of Battery F:

Capt. Josiah Burton took command of Battery F in March 1864 when John Cheney was promoted to major. Burton continued in that capacity until the battery was disbanded February 1865. Burton was discharged March 7, 1865. Lieut. John Risley and Lieut. Jefferson Whaley also served in Battery F until its disbandment.
Lieut. Samuel Smyth transferred to Battery A and became its captain. He was mustered out March 28, 1865.

Lieut. Theodore Raub of Battery F was attached to Battery A under Smyth's command in July 1864 during the Atlanta Campaign. On July 22, 1864 four guns in Smyth's Battery were overrun and captured. Lieut. Raub commanded 2 of those guns. The official report of Maj. Maurice, chief of artillery, 15th Army Corps relates that Theodore Raub "was killed outright while fighting the exultant enemy with his sword."

Appendix A - 1887 Battery F Reunion at Dixon, IL

1) George Loveland
2) Clay Hunter
3) W. H. Prescott
4) A. Gage
5) Adam Shear {Scheer}
6) Alex Turner
7) John J. Cox
8) Seth Thomas
9) Jacob Hoffman

10) Maj. J. T. Cheney
11) John G. Fiss
12) Hiram Hetler
13) Chas. Huff {Hough}
14) Milton Santee
15) John Powell
16) H. Q. Chapin
17) Henry Chappell
18) Michael Kearns

19) Henry Menchin
20) Richard Petty
21) George W. Goodwin
22) Dan C. Bressie
23) Nathan G. Eads
24) Jerry Mosteller
25) John Hughes
26) Elijah Vance
27) George Farrell

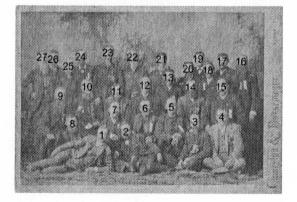

Appendix B - Roster of Battery F, 1st Illinois Light Artillery

This roster is based principally on the work of the Illinois USGenWeb Project, supplemented by information from the State of Illinois - Illinois Civil War Veterans Database, and the American Civil War Soldiers database.

Name	Residence	Muster In	Rank	Remarks
AIRD, Frank	Brooklyn	Oct 11, 1864	Recruit	Transferred to Battery I
AYERS, Henry W.	Dixon	Dec 28, 1863	Recruit	Transferred to Battery I
BABBITT, Franklin H.	Dixon	Jan 4, 1864	Recruit	Transferred to Battery B
BAKER, Augustus	Jacksonville	Sep 16, 1862	Recruit	Transferred to Battery E
BALL, James	Dixon	Aug 22, 1862	Recruit	Transferred out Jun 9, 1863
BENN, Henry L.	Grand Detour	Feb 25, 1862	1st Lt.	Resigned Sep 2, 1862
BENNETT, Frederick	Dixon	Feb 25, 1862	Private	Discharged Jan 4, 1865
BERRINGER, Lloyd	Brooklyn	Feb 25, 1862	Corporal	Re-enlisted as veteran
		Feb 28, 1864	Corporal	Mustered out Apr 11, 1865
BERRINGER, Obadiah	Brooklyn	Feb 25, 1862	Private	Discharged Jan 4, 1865
BLACK, William M.	Palmyra	Jan 4, 1864	Recruit	Transferred to Battery I
BLAIR, John	Jacksonville	Aug 2, 1862	Recruit	Promoted to corporal
		Sep 18, 1862	Recruit	Died at Marietta, GA., Oct 8, 1864
BLAIR, William	Springfield	Sep 16, 1862	Recruit	Transferred to Battery A
BOARDMAN, John D.	Dixon	Jan 4, 1864	Recruit	Transferred to Battery I
BOOTH, Reuben	Maluglin's Gr.	Feb 25, 1862	Private	Discharged Jan 4, 1865
BOSSACK, John W.	Jacksonville	Sep 16, 1862	Recruit	Transferred to Battery E
BRADWAY, Amos J.	Rock Creek	Feb 25, 1862	Private	Discharged Jan 4, 1865 as artificer

Name	Place	Date	Rank	Action
BRADWAY, Sylvanus	Dixon	Sep 16, 1862	Recruit	Transferred to Battery E
BRALEY, Esrick H.	Prophetstown	Feb 25, 1862	Private	Mustered out Mar 7, 1865
BRAMHALL, John	Elkhorn Grove	Feb 25, 1862	Private	Deserted
BRESSIE, Daniel	Dixon	Sep 1, 1862	Recruit	Mustered out Feb 22, 1865
BRIDGES, C. P.	Nashua	Feb 25, 1862	Private	Disability discharge Jun 26, 1862
BRIERTON, Henry E.	Dixon	Sep 1, 1862	Recruit	Transferred to Battery E
BRINK, Walton C.	Hanover	Sep 20, 1864	Recruit	Died at Nashville, TN Nov 8, 1864
BROCK, Andrew	Springfield	Apr 30, 1862	Recruit	Disability discharge Oct 24, 1862
BROWN, John	Morrison	Jan 4, 1864	Recruit	Transferred to Battery E
BROWN, Joseph	Sterling	Feb 25, 1862	Private	Died at Sterling, IL July 24, 1862
BROWN, Thomas	Grand de Tour	Jan 4, 1864	Recruit	Transferred to Battery B
BURKETT, Calvin	Dixon	Sep 1, 1862	Recruit	Discharged
BURR, Benjamin	Dixon	Aug 22, 1862	Recruit	Transferred to Battery A
BURR, Lionel C.	Dixon	Jan 4, 1864	Recruit	Transferred to Battery A
BURTON, Josiah H.	Dixon	Feb 25, 1862	1st Lt.	Promoted to captain Feb 13, 1864
BURTON, Josiah H.	Dixon	Mar 16, 1864	Captain	Mustered out Mar 7, 1865
BYMASTER, Lewis	Grand Detour	Feb 25, 1862	Private	Promoted to sergeant; discharged Jan 4, 1865
CAREY, Benjamin	Dixon	Feb 25, 1862	Private	Discharged Jan 4, 1865
CAREY, George	Dixon	Feb 25, 1862	Private	Discharged Jan 4, 1865
CARR, Elijah P.	Grand Detour	Feb 25, 1862	Private	Deserted
CHAFFEE, William W.	Rock Creek	Oct 11, 1864	Recruit	Transferred to Battery I
CHAPIN, Horatio O.	Jacksonville	Sep 16, 1862	Recruit	Transferred to Battery A
CHAPMAN, John B.	Menomonee	Oct 16, 1864	Recruit	Transferred to Battery I
CHAPPELL, Henry	Dixon	Feb 25, 1862	Private	Disability discharge

Name	Residence	Date	Rank	Remarks
CHENEY, John T.	Dixon	Dec 28, 1863	Recruit	Reenlisted in Battery F; transferred to Battery B
		Feb 25, 1862	Captain	Promoted to major; left Battery F, Feb 13, 1864
		May 20, 1864	Major	
CHRISTIANCE, Cornelius	Brooklyn	Feb 25, 1862	Private	Promoted to sergeant; mustered out Mar 7, 1865
CHRISTIANCE, G. W.	Brooklyn	Feb 25, 1862	Private	Discharged Jan 4, 1865
CHRISTIANCE, Wm. H.	Brooklyn	Oct 11, 1864	Recruit	Transferred to Battery I
CLARK, George	Chambers' Gr.	Feb 25, 1862	Private	Re-enlisted as veteran
	Chambers' Gr.	Feb 28, 1864	Veteran	Transferred to Battery E
CLINK, Homer H.	Palmyra	Dec 28, 1863	Recruit	Died at Rome, GA
COBB, Daniel	Viola	Feb 4, 1864	Recruit	Transferred to Battery B
COLTON, Josiah	Rock Creek	Oct 11, 1864	Recruit	Transferred to Battery E
CONNELLON, Owen	Rock Creek	Oct 11, 1864	Recruit	Transferred to Battery I
CONRAD, George	Jacksonville	Sep 16, 1862	Recruit	Transferred to Battery E
CONWAY, Franklin	Palmyra	Dec 14, 1863	Recruit	Transferred to Battery B
COOPER, William M.	Jacksonville	Sep 16, 1862	Recruit	Promoted 1st lieutenant Battery I
CORMANY, Jacob E.	Mt. Carroll	Jan 4, 1864	Recruit	Transferred to Battery B
COX, John J.	Virden	Feb 25, 1862	Private	Mustered out Mar 7, 1865
CURTIS, Charles W.	Dixon	Sep 1, 1862	Recruit	Disability discharge Feb 22, 1863
DAILY, Thomas	Rock Creek	Jan 11, 1864	Recruit	Transferred to Battery I
DECK, John W.	Palmyra	Dec 28, 1863	Recruit	Transferred to Battery I
DEYO, Laureston	Dixon	Jan 4, 1864	Recruit	Transferred to Battery B
DOCTOR, Valentine	Brooklyn	Feb 25, 1862	Private	Re-enlisted as veteran
	Melugin	Mar 14, 1864	Veteran	Promoted to corporal; mustered out Apr 11, 1865
DONIVAN, James	Wapella	Nov 30, 1863	Recruit	Transferred to Battery E

Name	Residence	Date	Rank	Remarks
DRISCOLL, David	Springfield	——	Recruit	Deserted
EADS, Nathan G.	Springfield	Jan 5, 1865	Recruit	Mustered out Mar 1, 1865
EDSON, Eliphalet B.	Dixon	Sep 1, 1862	Recruit	Promoted corporal; disability discharge Dec 24, 1862
ELWERT, William	Dixon	Aug 22, 1862	Recruit	Deserted Oct 11, 1862
EMMERT, Albert R.	Mt. Carroll	Jan 4, 1864	Recruit	Transferred to Battery B
EYRE, Alfred	Palmyra	Dec 28, 1863	Recruit	Transferred to Battery B
FAIRCHILDS, Samuel	Brooklyn	Oct 11, 1864	Recruit	Transferred to Battery I
FARRELL, George W.	Dixon	Jan 4, 1864	Recruit	Transferred to Battery B
FERGUSON, Harvey	Dixon	Jan 4, 1864	Recruit	Transferred to Battery B
FINK, Joseph	Menomonee	Oct 16, 1864	Recruit	Transferred to Battery I
FISS, John G.	Chambers' Gr.	Feb 25, 1862	Private	Mustered out Mar 7, 1865
FORD, John	St. Louis, MO	Mar 14, 1862	Recruit	——
FULLER, Frederick E.	Brooklyn	Feb 25, 1862	Private	Disability discharge Apr 14, 1862
GAGE, Alonzo D.	Dixon	Dec 28, 1863	Recruit	Transferred to Battery I
GARRISON, William H.	Northfield	Sep 20, 1864	Recruit	Transferred to Battery I
GATENBY, George	Jacksonville	Sep 16, 1862	Recruit	Transferred to Battery A
GILLETT, Charles S.	Washington	Jan 13, 1864	Recruit	Died Atlanta, GA Aug 3, 1864
GLEASON, Peter	Springfield	Apr 30, 1863	Recruit	Died Athens, IL Sep 22, 1863
GOODWIN, George W.	Dixon	Aug 22, 1862	Recruit	Transferred to Battery A
GORDON, Joseph	Thompson	Oct 11, 1864	Recruit	Died at Nashville, TN
GOSHEN, Henry	Sterling	Feb 25, 1862	Private	Killed at Atlanta, Ga., Aug 21, 1864
GRAFF, Henry	Dixon	Dec 22, 1862	Recruit	Deserted
GRAVES, John W.	Jacksonville	Sep 16, 1862	Recruit	Died at Lagrange, TN Mar 5, 1863
GROFF, Lewis	Menomonee	Oct 16, 1864	Recruit	Transferred to Battery I

Name	Location	Date	Rank	Notes
GROSH, John W.	Lanark	Jan 13, 1864	Recruit	Transferred to Battery E
GUNDERSON, Ole	Dixon	Feb 25, 1862	Private	Transferred out Oct 1, 1864
GUYLER, John	Jacksonville	Sep 16, 1862	Recruit	Transferred to Battery E
HAIGHT, Eugene N.	Springfield	Jan 5, 1865	Recruit	Died at Nashville, TN
HANSON, John	Polo	Feb 25, 1862	Private	Died St. Louis Jun 3, 1864
HARTFORD, Perry	Springfield	Apr 20, 1862	Recruit	Died at Pittsburg Landing Jul 12, 1862
HAYNES, John	Dixon	Feb 25, 1862	Private	Discharged Jan 4, 1865
HENDERSHOT, Hiram S.	Brookville	Oct 16, 1864	Recruit	Transferred to Battery I
HETLER, Hiram	Dixon	Aug 22, 1862	Recruit	Transferred to Battery A
HOFFMAN, Jacob	Palmyra	Feb 25, 1862	Private	Discharged Jan 4, 1865
HOLDEN, Frederick	Malugin's Gr.	Feb 25, 1862	Private	Mustered out Mar 7, 1865
HOLLISTER, Justin	Dixon	Sep 1, 1862	Recruit	Transferred to Battery A
HOREN, Charles	Springfield	Jan 5, 1865	Recruit	Mustered out Mar 1, 1865
HORN, Henry	Dixon	Feb 25, 1862	Private	Bugler; discharged Jan 4, 1865
HOUGH, Charles	Malugin's Gr.	Feb 25, 1862	Private	Discharged Jan 4, 1865
HOWE, A.. M.	Fair Haven	Feb 25, 1862	Private	Disability discharge Jan 4, 1863
HUGHES, John	Dixon	Sep 1, 1862	Recruit	Transferred to Battery A
HUNTER, Henry C.	Elk Horn	Jan 11, 1864	Recruit	Transferred to Battery A
HUNTER, James P.	Wysox	Jan 11, 1864	Recruit	Transferred to Battery A
JOHNSON, Theodore	Palmyra	Dec 28, 1863	Recruit	Transferred to Battery I
KANE, John		Jan 5, 1865	Recruit	Transferred to Battery B
KARSHNER, Michael	Malugin's Gr.	Feb 25, 1862	Private	Discharged Jan 4, 1865
KEARNS, Michael	Dixon	Feb 25, 1862	Private	Discharged Jan 4, 1865
KEISER, Edwin M.	Dixon	Jan 4, 1864	Recruit	Transferred to Battery B

Name	Place	Date	Rank	Remarks
KELLAN, Mart	Lodi	Feb 25, 1862	Private	Mustered out Mar 7, 1865
KEMPE, Warren	Pine Creek	Feb 25, 1862	Private	Promoted to sergeant; discharged Jan 4, 1864
KENNEDY, Charles Y.	Dixon	Feb 25, 1862	Private	Promoted to sergeant
	Dixon	Mar 14, 1864	Sergeant	Killed at Atlanta, GA July 21, 1864
KENNER, William H.	Elk Horn	Oct 11, 1864	Recruit	Transferred to Battery I
KNEPPER, German	Ogle	Jan 12, 1864	Recruit	Transferred to Battery B
KNIGHT, Milton C.	Sterling	Dec 31, 1863	Recruit	Transferred to Battery I
LAHEY, James	Dixon	Feb 25, 1862	Private	Mustered out Mar 7, 1865
LANE, George P.	Forreston	Feb 25, 1862	Private	Disability discharge Apr 28, 1863
LANG, A. V.	Daysville	Feb 25, 1862	Private	Transferred to Battery I
LANSING, Orrin	Jacksonville	Sep 16, 1862	Recruit	Transferred to Battery A
LEACH, Leander	Dixon	Feb 25, 1862	Private	Disability discharge 1862
LENNIHAN, Jeremiah	Dixon	Feb 25, 1862	Private	Re-enlisted as veteran
	Dixon	Feb 28, 1864	Veteran	Transferred to Battery B
LENTZ, Max	Jacksonville	Sep 16, 1862	Recruit	Transferred to Battery E
LEVITT, Jeremiah	Thompson	Oct 11, 1864	Recruit	Transferred to Battery I
LEWIS, George J.	Springfield	Sep 16, 1862	Recruit	Transferred to Battery A
LINDSEY, William O.	Freedom	Jan 5, 1864	Recruit	Transferred to Battery I
LITTLE, Thomas C.	Dixon	Aug 22, 1862	Recruit	Transferred to Battery A
LITTLE, Walter	Malugin's Gr.	Feb 25, 1862	Private	Discharged Jan 4, 1865
LOSEE, Joseph P.	Buffalo	Feb 25, 1862	Private	Discharged Jan 4, 1865
LOVELAND, George R.	Dixon	Jan 4, 1864	Recruit	Transferred to Battery B
LOVELAND, Willett O.	Dixon	Jan 5, 1865	Recruit	Transferred to Battery E
LOVELESS, Andrew J.	Dixon	Sep 1, 1862	Recruit	Transferred to Battery E

Name	Residence	Date	Rank	Remarks
LOVELESS, Joseph M.	Dixon	Sep 1, 1862	Recruit	Died, Memphis, Feb 3, 1863
LOWE, Charles	Dixon	Jan 25, 1864	Recruit	Transferred to Battery E
LYLE, John H.	Dixon	Feb 25, 1862	Private	Mustered out Mar 7, 1865
LYNCH, Alexander	Keokuk, IA.	Mar 1, 1862	Recruit	Transferred out
MANN, John	Malugin's Gr.	Feb 25, 1862	Private	Disability discharge Jul 3, 1863
MARKS, James	Jacksonville	Sep 16, 1862	Recruit	Disability discharge June 25, 1864
MARTIN, Edward	Jacksonville	Sep 16, 1862	Recruit	Transferred to Battery E
McCLOUD, Stephen	Nashua	Feb 25, 1862	Private	Disability discharge May 22, 1863
McCOY, Martin	Springfield	Apr 30, 1862	Recruit	Transferred to Battery E
McELROY, Frank	Malugin's Grove	Feb 25, 1862	Private	Deserted Jul 4, 1862
McMANUS, Michael	Springfield	Apr 30, 1864	Recruit	Died at Springfield, IL Apr 8, 1864
MEAD, Charles A.	Woodland	Jan 11, 1864	Recruit	Died at Marietta, GA Sep 8, 1864
MENCHIN, Henry	Elkhorn Grove	Feb 25, 1862	Veteran	Re-enlisted as Veteran
MILLER, Silas	Freedom	Jan 8, 1864	Recruit	Transferred to Battery I
MINTER, John	Jacksonville	Sep 16, 1862	Recruit	Transferred to Battery B
MITTS, Thomas J.	Springfield	Jan 5, 1865	Recruit	Transferred to Battery A
MOON, Clark W.	Dixon	Oct 2, 1862	Recruit	Mustered out March 1, 1865
MORGAN, Edward	Menomonee	Oct 16, 1864	Recruit	Transferred to Battery A
MOSHER, Alphonso	Hume	Feb 25, 1862	Private	Transferred to Battery I
MOSHER, Edward	Hume	Feb 25, 1862	Private	Discharged for disability
MOSTELLER, Jeremiah	Dixon	Sep 1, 1862	Recruit	Discharged Jan 4, 1865
MURAT, Edward	Jacksonville	Sep 16, 1862	Recruit	Transferred to Battery A
MURPHLETT, P. T.	Prophetstown	Feb 25, 1862	Private	Died. wounds, Marietta, GA
				Died Springfield, IL Feb 18, 1862

Name	Residence	Date	Rank	Notes
NIGHTLINGER, John	Sublette	Feb 25, 1862	Private	Discharged Jul 20, 1862
O'BRIEN, Edward	Dixon	Feb 25, 1862	Sergeant	Died of wounds at Marietta, GA Sep 8, 1864
O'CONNER, Henry	Jacksonville	Sep 16, 1862	Recruit	Died Memphis, TN Nov 25, 1863
OCHA, Lewis	Jacksonville	Sep 16, 1862	Recruit	Drowned at St. Louis, MO Sep 19, 1862
OTT, Philip	Jacksonville	Sep 16, 1862	Recruit	Transferred to Battery A
OVERCUTTER, Henry	Jacksonville	Sep 16, 1862	Recruit	Transferred to Battery A
PARKER, S. E.	Brooklyn	Feb 25, 1862	Private	Died, Memphis, Feb 27, 1864
PATRICK, Shepard G.	Dixon	Jan 21, 1864	Recruit	Transferred to Battery E
PEACOCK, Henry L.	Dixon	Jan 4, 1864	Recruit	Promoted to corporal; mustered out Apr 11, 1865
PEIRCE, Franklin O.	Brooklyn	Oct 16, 1864	Recruit	Transferred to Battery I
PETTIT, Daniel	Freedom	Oct 11, 1864	Recruit	Transferred to Battery I
PETTY/PETTEE, Richard	State of Miss.	Aug 1862	Recruit	Transferred to Battery E
PHILLIPS, William	Springfield	Jan 5, 1865	Recruit	Mustered out Mar 1, 1865
POTT, Henry R.	Boynton	Oct 3, 1864	Recruit	Transferred to Battery I
POWELL, John	Zanesville	Feb 25, 1862	Recruit	Re-enlisted as veteran
		Feb 28, 1864	Veteran	Promoted to corporal; mustered out Apr 11, 1865
PRESCOTT, William H.	Woosung	Feb 25, 1862	Private	Discharged Jan 4, 1865
PURDY, Elden	State of Wis.	Oct 16, 1864	Recruit	Transferred to Battery I
RAUB, Theodore W.	Dixon	Feb 25, 1862	Sergeant	Promoted to lieutenant
	Dixon	Mar 15, 1864	2nd Lt.	Killed in battle Jul 22, 1864
REARDON, John	Palmyra	Feb 25, 1862	Private	Re-enlisted as veteran
	Palmyra	Feb 28, 1864	Veteran	Transferred to Battery B
REED, Samuel B.	Mendota	Apr 30, 1862	Recruit	Killed, Atlanta, Jul 20, 1864
RENLAND, Peter	Springfield	Jan 5, 1865	Recruit	Promoted to corporal; mustered out Mar 1, 1865

Name	Place	Date	Rank	Notes
REUBENDALL, Franklin	Brookville	Feb 25, 1862	Private	Re-enlisted as veteran
	Rockville	Feb 28, 1864	Veteran	Transferred to Battery E
RHEAM, Frederick	Jacksonville	Sep 16, 1862	Recruit	Transferred to Battery E
RICHARDSON, William	Dixon	Feb 25, 1862	Private	Re-enlisted as veteran
	Dixon	Feb 28, 1864	Veteran	Promoted to sergeant; mustered out Apr 11, 1865
RICHEY, Robert	Brooklyn	Feb 25, 1862	Sergeant	Re-enlisted as veteran
	Brooklyn	Mar 14, 1864	Veteran	Promoted to lieutenant
	Brooklyn	Sep 8, 1864	2nd Lt.	Mustered out Mar 7, 1865
RIPLEY, John	Hyde Park	Sep 19, 1864	Recruit	Transferred to Battery I
RISLEY, Ezra B.	Springfield	Sep 18, 1862	Recruit	Disability discharge Mar 7, 1864
RISLEY, John W.	Jacksonville	————	Recruit	Promoted to 2nd lieutenant
		Aug 19, 1862	2nd Lt.	Promoted 1st July 23, 1864
		————	1st Lt.	Mustered out Mar 7, 1865
ROGERS, James	Jacksonville	Sep 16, 1862	Recruit	Transferred to Battery A
ROHRER, Amos	Dixon	Feb 25, 1862	Private	Discharged Jan 1, 1863
SAMPSON, Ichabod	Thompson	Oct 11, 1864	Recruit	Transferred to Battery I
SANTEE, Emery M.	Dixon	Jan 4, 1864	Recruit	Transferred to Battery B
SAUCE, Nicholas	Menomonee	Oct 16, 1864	Recruit	Transferred to Battery I
SCHEER, Adam	Dixon	Aug 22, 1862	Recruit	Transferred to Battery A
SCHUYLER, Elam A.	Springfield	Jan 5, 1865	Recruit	Discharged Mar 1, 1865
SCULLEN, William H.	Lee Center	Jan 19, 1864	Recruit	Transferred to Battery I
SEWELL, Luman A.	Daysville	Feb 25, 1862	Private	Discharged Jan 4, 1865
SHELLY, Thomas	Malugin's Gr.	Feb 25, 1862	Private	Discharged Jan 4, 1865
SHELTERS, Edward	Dixon	Aug 22, 1862	Recruit	Transferred to Battery E

Name	Residence	Date	Rank	Notes
SHERMAN, Luther	Mendota	Feb 25, 1862	Private	Deserted Jul 24, 1862
SHICK, Rush R.	Dixon	Feb 28, 1864	Veteran	Promoted to corporal; mustered out Apr 1865
SHICK, Rush	Palmyra	Feb 25, 1862	Private	Re-enlisted as Veteran
SHOEMAKER, William A.	Savannah	Jan 11, 1864	Recruit	Transferred to Battery E
SHORT, Henry W.	Palmyra	Dec 14, 1863	Recruit	Transferred to Battery B
SINDORF, Christian	Dunleith	Oct 16, 1864	Recruit	Transferred to Battery I
SINGLETON, John H.	Jacksonville	Sep 16, 1862	Recruit	Transferred to Battery A
SNAIL, John J.	Dixon	Aug 22, 1862	Recruit	Transferred to Battery A
SNYDER, Lawrence	Jacksonville	Sep 16, 1862	Recruit	Transferred to Battery E
SNYDER, William C.	Dixon	Aug 22, 1862	Recruit	Promoted to sergeant; transferred out Jul 25, 1864
STETLER, Perry	China	Feb 25, 1862	Private	Discharged Jan 4, 1865
STEWART, William A.	Dixon	Dec 28, 1863	Recruit	Died at Stephenson, AL Feb 18, 1865
STOCK, Daniel C.	Hardin	Feb 25, 1862	Private	Disability discharge Jun 11, 1862
SWEET, Amos	Brooklyn	Oct 11, 1864	Recruit	Transferred to Battery I
SMTH/SMITH, Samuel S.	Elkhorn	Feb 25, 1862	2nd Lt.	Promoted 1st lieutenant
	Elkhorn	Sep 2, 1862	1st Lt.	Promoted to captain and transferred to Battery A
TAYLOR, Alonso O.	Nashua	Feb 25, 1862	Private	Promoted to corporal; disability discharge
TAYLOR, James E.	Dixon	Feb 25, 1862	Private	Discharged Jan 4, 1865
TAYLOR, Lewis	Mt. Carroll	Jan 13, 1864	Recruit	Transferred to Battery B
THOMAS, Seth	Sterling	Feb 25, 1862	Private	Mustered out Mar 7, 1865
THOMAS, Van J.	Palmyra	Jan 4, 1864	Recruit	Transferred to Battery B
THOMPSON, William J.	Thompson	Oct 11, 1864	Recruit	Transferred to Battery I
THOMPSON, N. H.	Dixon	Feb 25, 1862	Private	Promoted to corporal; died Mound City Aug 24, 1862
THOMSON, James	Palmyra	Feb 25, 1862	Private	Discharged Jan 4, 1865

Name	Place	Date	Rank	Notes
THORNSBURY, James	Jacksonville	Sep 16, 1862	Recruit	Transferred to Battery A
TOBER, Joseph	Springfield	Apr 30, 1862	Recruit	Died, Nashville, Dec 31, 1864
TOMBOW, John	Palmyra	Dec 14, 1863	Recruit	Transferred to Battery B
TRACY, Henry	Daysville	Feb 25, 1862	Private	Died at Camp Sherman, MS Sep 26, 1863
TURNER, Alexander	Dixon	Jan 25, 1864	Recruit	Transferred to Battery E
UPHAM, James T.	Dunleith	Oct 16, 1864	Recruit	Transferred to Battery I
UTT, William H.	Lodi	Feb 25, 1862	Private	Re-enlisted as veteran
		Feb 28, 1864	Veteran	Transferred to Battery E
VANCE, E. P.	Jacksonville	Sep 16, 1862	Recruit	Transferred to Battery E
VANCE, James	Jacksonville	Sep 16, 1862	Recruit	Transferred to Battery E
VESPER, James M.	Dixon	Feb 25, 1862	Sergeant	Discharged Jan 4, 1864
WADE, Thomas	Dixon	Jan 21, 1864	Recruit	Transferred to Battery E
WAGNER, Addison	Dixon	Feb 25, 1862	Private	Discharged Jan 4, 1865
WEAVER, George	Springfield	Jan 5, 1865	Recruit	Discharged Mar 1, 1865
WELSH, Edwin A.	Harmon	Oct 11, 1864	Recruit	Transferred to Battery I
WELSTEAD, John H.	Elkhorn Grove	Feb 25, 1862	Private	Artificer; discharged Jan 4, 1865
WHALEY, Jefferson F.	Malugin's Gr.	Feb 25, 1862	1st Serg.	Promoted 2nd lieutenant
		Sep 2, 1862	2nd Lt.	Promoted 1st lieutenant
		Apr 19, 1864	1st Lt.	Mustered out May 7, 1865
WHALEY, Johnson	Brooklyn	Feb 25, 1862	Private	Disability discharge Jan 13, 1863
WHITE, Earl A.	Dixon	Feb 25, 1862	Private	Artificer; disability discharge Oct 24, 1862
WHITE, Harvey	Branch M., WS	——	Recruit	Transferred from Battery I, re-enlisted as veteran
		Feb 28, 1864	Veteran	Transferred to Battery E
WHITE, James F.	St. Paul, MN	Oct 16, 1864	Recruit	Transferred to Battery I

Name	Residence	Date	Rank	Notes
WILLIAMS, Charles W.	Cherry Grove	Oct 11, 1864	Recruit	Transferred to Battery I
WILLIAMS, Richard	Thompson	Oct 11, 1864	Recruit	Transferred to Battery I
WILLIAMS, Thomas	Rock Creek	Feb 25, 1862	Private	Died, Memphis, Nov 14, 1862
WILLIS, James D.	Zanesville, OH	Feb 28, 1862	Recruit	Deserted July 7, 1862
WINTERS, John	Woodland	Jan 14, 1864	Recruit	Transferred to Battery B
WITHINGON, Nathaniel	Jacksonville	Sep 16, 1862	Recruit	Transferred to Battery E
WITTEE, Henry	Elkhorn Grove	Feb 25, 1862	Private	Re-enlisted as veteran
		Feb 28, 1864	Veteran	Transferred to Battery I
WOOD, William T.	Dixon	Jan 4, 1864	Recruit	Transferred to Battery B
YATES, John Q	Dixon	Feb 25, 1862	Sergeant	Promoted 2nd lieutenant but not mustered
			Sergeant	Re-enlisted as veteran
		Mar 14, 1864	Sergeant	Mustered out Apr 11, 1865
YOUNGS, Albert	Brooklyn	Feb 25, 1862	Private	Discharged Jan 4, 1865

Appendix C - Letters from Mary (Briggs) Cheney

Of the many letters Mary Cheney wrote to her husband during the Civil War, only three survive. These would also have been the last ones she wrote as they are dated December 16, 19, & 22, 1863. John Cheney left the front to return home on recruiting service Dec 22, 1863, i.e., before he would have received any of these. He remained at home through Mary's death in April 1864.

Dixon
Dec. 16th 1863

My dear Husband,

This is a wild stormy night, wind blowing hard and snow flying in every direction. Oh John how I long for you to be here with us. I feel so lonely tonight. I was hoping to get a letter from you today but was doomed to disappointment. Pers came here this afternoon and my heart beat fast. I thought he surely had a letter for me. He had, but not from you my own dear John. The letter he brought was from Brother James. His health is improving. His family are all well.

Sarah Cheney is going to Maryland to spend the winter. Her health is improving slowly. Marg is over to Lib's. We have fixed a good lid on some chairs for Royce, and Roxie is going to sleep downstairs with me. Royce has gone to bed. Roxie is sitting on the floor behind the stove. Gracie is sitting here by the table with a pen and paper and is writing to "my papa." I told her I wanted to undress her and put her to bed. She said "well I fant (shant) go till I get my writing done."

Sunday and Monday we were fearful she was going to have diphtheria, but I commenced in season to doctor her and have prevented it. She has swabbed her throat as well as a child of ten years could. Every few minutes she says, "Ma let me fob my throat a little now." She has seemed as well as usual today; been full of fun and play.

Night before last poor Jed came home sick. Has been sick so he could not work more than a week. His lungs are in a very bad condition. Lib is fearful he will have quick consumption. Lib and Tate were terrible blue this morning about him. I think he will get better with proper care and I guess he will get that. I pity him. He tries hard to get along but bad luck attends him.

Dearest you should see the things (men I will not call them) who are rushing to the Provost Marshal's Office to get exemptions from the draft. Several carloads arrive every day. This morning Pers knocked one down. He stayed at Pers' all night and had breakfast. When he came to settle his bill found fault with the price. Pers told him it was 25 cts. cheaper than any other hotel in town. One word led to another and finally to end the thing Pers knocked him down. Pers received another letter from Tom this week. It was very different from the other two. Tom wrote that Pers misunderstood his meaning. Meant no abuse to anyone, simply asked a few questions. I don't think plain English need to be misunderstood, and it was not. The fact is, Pers wrote Tom and made him ashamed of what he had before written. Pers and Hat are expecting to start for the East Monday night. They have passes to Boston and back.

Dearest do come home soon as you can get away. We all want to see you so much. Sometimes I get nervous thinking about you. I hardly know what to do with myself. Mrs. Burton says that Burton shall never be commissioned captain of the battery if she can prevent it. For she has lived alone as long as she wants to and when his time is out she wants him to come home. Monday there were four men enlisted to join your battery. Henry Chappell thinks of enlisting again. Will go to the battery if he does. Wish I could enlist. I too would go to the battery about as quick as cars could carry me. Would start tonight stormy as it is. Well my love I will bid you good night, read your last letter again and retire. Love to Jim.

Thine ever,
Mary

~ ~ ~ ~ ~

Dixon
Dec. 19th 1863

My dear Husband,

Another week has passed and I have received no letter from you. I was sadly disappointed today. I fully expected to get a letter but I know that you write every opportunity. I must be patient and wait but the time seems so long. Only think John three weeks have passed since the last letter that I received from you was written. God only knows where you have been since that time and as you used to say "He won't tell." Oh John how I do want to see you. Don't you think you can get a leave of absence and come home for a while? I know it would be very hard for us to part again but I do want to see you so much. I cannot endure the thought of living this long cold winter without even seeing you. I should not urge you from duty, but you did not come last summer and the other officers did. I should think that you might get a leave now. I mean after the roads get so that you cannot march. I have dreamed several times recently of you being here at home and we were so happy. And then to awaken and find it all a dream, I tell you dear John it made me feel blue enough. But after this Rebellion is crushed and we again reunited, our joy will more than repay us for all we have endured for our country's cause, will it not? I know that we have much to be thankful for. When I think of the many homes made desolate since this cruel war commenced, I feel that so long as your life is spared I ought not complain at living separated from you while you are acting from a sense of duty and doing all you can toward crushing this Rebellion. I don't complain but it is very hard to be separated so long from those we love. This war cannot last forever if we continue to be successful. I should think the Rebels would begin to think their race was almost run.

I was told today that Hank Chappell and eleven others had enlisted to go to your battery. Its reputation must be good. Col. Gorgas[i] has an office here and is recruiting for the 13th. Don't know how he succeeds. Jed is better than when I wrote you on Wed. but he is low-spirited and sometimes says he never should be any better. He was up and dressed a part of yesterday and today. His lungs are in a bad condition, but I think he will get over this sickness. Lib and Tate you know are apt to look on the dark side, and I should never think a person was going to die because they thought so. Jed is very careless and may step out, but I don't believe he will if he will only follow the old doctor's directions and be careful. Pers and Hat will doubtless start Monday morning for the East. They are intending to be gone about a month. Mother is going up to the Waverly to take charge of the work, but will not be able to do as much as she will want to on account of her hand. Gracie is quite well again. This has been a very unpleasant week. The sun has not shone a single day and it is very cold. There is plenty of snow for sleighing now and if you were here we would take a ride. Pers received a letter from Sam yesterday. He was about starting for New Orleans with a squad of 400 men. He and ten others from his regiment was ordered home on recruiting service. He did not remain at Holderness a few days. I will get his letter and send to you. While I write, Roxie and Royce are playing muggins. Royce is rather too much for Roxie. The fire is getting low and I will bid you good night dearest.

---

[i] Col. Adam B. Gorgas of Dixon, IL, HQ, 13th Illinois Infantry

Sunday Evening. Well dear John I have just been up to say good-bye to Hat. I gave her ten dollars to give to Mother for a Christmas gift. She could not find Sam's letter. Tom's wife[i] has another boy born on the 15th. Sam's wife[ii] is there nursing Lib.

There is a teacher of penmanship here and Lib and I think some of taking lessons. Need enough of it, isn't there? Our darling little Gracie stands by my side and says "tell Papa Ma, that I went up to the Waverly with my aunt on yesterday." Jed is a little better today. Oh my dear John if I do not get a letter soon I don't know what I shall do. The time seems so long without your kind words of cheer. Angels guard you is my earnest prayer.

Thine truly,
Mary

Love to the boys.

~ ~ ~ ~ ~

Dixon
Dec. 22, 1863

My dear Husband,

It is Tuesday evening, the children have gone to bed. Roxie and I are alone and lonely enough we[iii] are feeling tonight. I went up to the office today as usual and came home without a letter. I kept the tears back until I reached home, then went into your room and had a good cry. Oh the hours of heartache this awful war is causing. We must each have a share. Were it not for the good that will result from it, I should be tempted to give up in despair. I have waited and watched on hour anxiously from day to day for tidings from you, and have as often been disappointed. But dearest with the knowledge that it is no fault of yours, I am comforted.

John I am not in a mood tonight to write to a soldier boy, but thought that by writing I might feel better. We are all enjoying unusual health except Royce. He has a cold. He has soaked his feet, taken a dose of medicine and doubtless by morning will be feeling quite smart. Tonight the ladies of the Episcopal Church have a fair and festival for the benefit of their church. Christmas Eve there is another festival to raise funds for the bridge – filling the piers I believe. I was notified

---

[i] Elizabeth (Keys) Cheney is the wife of Tom Cheney, brother of John Cheney
[ii] Mary (Moulton) Cheney is the wife of Sam Cheney (Sam is John's brother)
[iii] Roxanna's husband Pvt. James Fitch, 127th Illinois Infantry was also away at war

today that I was on a committee for waiting upon the tables. I declined serving. If it had been for the soldiers or war widows, I would have gone, but I know there will be enough attending the hall to take care of the tables. There is not pleasure for me at such gatherings.

Next Monday fifteen fine young men leave Dixon to join your battery, and the first of January, seven more go. Perhaps you may see them ere you receive this. You will have enough when they all get there to have two more guns[i] won't you?

Mrs. Burton told me today that Burton wrote he thought they would winter at Bridgeport, Ala. where they were when he wrote last. Jed is getting better slowly. He has not much patience. Yesterday I bought a book for Royce and a few little things for Gracie's stocking. She has as much to say about old "Fanta Claus" as any of them. You must make ready to give her an outfit soon as you get home – for "her papa will buy her a little stove and table with 'ittle dishes on and a 'ittle wash tub and every thing else she sees she will have foon (soon) as her Papa comes." I hope her expectations may soon be realized at least this far, viz. that her Papa may soon come home. There is not a day passes that she does not talk about you.

It seems odd not to see Pers and Hat at the Waverly. I don't think they will be gone longer than four weeks. Dearest I feel so much better than when I commenced this letter, and could I write anything worth the reading don't know how long I might be tempted to write. Capt. Marble is yet in town. I think he manages to have an easy time of it. I forgot to write the news in my last, viz. Pers and Dana knocked down four of the <u>noble</u> <u>patriotic</u> <u>exemption</u>[ii] <u>things</u> last week. I declare I am glad they were not women for I should be ashamed of my sex. Those who enlist now get a liberal bounty (over five hundred dollars) so their families can be left quite comfortable. I will bid you good night my darling husband and God bless you. Love to Jim.

Thine,
Mary

---

[i] Have enough men to go from being a 4-gun to a 6-gun battery
[ii] Exemption from the draft

Appendix D - Richard Petty

This appendix provides additional information on the pre-war history of Richard Petty

Early History

Richard Petty's pension file provides information on his date and place of birth and marriage. A Grundy County Illinois history includes a biography on him. That biography appears to be the source for similar information in Petty's obituary. None of those sources report his status as a former slave. Quoting form the Grundy County biography:

> ... He was born in Limestone County, Ala., August 10, 1842, son of Abner and Kittie (Carrington) Petty, the former born in England and the latter in Virginia. The father died when his son Richard was a child, but prior to his death made a number of changes moving from Alabama to Mississippi when Richard was eighteen months old, and later to Arkansas where he bought a farm, but within a year returned to Mississippi. Richard Petty grew up in the rural districts of Mississippi...

The 1850 Census has two Abner Petty's in Mississippi – one in the northern division of DeSoto County and one in the southern division of Carroll County. The enlisted men of Battery F stated that Richard Petty was from Senatobia, MS which is in the northern division of DeSoto so that Abner is a logical choice. There is nothing obvious to connect Richard with the Carroll County Abner Petty.

The DeSoto County Mississippi Abner Petty household shows Abner born about 1797, wife Elizabeth born about 1807 and children George 1820, Reuben 1831 and John 1833. All in the household are listed as born in Alabama. Following the notion that Abner was Richard's owner as well as his father, neither Richard nor Richard's mother Kittie, i.e., both slaves, would be listed as part of Abner Petty's family.

This Abner Petty is not shown in the Census as being born in England, i.e., that point does not agree with the Grundy County biography on Richard Petty. However place of birth is often in error in census data.

In this case the Alabama listing is likely wrong. The Mississippi Territory (Mississippi and Alabama) was not opened for settlement until 1798. This Abner Petty was born about 1797, making it improbable he was in fact born in Alabama. The census information may hint that he came to Mississippi from Alabama which would be consistent with Richard Petty's biography.

Abner Petty of Desoto County owned 16 slaves in 1850. Slave census schedules don't list the slave's name but do list age, sex and a designation of color as black or mulatto. Mulatto in this context does not have its current meaning (half white, half black). Rather it was an inexact indication of light skinned as opposed to dark skinned. An apparently white slave would have been rated mulatto.

The 1850 Census Slave Schedule shows that one of Abner Petty's 16 slaves was a 9-year-old mulatto boy. This census was taken September 19, 1850 at which time Richard Petty was age 9.

Abner Petty died in DeSoto County, MS. His will was recorded on May 2, 1853. At that date Richard Petty was 10 years old, i.e., the date qualifies for Richard's father to have died when "Richard was a child" as mentioned in the Grundy biography.

It is not known for sure that this Desoto County Abner Petty was the father and owner of Richard Petty, but he seems a reasonable match.

Mississippi 50th Infantry

Richard Petty's biography includes a perplexing statement. It says Petty

> ... "in the spring of 1861 enlisted in the Fiftieth Mississippi Volunteer Infantry, but after a year of service was detailed to take back a number of sick. He then enlisted in Battery F First Illinois Artillery."

On the face of it that story does not hold. There never was a 50th Mississippi regiment. While the biography may simply contain an error in the regiment number, there were no Union Mississippi regiments at the time indicated. A Mississippi regiment in the spring of 1861 would have been Confederate. It seems odd that Petty would relate in his biographical sketch a story that implies a seemingly casual change in loyalties, although instances of soldiers switching sides did occur.

I have not located Richard Petty's name in any lists of soldiers from DeSoto County or in Confederate units that drew soldiers from DeSoto. It is possible a record exists that I have not found. The logical explanation is that as a slave Petty would not have been enrolled in a Confederate unit at that time.

One speculative scenario is that in the spring of 1861 Richard's owner enlisted in a Confederate Mississippi regiment – possibly the Fifteenth rather than Fiftieth. That soldier could have taken his slave Richard, age 19, along as a personal servant. That soldier could have returned home sick with Richard in the spring of 1862. Then in the summer of 1862 Richard ran away.

Photo close-up of Richard Petty at the 1887 reunion at Dixon, Illinois

Appendix E - Frequently Mentioned People

Family in Dixon, Illinois
- Mother – Nancy (Franklin) Briggs, mother of Mary Briggs Cheney
- Mary – Mary (Briggs) Cheney – John Cheney's wife
- Gracie – Grace Cheney the approximately 2-year-old daughter of John & Mary Cheney
- Royce – Royce Cheney the approximately 11-year-old son of John & Mary Cheney
- Lib – Elizabeth (Briggs) Vesper, wife of Sergt. James Vesper; Elizabeth is the sister of Mary (Briggs) Cheney
- Marg – Margaret Briggs, the sister of Mary (Briggs) Cheney
- Ruth – Ruth (Briggs) Shepard, the sister of Mary (Briggs) Cheney
- Jed and Tate – young men, say teenagers, related in some way to the Cheney or Briggs families
- Pers – Person Cheney, John Cheney's brother. Pers did not enlist in the army due to his health. He was proprietor of the Waverly House Hotel.
- Hat – Harriet Cheney, the wife of Pers Cheney

Family in New Hampshire
- Father – Person Cheney Sr., of New Hampshire, John Cheney's father
- Mother – Ann (Morrison) Cheney of New Hampshire, John Cheney's mother
- Daniel – Daniel Cheney of Holderness, NH, brother of John Cheney, a lieutenant in the 12th NH Infantry
- Sam – Samuel Cheney of Holderness, NH, brother of John Cheney, a sergeant then lieutenant in the 12th NH Infantry
- Tom – Thomas Cheney of Holderness, NH, the brother of John Cheney, a lieutenant in Co. A, 6th NH Infantry

Officers in Battery F, 1st Illinois Light Artillery
- Lieut. Benn – Henry L. Benn of Grand Detour, IL
- Lieut. Burton – Josiah H. Burton of Dixon, IL
- Sergt./Lieut. Raub – Theodore W. Raub of Dixon, IL
- Sergt./Lieut. Richey – Robert Richey of Brooklyn, IL

- Lieut. Risley – John W. Risley of Jacksonville, IL
- Lieut. Smyth – Samuel Smyth of Elkhorn, IL
- Sergt./Lieut. Whaley – Jefferson F. Whaley of Brooklyn, IL
- Sergt./Lieut. Yates – John Q. Yates of Dixon, IL

Friends/Relatives in Battery F
- Charlie – Pvt. later Sergt. Charles Y. Kennedy of Dixon, IL. "Mrs. Kennedy" is his mother
- Jim – Sergt. James M. Vesper of Dixon, IL, the husband of Lib (Briggs) Vesper
- Joseph – Pvt. Joseph Brown of Sterling, IL. His mother, and probably he, had at one time lived with the John Cheney family, probably at the Waverly House.

Frequently Mentioned Officers in Other Units
- Capt. Bouton – Edward Bouton of Chicago, Battery I, 1st Illinois Light Artillery
- Capt. Cogswell – William Cogswell of Ottawa, IL, Cogswell's Battery, Independent Illinois Light Artillery
- Col. Hicks – Stephen G. Hicks of Salem, IL, HQ, 40th Illinois Infantry

Bibliography

General Civil War:

American Civil War Regiments, Kingston, MA: Historical Data Systems Inc. 1999 (accessed via Ancestry.com).

American Civil War Soldiers, Kingston, MA: Historical Data Systems Inc. 1999 (accessed via Ancestry.com).

Castel, Albert, *Decision in the West: The Atlanta Campaign of 1864*, Lawrence, Kansas: University of Kansas Press, 1992.

Database of Illinois Civil War Veterans, Illinois State Archives On-Line Databases.

Hazlett, James C., Olmstead, Edwin, and Parks, M. Hume (eds.) *Field Artillery Weapons of the Civil War*, Newart: University of Delaware Press, 1983.

Long, E. B. (ed), *Personal Memoirs of U. S. Grant*, NY: Da Capo Press, 1982.

McPherson, James M., *For Cause and Country: Why Men Fought in the Civil War*, NY: Oxford University Press, 1997.

Nosworthy, Brent, *The Bloody Crucible of Courage – Fighting Methods and Combat Experience of the Civil War*. NY: Carroll & Graf, 2003.

Official Records of the Union and Confederate Armies, Washington: Government Printing Office, 1880-1901.

Regimental and Unit Histories 1861-1866, Illinois Adjutant General's Report, State of Illinois Archives, 1886.

General Family History:

Hay, Nancy, *Family Papers*, unpublished manuscripts.

United States Census 1790-1930, Index and Images, Ancestry.Com.

Vital Records, Birth, Death, Marriage, State Offices in Illinois, Iowa, and California.

Cheney and Briggs Family in New Hampshire:

Pope, Charles, H., *Cheney Genealogy*, Boston: Barta Press, 1897.

Runnels, M. T., *History of Sanbornton, NH, Vol II Genealogies*, Boston: Alfred Mudget and Sons, 1881.

Cheney Family in Illinois:

Bateman, Newton and Selby, Paul, *Historical Encyclopedia of Illinois.* Chicago: Munsell Publishing Company, 1904.

Dixon Telegraph (newspaper). Dixon, IL, Jan. 20, 1876; Feb. 3, 1876.

History of Dixon and Lee County. Dixon, IL: Dixon Telegraph Print 1880.

History of Lee County, Chicago: H. H. Hill and Company, 1881.

Holland's Dixon City Directory for 1869-70. Chicago: Western Publishing Company, 1870.

Portrait and Biographical Records of Lee County Illinois. Chicago: Biographical Publishing Company, 1892.

Proceedings of the First Reunion Battery F, 1st Illinois Light Artillery, Dixon, IL: pamphlet, 1887.

Sixth Annual Reunion of Battery F 1892, Sterling, IL: Gem Printing House, 1892.

Cheney Family in Iowa and Ohio:

Evening Telegraph (newspaper). Dixon, IL. Oct. 17, 1901; Oct. 25, 1901.

Federal Pension Records, *John Cheney*, National Archives, Washington, DC.

History of the Counties of Woodbury and Plymouth Iowa, Chicago: A. Warner and Company, 1890-91.

Sioux City General Directory, Detroit: R. L. Polk and Company, 1881, 1882, 1883, 1887, 1889, 1890, 1891, 1895, 1896.

Richard Petty and Passing as White:

DeSoto County Mississippi, Will Book 1, page 38, Hernando, MS, *Will of Abner Petty*, May 2, 1853.

Federal Pension Records, *Richard Petty*, National Archives, Washington, DC.

Graham, Lawrence O., *Our Kind of People*, NY: Harper Perennial, 1999.

History of Grundy County (Iowa), Chicago: Munsell Publishing Company, 1914.

Morris Daily Herald, newspaper, Morris, IL, Nov 26, 1928.

Olmsted, Frederick L., *The Cotton Kingdom*, NY: Da Capo Press, 1996.

Quarles, Benjamin, *The Negro in the Civil War*, NY: Da Capo, 1989.

Smyth, Samuel, *Papers 1862-1865*, manuscript, William Miles Collection, Davidson Library, University of California, Santa Barbara.

People Index
See also the roster of Battery F in Appendix B

Henry, 25, 287, 288
Cheney
  Abigail (Morrison), 8
  Allison, 233
  Ann (Morrison), 8, 34, 136,
    137, 219, 294
  Daniel, 91, 117, 127, 173,
    176, 236, 257
  Elizabeth (Keys), 289
  Grace, 11, 19, 54, 72, 110,
    118, 213, 214, 264, 268,
    270, 294
  Harriet, 16, 22
  Mary (Moulton), 257, 289
  Moses, 8
  Person, 8, 11, 16, 17, 22,
    25, 26, 32, 34, 35, 36, 38,
    47, 48, 53, 60, 65, 66, 68,
    71, 78, 83, 96, 99, 117,
    118, 134, 136, 137, 142,
    145, 150, 166, 171, 181,
    213, 236, 257, 258, 267,
    286, 287, 288, 290, 294
  Royce, 10, 11, 13, 15, 16,
    17, 18, 19, 20, 21, 22, 24,
    25, 33, 36, 44, 49, 51, 54,
    55, 57, 65, 71, 72, 73, 83,
    84, 107, 109, 118, 155,
    156, 166, 170, 173, 174,
    175, 178, 179, 181, 191,
    213, 214, 215, 217, 228,
    232, 234, 236, 237, 238,
    240, 241, 242, 246, 248,
    249, 250, 251, 252, 254,
    255, 256, 259, 262, 264,
    265, 268, 286, 288, 289,
    290, 294
  Samuel, 91, 117, 127, 142,
    176, 236, 244, 248, 288,
    289
  Thomas, 49, 60, 63, 65, 91,
    117, 246, 257, 287, 289
Christiance
  Cornelius, 114
Cocherill
  Joseph, 197

Cogswell
  William, 23, 34, 51, 89, 92,
    93, 94, 97, 100, 106, 126,
    138, 141, 143, 146, 152,
    163, 164, 167, 171, 175,
    215
Cooper
  Edgar, 226
Coyle
  John, 47
Cudney
  Albert, 192
Curry
  Amos, 133
Davis
  John, 32, 35
DeGress
  Francis, 221
Dement
  Henry, 74, 158, 159
Dysart
  Alexander, 33, 34
  John, 133
Eddy
  Henry, 215
Edson
  Eliphalet, 126
Elting
  William, 215
Forsyth
  Frances, 34
Franklin
  Billy, 159, 166
Godown
  John, 138
Goodwin
  George, 89
Gorgas
  Adam, 159, 288
Goshen
  Henry, 166, 261
Graves
  John, 121, 143
Griffith
  Henry, 232
Hatch

Shaw
Albert, 101, 102
Shepard
Ruth (Briggs), 11, 178, 294
Smyth
Samuel, 29, 30, 34, 44, 49,
65, 66, 110, 111, 121,
124, 126, 131, 136, 146,
171, 173, 175, 177, 187,
207, 234, 235, 239, 258,
272, 295, 298
Snyder
Edward, 75, 86, 87, 157,
158
William, 83, 134
Sprouse
William, 147
Stevens
John, 18, 32
Stewart
Owen, 197
Taylor
Ezra, 195, 197, 217, 257
James, 172
Thomas
Seth, 107
Thompson
N H, 66, 67, 69, 70, 71, 74,
75
Vesper
James, 11, 46, 48, 50, 76,
78, 211, 294

Lib (Briggs), 10, 11, 22, 26,
34, 46, 48, 49, 53, 67, 69,
71, 72, 76, 83, 171, 178,
211, 213, 229, 239, 254,
259, 261, 286, 288, 289,
294
Walcutt
Charles, 125, 135, 239
Waterhouse
Allen, 85, 185, 217
Watson
James, 216
Whaley
Jefferson, 26, 79, 107, 110,
111, 114, 115, 124, 139,
146, 171, 175, 177, 187,
207, 262, 272, 295
Willard
Charles, 50
Williams
Martin, 133
Woodbury
Henry, 94, 168
Wright
Charles, 229
George, 219, 239
Mary (Cheney), 229
Wyman
John, 101
Yates
John, 83
Richard, 13, 52, 53, 83, 95,
99, 153

Map

Dixon

Illinois

Decatur
Springfield

St. Louis
MO

Cairo

Kentucky

Knoxville
Maryville

Tennessee

La Grange
Grand Junction

Chattanooga

Memphis Shiloh

Graysville
Trenton

Corinth
Davis Iuka
Mill

Big Shanty/
Kennesaw
Dallas
Atlanta

Holly Springs

Vicksburg
Black River
Jackson

Alabama

Georgia

Mississippi

Printed in the United States
38120LVS00006B/175-252

9 781589 397675